An Introduction to Buddhist Psychology

Padmasiri de Silva
Research Fellow
Monash University
Clayton
Australia

Foreword by John Hick

Fourth Edition

palgrave
macmillan

First edition 1979
Second edition 1991
Third edition 2000

Fourth edition published 2005 by
PALGRAVE MACMILLAN
Houndmills, Basingstoke, Hampshire RG21 6XS and
175 Fifth Avenue, New York, N. Y. 10010
Companies and representatives throughout the world

PALGRAVE MACMILLAN is the global academic imprint of the Palgrave Macmillan division of St. Martin's Press, LLC and of Palgrave Macmillan Ltd. Macmillan® is a registered trademark in the United States, United Kingdom and other countries. Palgrave is a registered trademark in the European Union and other countries.

ISBN-13: 978–0–230–00331–6 hardback
ISBN-10: 0–230–00331–1 hardback
ISBN-13: 978–1–4039–9245–1 paperback
ISBN-10: 1–4039–9245–2 paperback

This book is printed on paper suitable for recycling and made from fully managed and sustained forest sources.

A catalogue record for this book is available from the British Library.

Library of Congress Cataloging-in-Publication Data
De Silva, Padmasiri, 1933–
An introduction to Buddhist psychology / Padmasiri de Silva.—4th ed.
p. cm. — (Library of philosophy and religion)
Includes bibliographical references and index.
ISBN 1–4039–9245–2
1. Buddhism—Psychology. I. Series

BQ4570.P76D47 2005
294.3'422—dc22

Printed and bound in Great Britain by
CPI Antony Rowe, Chippenham and Eastbourne

Library of Philosophy and Religion

General Editor: **John Hick**, Fellow of the Institute for Advanced Study in the Humanities, University of Birmingham

This series of books explores contemporary religious understandings of humanity and the universe. The books contribute to various aspects of the continuing dialogues between religion and philosophy, between scepticism and faith, and between the different religions and ideologies. The authors represent a correspondingly wide range of viewpoints. Some of the books in the series are written for the general educated public and others for a more specialised philosophical or theological readership.

Selected titles:

Masao Abe
BUDDHISM AND INTERFAITH DIALOGUE
ZEN AND WESTERN THOUGHT

Dan Cohn-Sherbok
ISLAM IN A WORLD OF DIVERSE FAITHS (editor)
ISSUES IN CONTEMPORARY JUDAISM

Stephen T. Davis
LOGIC AND THE NATURE OF GOD

Padmasiri de Silva
AN INTRODUCTION TO BUDDHIST PSYCHOLOGY

Clement Dore
MORAL SCEPTICISM
GOD, SUFFERING AND SOLIPSISM

J. Kellenberger
INTER-RELIGIOUS MODELS AND CRITERIA

Adil Özdemir and Kenneth Frank
VISIBLE ISLAM IN MODERN TURKEY

Chakravathi Ram-Prasad
KNOWLEDGE AND LIBERATION IN CLASSICAL INDIAN THOUGHT

Joseph Runzo
IS GOD REAL?

Ninian Smart
BUDDHISM AND CHRISTIANITY

Michael Stoeber
RECLAIMING THEODICY
Reflections on Suffering, Compassion and Spiritual Transformation

Roger Teichmann
ABSTRACT ENTITIES

Donald Wiebe
BEYOND LEGITIMATION

Richard Worsley
HUMAN FREEDOM AND THE LOGIC OF EVIL

Library of Philosophy and Religion
Series Standing Order ISBN 0–333–69996–3
(*outside North America only*)

You can receive future titles in this series as they are published by placing a standing order. Please contact your bookseller or, in case of difficulty, write to us at the address below with your name and address, the title of the series and the ISBN quoted above.

Customer Services Department, Macmillan Distribution Ltd, Houndmills, Basingstoke, Hampshire RG21 6XS, England

---

TO THOSE WHO LIKE

'the simple things in life'

Contents

Foreword

Buddhism is the most psychologically interested of the great world religions. For when, some twenty-five centuries ago, Gotama the Buddha experienced the ultimate liberation which is *nirvana* and became one of mankind's supreme teachers, he did not point upwards or outwards to God or gods but inwards to the intricate dynamics of our mental and spiritual life. For Buddhism 'the proper study of mankind is man': it is through coming to realise what we are and – equally importantly – what we are not, that we may eventually attain to that which the east calls liberation and the west salvation. Through its founder's teaching, treasured and amplified by generations of his followers, Buddhism has developed the extraordinarily astute and penetrating analysis of human nature and the human condition on which its guidance towards liberation is based. Its central no-soul (*anatta*) doctrine, according to which a human self is not an enduring psychic entity or substance but a karmic process, a patterned flow of change through time, remains one of the great options for thought, and one which we dare not write off. Again, we cannot ignore the Buddhist account of the 'grasping' or incessant desiring which keeps the individual karmic process going, not only through a lifetime but, according to the Buddha's teaching, through a long succession of lives. In addition to this, the Buddhist tradition has important things to say about the ways in which we perceive our world; about our emotional and volitional life; about our sexuality, our social nature, and our aggressiveness; about the thin façade of the surface personality; and about the very important ethical implications of this Buddhist understanding of man.

These topics are of course discussed – some more extensively than others – in the literature on Buddhism. But it is surprising that there has been no book in English covering the field of Buddhist psychology as such since the early work of Mrs C. A. F. Rhys Davids, *Buddhist Psychology* (London, 1914). There is thus a gap in the available literature at this point, a gap which Dr de Silva has filled in the present book. This will not be the last word on Buddhist psychology; but it opens the subject up again, and in doing so it provides a much-needed point of entry for the student of Buddhism.

Dr Padmasiri de Silva is the Head of the Department of Philosophy at the Peredeniya campus, near Kandy, of the University of Sri Lanka (Ceylon). He is himself a Buddhist, thoroughly versed in the Pāli literature, as well as having studied the various western schools of psychology. He is the author of a study of *Buddhist and Freudian Psychology* (Colombo, 1973), and of *Tangles and Webs: Comparative studies in Existentialism, Psychoanalysis and Buddhism* (Kandy, 1974). He stands within the Theravada tradition, which claims to represent original Buddhism in its distinction from the Mahayana movement which started to develop at about the beginning of the Christian era and which elevated the figure of the Buddha himself from a great human teacher to the level of cosmic saviour. Dr de Silva bases his discussion on the Pāli scriptures of the Theravada tradition rather than the Sanscrit literature of the Māhayana; and so we find in his pages, for example, the word *nibbana*, which is the Pali equivalent of the (to most of us in the west) more familiar Sanscrit term *nirvana*.

Dr de Silva's book will be a valuable resource for the comparative study of religion, and in particular the study of Buddhism, in both west and east.

JOHN HICK

Preface to the First Edition

The discourses of the Buddha provide apparently simple but in fact sophisticated and stimulating discussions relating to diverse facets of man's life: his codes of personal conduct, the ideal of the virtuous life, the nature of man and the universe, the riddle of life and death, the nature of human reasoning and sensory experience, and man's search for wisdom, knowledge and truth. Above all, the discourses delve into a yet more fascinating sphere of the human mind – the underworld of man's submerged and conflicting desires, the nature of his emotions and the paths of human personality development, and it is upon this group of issues centring on the psychology of Buddhism that this book focuses.

For over ten years I have made studies of diverse aspects of the psychology of Buddhism. It was at the invitation of Professor John Hick, the Editor of this series, that some attempt was made to put together all the material collected over the years and weld them to more recent findings. The present work is thus concerned with the systematisation and interpretation of the psychological questions raised within the discourses of the Buddha.

Among serious students of Buddhism psychology is a badly neglected field, and I hope this venture will stimulate a greater degree of interest in the psychological foundations of Buddhism. Among the more clinically oriented psychologists and psychiatrists in the west, there is a growing interest in what may be called 'Asian psychology'. It would be necessary to break through the misty atmosphere that surrounds this term, and present in prosaic terms, and if possible in a modern idiom, some specific schools of traditional psychological enquiry. Thus this book is addressed to both the student of Buddhism and the student of psychology interested in Asian thought.

I am grateful to all those who assisted me by valuable discussion. I owe a special debt of gratitude to the Venerable Nyanaponika Maha Thera, who went through the first draft and made important suggestions. I am also grateful to my friends Mr P. D. Premasiri and Mr G. Samararatne for their comments.

When Dr Jerry D. Boucher of the East-West Center invited me to participate in the collaborative research project on emotion and culture, a fresh breeze of life invigorated my attempt to work out a Buddhist theory of emotions. While I have written here a fairly long account of Buddhist thinking in that area, the unexpected encounter with the work of Jerry Boucher has already provided me with a challenging base for future research. I am grateful to him for having opened out these exciting horizons for me.

Finally, this work would never have reached happy completion but for the warm encouragement I received from my wife, Kalyani. But she has done more – she has given shape and substance to those 'simple things in life' which feature on the dedication page of this volume.

University of Sri Lanka PADMASIRI DE SILVA
September 1977

Preface to the Second Edition

It is a gratifying experience to look back after ten years with a great feeling of satisfaction and find that the objectives with which this work was written have been achieved. It was my original intention to write an intelligible and clear presentation of the early Buddhist reflections on human psychology, so that this would be available for a broad spectrum of readers, ranging from the academically oriented scholar to the diverse types which come under the rubric of the 'general reader'. The responses that I received over the years from these different types of readers have been encouraging. I am very happy to assist the publishers to bring out this new edition with an additional chapter.

I had the opportunity of using the book as a text for courses which I taught in a number of foreign universities, and I also kept in touch with number of teachers who were using it as a course text. This new edition will, I hope, preserve interest in the subject and generate further creative work in the area of Buddhist psychology.

There has also been a growing interest, in recent times, in the Eastern spiritual traditions, particularly among psychologists and therapists trained in the West. Although the therapist is often drowned by the 'drama of neurosis', there has been a change of attitude; they now are prone to consider psychotherapy more as a 'way of life' than as a 'form of treatment'. These changing vistas in the study of mental sickness and health are of great interest, and in the new edition I have added a new chapter which examines the therapeutic stance of Buddhism. I am glad that the book will be available again to interested readers.

Padmasiri de Silva
National University of Singapore
October 1990

Preface to the Third Edition

The growing academic interest in Eastern spiritual traditions and their therapeutic resources is the background that sustained the positive response for two editions of this book for over two decades. But as this work moves into the twenty-first century, there is a new dimension in the emerging interest in Buddhist psychology. Outside academia, there is a growing interest among some people in the therapeutic appeal of Buddhist psychology, and these interests converge on the need to make their routine lives more coherent and meaningful and their professional lives more robust and vibrant.

During the last two years, I have moved to places outside the universities, given regular talks and occasional courses at the Buddhist temples, centres for adult education, talks at youth seminars and professional bodies. I have found my book a useful guide to expand and sustain interest in the perennial psychological insights of the Buddha among all these interested groups. While I look forward to working in these fresh pastures and exciting contexts in the years ahead of us, I am sure other teachers of Buddhist psychology will respond to these emerging trends.

Macmillan, and especially Mr. T. M. Farmiloe, have been over the years, more than a publisher. I consider them as great friends of an author. They recently brought out a splendid publication of my new work, *Environmental Philosophy and Ethics in Buddhism.* This is a work that builds a vital link between Buddhist psychology and ethics. I express my deep sense of gratitude to my publishers and also to academics and lay readers who have given me encouragement and confidence to continue writing over the years. A very special expression of thanks is due to Charmian Hearne of the publishers, and also to the copy-editor Lesley Steward, for the speedy and smooth production of this work.

I have added a new chapter on the mind–body relationship. We need to re-affirm the Buddhist perspective on the mind–body relationship, not only because philosophers are clarifying these problems at the turn of this century, but also as therapeutic concerns in the emerging field of behavioural medicine, as well as meditation and healing have presented the body–mind relationship in new and refreshing perspectives. It is with a great sense of fulfilment that I assist the publishers to bring out a third edition of the book.

Padmasiri de Silva
Monash University

Preface to the Fourth Edition

In writing this preface to the fourth edition of the present work, it is necessary to mention that this edition celebrates twenty-five years of wide and consistent circulation of the book.

The most significant change of recent times in the field of Western psychology and therapy is the gradual fading of the rivalries that existed between cognitive psychology and behaviourism. Even among a number of other schools of psychology and therapy in the West there has been meaningful points of convergence. Not only have we witnessed the emergence of cognitive behaviour therapy (CBT) but these schools have also integrated Buddhist mindfulness practice to their therapies. The work on behaviour modification and mindfulness practice by Padmal Silva, the relatively recent development of mindfulness based cognitive therapy by Segal, Williams and Teasdale, Erich Fromm's posthumus publication, *Art of Listening* and Mark Epstein's work, *Thought Without a Thinker* – all these trends in Western therapy point to a significant domain of convergence of Western systems of therapy and Buddhist practice. These Western traditions have broken off from their insularity and generated new trends of therapy. A new chapter to this book, entitled 'A Holistic Perspective on Emotion Theory and Therapy in Early Buddhism', discusses the enormous significance of these changes for the development of Buddhist psychology.

I wish to express my gratitude to the teachers of Buddhist psychology and students, as well as the general reader across the world, for having sustained a continuous interest in this work. I wish to also express my gratitude to Palgrave Macmillan publishers for undertaking the publication of a fourth edition of this book and especially the staff at Palgrave in charge of editing and publishing this work.

Padmasiri de Silva
School of Historical Studies
Monash University, Australia

1 Basic Features of Buddhist Psychology

Though the discipline of psychology is a well developed empirical science in the west today, few psychologists have dipped into the religious and philosophical literature of the east. Yet the analysis of psychological phenomena in the discourses of the Buddha offers significant insights into the nature of consciousness and the psychology of human behaviour. In fact Robert H. Thouless, the Cambridge psychologist, distinctly comments on the contemporary relevance of the psychological reflections of the Buddha: 'Across the gulf of twenty-five centuries we seem to hear in the voice of the Buddha the expression of an essentially modern mind.'[1]

Though the discourses of the Buddha are very rich in the use of psychological terminology as well as psychological analysis, this facet of the doctrine has been a badly neglected field, except for the pioneering work done by Mrs C. A. F. Rhys Davids.[2] In more recent times, a western psychologist who made a study of the psychology of *nirvana* says:

> Anybody with a good knowledge of psychology and its history who reads the Pāli nikayas must be struck by the fact that the psychological terminology is richer in this than any other ancient literature and that more space is devoted to psychological analysis and explanations in this than in any other religious literature.[3]

Apart from the contemporary significance of the psychological analysis in Buddhism, a comprehensive grasp of the entire doctrine of the Buddha cannot be arrived at without extensive study of the Buddhist concepts of mind, cognition and motivation, and of the nature of emotion and personality. It will also be seen that the psychological facets of Buddhism are closely interwoven with its more philosophical and ethical aspects. For these reasons, it would be worthwhile to abstract the psychological facets of the doctrine, systematise them and present the findings within a framework and in an idiom that would interest the psychologist today. However, before we go directly into the material in the discourses of the Buddha pertaining to psychological analysis, it is necessary to find out in what way the psychology of Buddhism is related to the other parts of the doctrine.

A close study of the discourses of the Buddha [4] will reveal that the psychological analysis found there is interlocked with the general philosophical facets of the doctrine. The basic aspects of the philosophy of early Buddhism would fall into the following areas: theory of knowledge, ethics, theory of society and theory of reality. While the material relating to the psychology of consciousness and behaviour may be isolated for the purposes of study, its distinctive quality has to be grasped in relation to the other facets of the doctrine.

At a time when psychology is struggling to emerge as an autonomous discipline, shedding its old links with philosophy, our attempt to go in the opposite direction may seem a retrogade step. However, today there is an equally significant move within the behavioural sciences to break through the parochial fences and seek a more comprehensive picture of man and human nature. In the field of psychology Carl Rogers, for instance, has emphasised the necessity to develop a methodology which, while upholding the precision and the formal elegance of the behavioural sciences , will not turn a blind eye to the subjective experiences of individuals.[5] Philosophers have also pointed out that the attempt to bring together the analysis of mental concepts and ethics will lead to the 'mutual enrichment of both fields'.[6]

ETHICS AND PSYCHOLOGY

The doctrine of the Buddha clearly accommodates the interlacing of the psychological and the ethical aspects of behaviour. Closest to this in the history of western ethics would be Aristotle's *Nicomachean Ethics*. The development of virtue is not merely blind adherence to rules, but the development of a certain type of skill (*kusala*). Virtue has to be developed by the cultivation of good habits and continuous self-analysis.

Buddhist ethics is not limited to the analysis of ethical concepts and theories, but also recommends a way of life and patterns of conduct. This practical orientation in Buddhist ethics is well grounded in an understanding of the psychological factors that obstruct as well as promote the living of a virtuous life. Buddhist ethics has been summed up in the words 'Not to do any evil, to cultivate the good and to purify one's mind . . .'[7] The cultivation of the good and the purification of the mind go together. A close study of Buddhist ethics would show that it betrays a significant link with psychology.

On the side of the psychology of Buddhism, too, we discern the use of psychological terms coloured by ethical overtones. To cite an instance, according to Buddhist psychology there are six roots of motivation: greed, hatred, delusion and their opposites liberality, kindness and wisdom. The first three roots of motivation are referred to by the term *akusala* and the other three by the term *kusala*. These two words, *kusala* and *akusala* are sometimes rendered by the purely ethical terms good and bad, or by the psychologically oriented terminology of wholesome and unwholesome or skilful and unskilful. In general, apart from the ethical overtones of the psychological vocabulary, the types of psychological phenomena selected by the Buddha for prolonged discussion and analysis are those that have a relevance to the ethical and spiritual quest in the doctrine. The Buddha's recommendations regarding what is 'desirable' depend on a factual grasp of what in fact is 'desired' by man. Thus the therapeutic recommendations of the Buddha concerning what is desirable are based on a deeper understanding of what people are prone to desire, their 'native beat'[8] and the potentiality for changing and directing their behaviour towards a desirable ideal. In this manner the ethical quest in Buddhism cannot be severed from its psychological foundations.

SOCIAL ETHICS AND HUMAN NATURE

While the kind of human community that the Buddha considers as ideal is based on ethical recommendations, the analysis of social behaviour is linked to the psychology of Buddhism. In analysing the foundations of social harmony and the roots of conflict, a significant place is given to the psychological make-up of the individual. As an initial method of settling disputes the Buddha requires that people practise the art of diligent self-analysis and search for the roots of discord within themselves, for this is the surest way of minimising social tensions.

The psychological foundation of social well-being has been aptly described thus:

> According to the Buddha the conditions to which a man as a social being is subject are to a large extent psychological; in any case they are not merely physical and environmental, although he himself regarded the presence of satisfactory conditions for physical life (*patirūpadesa vāsa*) as a great blessing.[9]

It is also necessary to emphasise that the aim of Buddhism's attempts to understand the workings of the human mind is not merely to understand the individual psyche, but through understanding the underlying principles to explain the patterns of social interaction. The social ethics of Buddhism is based on these wider dimensions of the psychology of human behaviour. Greed, hatred and delusion as roots of unwholesome actions have social dimensions. The evil impact of greed and hatred is not limited to cases where people become the passive victims of these impulses, rather they generate the climate which feeds the acquisitive personality (*rāga carita*) and the aggressive personality (*dosa carita*). If we are dominated by the craving to collect, hoard and possess things, we excite the same tendencies in others and unknowingly exalt this personality type as the most infectious social symbol. The evil generated by men with greedy dispositions is well described in the Buddhist scriptures as leading to passion, avarice, wickedness, quarrelling and strife.[10]

Emotions like greed, envy, jealousy, pride and fear—all derive significance from an interpersonal context, and if we do not want to spread the seeds of discord, we have to begin with ourselves and then try to foster the same spirit in others. It is upon these foundations of healthy ethical values that meaningful social structures can then be built. Thus it may be said that, while presenting the necessary psychological foundations for the building of a healthy society, the Buddha cuts across the somewhat exaggerated dichotomy between the individual and society. It is said, 'Protecting oneself one protects others, and protecting others one protects oneself' (*attānaṃ rakkhanto paraṃ rakkhati, paraṃ rakkhanto attānaṃ rakkhati*).[11]

While certain anti-social impulses that lead to the moral degradation of society should be eliminated, the Buddha recommends the development of the socially valuable psychological qualities of self-control (*dama*), mental calm (*sama*) and restraint (*niyama*).[12] In another context, where the Buddha discusses the factors affecting society, he says that the economic factor of poverty, the bodily proclivity to sickness and the psychological factor of craving all have to be taken into account.[13]

In general it may be concluded that the Buddhist social ethic has both a negative and positive aspect: on the negative side the control of personality factors and practice of an ethical code that will lessen social conflicts, and on the positive side the development of a healthy personality type and a code of living which will promote the building up of a good society. This vision of society is backed by a concept of human nature which is neither excessively gloomy nor purely utopian. The Buddha compares the mind to a piece of gold ore, temporarily disfigured by defilements of iron, copper, tin, silver and lead.[14] This does not mean that the Buddhist view of man is an idealised one. The Buddha gives a realistic picture of human nature, accepting that human beings possess the capacity for both good and evil.

THE THEORY OF KNOWLEDGE

The conflicting welter of metaphysical theories up to the time of the Buddha and during his lifetime raise doubts as to their grounding in truth. The name given to that branch of philosophy which explores the concepts of knowledge, truth and meaning is 'theory of knowledge', a sub-field of philosophy which has in general enjoyed a sense of autonomy and clearly demarcated its status and limits; and this seems to be the case with the philosophy of Buddhism, too.

But there are a few other interesting points in relation to Buddhism. The means of knowledge broadly fall into the two categories of reason and experience, experience again being sub-divided into sense experience and higher intuitive experience.[15] The use of reason and sense experience are generally within the scope of an average human being, but only those who have developed their intuitive skills can use that path to knowledge. The emergence of this kind of skill is not a mystery in Buddhism, it is the product of the kind of training a person undergoes. The Buddha lays down the path that a person should follow, the psychological and spiritual transformation necessary for the emergence of intuitive knowledge. In fact a better term than 'knowledge' to describe the emergence of such insights would be 'realisation'. This is an epistemological concept somewhat alien to current thinking in the west.

There is also an analysis of the forms of sensibility and the development of our conceptual structure which sounds like a facet of what is called genetic epistemology today. The worldly person's predilection and bondage to certain concepts limits his experience, and the higher forms of experience in Buddhism go beyond concepts and discursive reasoning. The limitations in the categories through which we seek knowledge are ultimately traced to craving and ignorance. This aspect of Buddhism cannot be neglected: 'Thus in its analysis of the concept, Buddhism does not stop at the linguistic or logical level, but delves deeper into its psychological main-springs.'[16] These aspects of Buddhism that cut across the established divisions of philosophical enquiry might turn out to be an interesting eye-opener to one in search of a new model of epistemology.[17] The methodological issues which are discussed in this chapter are also related to the field of epistemology.

THE THEORY OF REALITY

The nature of psychological phenomena cannot be completely separated from the underlying concept of reality in Buddhism. Questions pertaining to the structure of the universe and the nature of man raise significant issues relating to physical and moral as well as psychological phenomena. However, Buddhism distinguishes the several realms in which the laws of the universe operate: physical laws (*utu-niyāma*), biological laws (*bīja-niyāma*), psychological laws (*citta-niyāma*), moral laws (*kamma-niyāma*) and laws pertaining to spiritual phenomena (*dhamma-niyāma*). While all the laws (except the last) operate within their respective fields, the last cuts across all the realms. Thus the field of psychological phenomena is a distinctive area of study, but when necessary it has to be placed within the wider realm of the general principle of causality as such. These patterns of events are neither deterministic nor indeterministic but present themselves as probable tendencies rather than inevitable consequences.[18]

Though man's actions may be conditioned by some of these laws he is not determined by any one of them. In general the Buddha opposed all forms of determinism, whether natural determinism (*svabhāva-vāda*), theistic determinism (*issara-kāraṇa-vāda*), karmic determinism (*pubbekata-hetuvāda*), or any other philosophy in which these facets may be combined.

In general the Buddhist theory of causation offers a *via media* between the extremes of determinism and indeterminism. According to strict determinism the present and the past are unalterable, but the Buddha upholds a concept of free will according to which an individual may to a certain extent control the dynamic forces of the past and present and also the course of future events. Man has free will (*attakāra*) and personal endeavour (*purisa kāra*) and is capable of changing both himself and the environment. This concept of the possibility for action binds man's activity especially in the realms of moral, spiritual and psychological behaviour—an image of man that stands against the background of our psychological analysis in this work.[19]

Any student of Buddhism who is keen to pursue the Buddhist theory of reality would find a very rich source of material in the suttas, where the Buddha impartially analysed the structure and claims to truth of a variety of metaphysical theories which existed at the time. The 'net of theories' presented in the *Brahma-jāla Sutta* presents a systematic breakdown of all the metaphysical theories discussed by the Buddha. There were in fact six prominent thinkers with whom the Buddha had discussions and debates: Makkhali Gosāla, who was a theist, and upheld the view that the world was created and guided by the will of God; Ajita Kesakambali, a materialist, who maintained that man was annihilated at death and that there was no base for the development of a virtuous life; Sañjaya Belaṭṭhiputta, a sceptic who believed that certain basic notions like belief in an after-life and moral responsibility could not be rationally demonstrated or verified; Pūraṇa Kassapa, a natural determinist and thus unable to see any meaning in distinguishing between good and bad; Pakudha Kaccāyana, who attempted to explain the nature of reality in terms of discrete categories and is referred to as categoralist; and finally Nigaṇṭha Nātaputta, a relativist who saw some truth in every point of view.

The critical evaluation of such theories belongs to the two branches of philosophy referred to as epistemology and metaphysics (or better termed 'theory of reality'). But the various theories which are examined in such discussions are germane to the framework in which studies regarding ethical or psychological phenomena are pursued; for instance the concept of freewill is of central importance to ethics and the status and nature of causal laws is of great relevance in understanding psychological phenomena.

Apart from the study of causal laws, basic doctrines like those of impermanence (*anicca*), suffering (*dukkha*) and egolessness (*anattā*) colour the discussion of psychological states in Buddhism. In fact the doctrine of egolessness is the key to the understanding of the Buddhist psychological analysis presented in this work. In western thought today, studies pertaining to the framework in which mental concepts are charted fall within the recent offshoot of philosophy known as 'philosophical psychology'; and empirical psychology, too, may initiate a further sub-field of enquiry which could be called 'meta-psychology'. In the area of psychological therapy questions have been raised regarding the image and theory of man on which therapeutic systems rest. The psychology of Buddhism, too, is clearly based on a theory of man and the universe.

THE THERAPEUTIC BASIS OF BUDDHIST PSYCHOLOGY

The psychology of Buddhism is different from that of any field of psychological enquiry pursued for its own sake, for the Buddha pursued theoretical questions only when they had a bearing on the predicament of the suffering man. The psychology of Buddhism is primarily designed to answer the question What are the causes of suffering (*dukkha*) and what is the way out of it? The therapeutic basis of the psychology of Buddhism provides interesting analogies to the philosophy of Buddhism.

When Wittgenstein attempted a 'therapeutic analysis of specific logical disorders', he left aside their psychological roots as being outside the strict delineation of the problem according to his methodology. While Buddhist analysis of the logical structure of intellectual puzzlement may separate this from its psychological roots, the two aspects do supplement each other within an integrated whole. When the Buddha was confronted with a bewildering variety of theories and ideologies, he not only subjected each to careful analysis in the light of logical criteria and experiential data, but also supplemented this study by pointing to the deep psychological roots that fed such misconceived theories, remarking that desires feed metaphysical theories and metaphysical theories feed desires.

To cite an instance, when the Buddha examines the dogma of personal immortality, he examines the linguistic and the logical roots as well as the emotional roots of the eternalist view (*sassata diṭṭhi*). There were of course at least two good reasons for doing this: if we take the belief in a permanent pure ego as an example, logically it is possible to demonstrate certain inner contradictions, yet in real life, in spite of intellectual conviction, one may not get rid of the spell such a concept will continue to exert.

The Buddha also showed the futility of mere intellectual discussion beyond a certain point. Logical clarification is useful only as a preliminary step, for there are certain views which can have the appearance of rationality and yet be false.[20] After a process of logical clarification, one should develop the powers of self-analysis, mindfulness and penetrative insight (*paññā*). An understanding of the psychological basis of wrong beliefs arrived at in this way will help a person to control his desires, eradicate bias and develop the foundations of insight. It is at this stage that he will see the world in a new way and experience a 'transformation of perspective'.

It is necessary to stress again that the Buddha does not pursue logical, metaphysical or psychological problems for their own sake. In the *Cūla-Māluṅkya Sutta*[21] the Buddha compares the metaphysician to a person wounded by an arrow, who before being attended asks such questions as Who aimed the arrow? To what caste does he belong? Is he tall or short, dark or fair? What sort of arrow is that?, etc. If he went on raising questions of that sort without attending to his wound, wounded man would die; and the man who wants to get rid of suffering is compared to the man who has to heal his wound. In the *Devadahasutta*,[22] too, the Buddha is compared to a physician. But since the philosophy and the psychology of Buddhism are 'therapy oriented', the resemblance between the Buddha and the physician does not end there. While its philosophy offers a way out for the intellectually puzzled, its psychology offers therapy for the emotionally disturbed.

Within the context of modern psychology the word 'therapy' is often used in the restricted sense of techniques for treating mental illness. But, during the last few decades the framework of therapy has widened: the narrow gap between the mentally sick and the healthy has been questioned; whole societies have sometimes been sick and psychologists like Fromm refer to the pathology of normalcy; and increasing numbers fall prey to the milder forms of behaviour disorders.

These widening concepts of therapy and their point of contact with Asian religions have already been voiced in works like *Zen and Psychoanalysis*[23] and our own *Buddhist and Freudian Psychology*.[24] Fromm says that even the work of Freud was not merely therapy for the mentally sick, but was concerned with the liberation of man from irrational anxieties and compulsions. There has also been a significant shift of interest in the type of patient. As Fromm says: 'Psychoanalysis shifted its emphasis more and more from the therapy of the neurotic symptoms to a therapy of difficulties in living rooted in the neurotic character.[25] Today's psychologists are interested in even wider problems of adjustment and patterns of social pathology. The fact that people in the highly industrialised, affluent countries are haunted by inner emptiness, and a sense of alienation and of lack of direction in their routine lives has called for a widening of the concepts and goals of psychotherapy. In the light of this need and of the changing vision of sickness and health, the Buddhist concept of therapy deserves serious consideration.

The Buddha says that man is so constituted that his condition generates conflicts, discontent and anxiety, and the strong roots of greed, hatred and delusion that sustain man's proneness to anxiety will only be completely stilled and eliminated with the attainment of *nibbāna*; though man may suffer from physical diseases from time to time, mental diseases will prevail until the roots of passion, animosity and ignorance are eliminated. Buddhism's formula for helping free man from his inbuilt anxiety can be interpreted at two levels: the recluse who renounces the world will seek the high goal of utter quietude and peace; the householder who makes a compromise with living and would find a life of complete renunciation impossible or difficult will seek the ideal of harmonious and righteous living (*samacariyā*, *dhammacariyā*).

MAIN PROBLEM AREAS IN THE PSYCHOLOGY OF BUDDHISM

If we glance at some of the recognised schools of psychology in the west, it will be seen that certain problem areas are central to their focus of study and research: Gestalt psychology is *mainly* interested in perception, Freudian psychoanalysis in motivation and personality, and Behaviourism in learning.

Since a dominating concern of the psychology of Buddhism is the need to probe to the roots of human suffering and present a way out of it, the study of the psychology of motivation and emotions is a central focus of analysis for the doctrine. In fact, the discussion of psychological phenomena in this work will centre mainly on the triad of motivation, emotion and personality. We shall examine in detail the theory of motivation, the basic drives and instincts, the nature of unconscious motives and in general the affective and conative dimensions of behaviour. The psychology of cognition will be taken up in the following chapter as a prelude to the study of motivation.

Even in the pioneering work of Mrs Rhys Davids a reference is made to the dearth of studies of the analysis of emotions and instincts in Buddhism,[26] and the the study of personality is an equally neglected field. However, there is some difficulty in working out the psychology of personality in the doctrine. One important reason for this is that in Buddhism the material pertaining to the philosophy of the 'person' and the psychology of 'personality' is interwoven. Perhaps this is due to the centrality of the doctrine of egolessness (*anattā*) and its link with both the psychology of personality and the philosophical analysis of the person concept. The question has even been raised whether a philosophical system which denies a permanent self makes provision for a study of personality. While our discussions of the Buddhist concept of personality go some way towards clarifying this point, it may be mentioned that a 'dynamic psychology' like Buddhism could offer a congenial base for such a study.

The central study pertaining to motivation, emotions and personality will be concluded by presenting the therapeutic structure of Buddhist psychology in a comparative perspective; here the psychological features of Buddhist therapy are presented in terms of four systems: Freudian psychoanalysis, the Humanistic psychology of Rogers and Maslow, Existential therapy and Behaviour therapy.

SOURCES FOR THE STUDY OF BUDDHIST PSYCHOLOGY

This book is mainly concerned with the systematisation and interpretation of the psychological enquiries in early Buddhism. The original discourses of the Buddha which are in the Pāli language fall into two groups – the main teachings of the Buddha contained in the *sutta piṭaka* and the rules of discipline for the monks referred to as the *vinaya piṭaka*. Third, we get the systematic exposition of the *sutta piṭaka*, referred to as the *abhidhamma piṭaka* which was the work of later systematisers, and, although noteworthy for its psychological analysis, sometimes goes beyond the original discourses of the Buddha.

The *abhidhamma* – primarily an attempt to collect the material pertaining to psychological analysis in the light of the original discourses of the Buddha – [27] should fascinate students of psychology, but it is very important for the student first to make an independent study of the discourses of the Buddha contained in the *sutta piṭaka*. In fact, any person interested in studying the original doctrines of the Buddha is advised to go to the *sutta piṭaka* first. Most of it has been translated into English, and the material in this work is also primarily drawn from the *sutta piṭaka*.

The *sutta piṭaka* may be divided into five sections:

The *Dīgha Nikāya* (Dialogues of the Buddha)
The *Majjhima Nikāya* (Middle Length Sayings)
The *Samyutta Nikāya* (Kindred Sayings)
The *Aṅguttara Nikāya* (Gradual Sayings)
The *Khuddaka Nikāya* (Division of Small Works)

We have made an attempt to present the material in as simple and lucid a way as possible. It is also designed in such a way that the student who does not have a knowledge of the Pāli language will be able to pursue any facets of the psychology of Buddhism with the help of the English translations. Such a student may take to the study of Pāli if he is stimulated to make a closer study of the sources by this encounter with Buddhist thought. Though a degree of sophistication regarding the Buddhist doctrine may be an initial advantage in following the main themes presented here, a student with an elementary knowledge of Buddhism should be able to make his way through the final chapter. It is also expected that the idiom and the framework within which the material is presented will facilitate the communication of these ideas to students of psychology interested in the psychological reflections of the Buddha.

SOME METHODOLOGICAL ISSUES

The significance of a system of psychology is not only evaluated in terms of the problems it discusses, but also in terms of the methods it advocates to examine and verify the statements, hypotheses and theories it presents. In view of the nature of the source material we have outlined, what are the techniques the Buddha advocates for analysing and testing the theories and statements pertaining to psychological phenomena in the early Buddhist scriptures?

In the *Saṅgārava sutta* there is a reference to three groups of thinkers: (i) the traditionalists (*anussavikā*), (ii) the rationalists and metaphysicians (*takkī vīmaṃsī*), (iii) the experientialists, who have personal experience of higher knowledge.[28] The Buddha also says that he belongs to the third group. The criterion for judging the truth of a theory does not rest on mere tradition, the use of logic or speculative reason. It has to be tested by experience; experience of course is not mere sense experience but also intuition and insight. The weight of tradition, the use of logic and reason have their limits and an appeal to experience is necessary.

While the use of reason is a good corrective to accepting things on hearsay or on authority, mere reasoning based on logic is not a sufficient criterion for testing a belief. But when we say that the Buddha makes an appeal to experience, it has to be clearly stated what the Buddha means by the term 'experience'. Apart from the information obtained by the avenues of the five senses – of the eye, ear, nose, tongue and bodily contact – the Buddha also considers 'introspection' as one of the most valuable techniques for acquiring knowledge and developing insight. Introspection itself is a whole dimension of experience, ranging from 'looking into your own mind' to the more penetrating insights that emerge at various levels of spiritual development. Thus it must be emphasised that the acceptance of such a technique would clearly differentiate the psychology of Buddhism from a behaviourist methodology which rejects introspection. But even psychologies in the west which accept 'introspection' as a viable method, will not fall in line with a technique of introspection which culminates in spiritual insight; nevertheless, the use of introspection at a more mundane level at least will be common to both Buddhism and its western counterpart.

The use of 'self-analysis' for a closer and unbiased view of one's own emotional make-up is recommended in Buddhism. The value of introspection is discussed in the *Anumāna sutta*.[29] In this sutta there is a reference to the person whose mind is intractable, who is difficult to instruct and unable to listen to others; such a person is in the thrall of evil desires, wrathful, a fault-finder, reproves others, disparages others, etc. In this context continuous reflection about one's own mental qualities is recommended:

> That person who is of evil desires and who is in the thrall of evil desires, that person is displeasing and disagreeable to me; and, similarly, if I were of evil desires and in the thrall of evil desires, I would be displeasing and disagreeable to others.[30]

This technique is referred as a method where 'self ought to be reflected by self' and 'self ought to be measured against self'.[31]

If a person who is in the prime of life and fond of ornaments ponders on his own reflection in a mirror which is quite clean, the moment he sees a speck of dust he will get rid of it.[32] The person who uses introspection to eliminate evil mental states will similarly be quick in getting rid of them.[33]

The metaphor of the mirror to describe the use of introspection is also found in the advice to Rahula.[34] This concept of looking at oneself by reflecting upon one's mental states (*paccavekkhati*) is a method which is often advocated for getting a true picture of oneself. Introspection is a crucial method for the Buddha, since self-knowledge is a primary concern of Buddhist psychology. Introspection may be used for getting at more abstract truths: one can look into one's mind as for instance, David Hume did, and discover only a series of impressions, ideas and feelings rather than any permanent self.

In western psychology introspection is often considered an unreliable technique for studying mental phenomena, since our private experiences cannot be checked by others. According to the Buddha introspection can be cultivated methodically, biases can be eliminated and our powers of reflection refined. When the development of the mind is pursued in a methodical manner, it is possible to achieve extra-sensory powers such as telepathy and clairvoyance.[35] The development of introspection at the higher levels of meditation is considered as the test of objectivity:

> Just as one person should objectively observe another, a person standing should objectively observe another, a person standing should observe a person seated or a person seated or lying down, even so, should one's object of introspection be well apprehended, well-reflected upon, well-contemplated and well-penetrated with one's knowledge.[36]

Introspection is of course primarily a technique of therapy and there are two kinds of meditation recommended by the Buddha: *samatha* (tranquillity meditation) and *vipassanā* (insight meditation). This insight meditation is basically a technique which develops introspective insight. There is a significant discussion of this in the *Aṅguttara Nikāya*:

> If cultivated, what profit does calm [*samatha*] attain? The mind is cultivated. What profit results from a cultivated mind? All lust is abandoned. If introspection [*vipassanā*] be cultivated, what profit does it attain? Insight is cultivated. If insight be cultivated, what profit does it attain? All ignorance is abandoned. A mind defiled by lust is not free: nor can insight defiled by ignorance be cultivated. Indeed, monks, this ceasing of lust is the heart's release [*cettovimutti*], this ceasing of ignorance is the release by insight [*paññāvimutti*].[37]

Although introspection is a crucial technique within the psychology of Buddhism, there are also appeals to behavioural tests. At the time of the Buddha there were no developed laboratory techniques, but the value of personal experience in the light of test situations is accepted by him. There is a reference to four ways of knowing a person's character: by living together with a person one can find whether a person is consistent in his actions and if so whether he is a virtuous person; in the same manner a person's integrity can be tested by having dealings with him; and a person's fortitude can be tested in a crisis situation and his wisdom in conversation.[38] The way a person acts in a particular situation or a series of similar situations over a certain length of time gives us an indication of the character of a person. It is also said of the Buddha that his preaching and actions are consistent (*yathāvādi tathākāri*).

THE CONCEPT OF MIND

An attempt has already been made to relate the psychology of Buddhism to the philosophy of Buddhism and its primary task of diagnosing and alleviating human suffering. We have also referred to the main problem areas of Buddhist psychology and the nature of the source material used in discussing Buddhist psychological concepts, as well as describing briefly some of the methods of psychological analysis. We shall conclude this chapter by making a brief review of the Buddhist concept of mind, a concept which will always lie in the background of our study of the psychology of Buddhism.

The Buddha denies the existence of any permanent entity whether we describe it as mind or consciousness. What we refer to as mind is really a psycho-physical complex (*nāma-rūpa*). *Nāma* is used to refer to the four non-material groups (*khandhas*): these are *vedanā* (feeling), *saññā* (sense-impressions, images, ideas, concepts), *saṅkhāra*(conative activity, dispositions) and *viññāṇa* (consciousness). The term *rūpa* refers to the four great elements: extension, cohesion, heat, and the material shape derived from them. The mental and physical constitutents form one complex, and there is a mutual dependency of the mind on the body and of the body on the mind.

All mental phenomena have to be understood in the light of causal laws, since they are causally conditioned. The law of dependent origination (*paṭiccasamuppāda*) shows the conditionality of all physical and mental phenomena. While the theory of dependent origination shows that all mental phenomena are causally conditioned (*paticcasamuppanna*), the doctrine of egolessness (*anattā*) points towards the fact that neither within nor outside the mental and physical phenomena is there an abiding substance.

These two doctrines provide the foundation for understanding the Buddhist concept of mind:

> Dependent origination is the doctrine of the Conditionality of all physical and psychical phenomena, a doctrine which, together with that of Impersonality (*anattā*), forms the indispensable condition for the real understanding . . . of the teaching of the Buddha.[39]

In the explanation of phenomena the first takes a synthetic approach and the second an analytic approach: the dependent origination analysis shows the dependence and the interdependence of phenomena, while in the other analysis such constituents of the personality as feeling, ideas, sense-impressions, consciousness, volition etc., are revealed in their differentiating characteristics.

The mind according to Buddhist psychology is a dynamic continuum which extends to an innumerable number of births. It consists of both a conscious and an unconscious mind, the unconscious mind containing the residue of emotionally charged memories which extend beyond one life-span. The question whether there are such things as memories which go beyond one's childhood in this birth to other past births has of course come under experimental investigation today.[40] This is a significant facet of Buddhist psychology which has not been absorbed or accepted by the recognised schools of western psychology. It might be of interest to find out what exactly Freud tried to convey by the term 'the archaic heritage of man', and Jung by the term 'Collective Unconscious'.[41]

The nature of the mind as a dynamic continuum is explained in the suttas with the help of a number of analogies and metaphors. Sometimes it is referred to as a stream of consciousness (*viññāṇa sota*); sometimes it is compared to the movements of a monkey moving from one branch to another not letting go of one till he clutches another; it is also compared to a fire which will last only as long as the fuel lasts, and so on.

FOUR ASPECTS OF THE CONCEPT OF MIND

The four non-material groups (*nāma*) need some detailed clarification, for these concepts will be referred to again when discussing further aspects of the psychology of Buddhism in the succeeding chapters. Also, the meaning of the terms *viññāṇa*, *saṅkhāra*, *vedanā* and *saññā* is often coloured by shifts of context and emphasis, so it will be useful to sort out the strands of meaning at this point. Additionally, these four concepts are seen as being the key to a comprehensive grasp of the nature of mental phenomena in Buddhism. In fact, there are some scholars who have even compared the Buddhist analysis to the tripartite division of the mind into cognition, conation and affection, a concept which has come down the stream of western thought since the time of Aristotle. It is true that contemporary psychologists in the west consider this a highly simplified picture which does not do full justice to the complexity of psychological phenomena. But others, like J. C. Flugel, feel that it may be used, with some caution, for ordering the very complex nature of our experience.[42]

Scholars who find the tripartite functions useful in understanding the Buddhist concept of mind consider feeling (*vedanā*) as the affective dimension of experience, disposition and volition (*saṅkhāra*) as the contative dimension, and perception (*saññā*) and consciousness (*viññāṇa*) as the cognitive aspect.[43] While this may be a useful way of charting out the dimensions of psychological experience and behaviour, it may not be very safe to put absolute reliance on it. In a deeper sense all four mental *khandhas* are present in all states of consciousness and experience. Thus a mental factor like volition is not a separate entity but is inseparably associated with other factors. In this manner, the three dimensions of experience are the product of abstract analysis, whereas all three aspects are found in all states of consciousness and behaviour.

Vedanā, the feeling-component of our experiences, is considered to be of three types: pleasant, painful and neutral. Feelings are classified into bodily and mental feelings and they are also related to the sense organs. Pleasant feelings excite man's attachment to objects and rouse latent sensuous greed. Painful feelings excite latent anger and hatred. The saint who seeks to master passions has to eliminate three features connected with these feelings: the tendency to attachment in pleasant feeling, the tendency to revulsion in painful feelings, and the tendency to ignorance in neutral feeling.

There is also an interesting ethical dimension that runs through the analysis of feelings. The question is raised as to whether there are pleasurable states devoid of attachment. At this stage distinctions are made between the pleasures of domestic life and the pleasures of renunciation, the pleasures of the senses and the delight which emerges from meditational states, and so on. But feeling as a part of the five attachment groups (*pañca upādānak-khandha*), cannot be severed from the projections of the ego. Feelings arise in association with sensory stimulation and the conceptual activity of the mind.

As has been said, *saññā* as one of the four non-material groups is often rendered as 'perception'. While others render it as 'conceptual activity', it appears that a translation of the term to fit every context and all its manifestations is not possible. The term *saññā* is also divided into *patigha-saññā* and *adivacana-saññā*: Sanna that arises out of contact with the sense organ is described as *patigha-saññā*. *Adivacana-saññā* is of a nominal character and includes sense images and concepts. Perception can be of six kinds: of visual form, of sound, of smell, of taste, of bodily sensation and of images.

Feeling and perception take place only in relation to the senses (*indriyas*) and these exist only in the physical body. The two other concepts, *saṅkhāra* and *viññāṇa*, are rooted deeper in the flux of *bhava* or *samsāric* continuity, and they are in some sense the cause for that continuity. Thus the two terms occur both with reference to the five *khandhas* (aggregate or groups) as well as in relation to the law of dependent origination. *Saṅkhāra and viññāṇa* occur in the *pañca-upādanakkhandha* analysis in the narrow sense of those dispositions and in acts of consciousness which manifest themselves only so far as the body and mind are together. But they also have a deeper significance as links in the formula of dependent origination. In the course of the analysis of the nature of consciousness in the subsequent chapters we shall refer to the role of *viññāṇa* both in relation to its position as one of the five aggregates as well as in its role as a link in the wheel of dependent origination.

In the context of sense perception there is a reference to six kinds of consciousness: visual consciousness deriving from the eye and material shapes; auditory consciousness from the ear and sounds; olfactory consciousness from the nose and smells; gustatory consciousness from the tongue and tastes; bodily consciousness derived through the body and touching; and mental consciousness deriving from the mind and mental states.[44] *Viññāṇa* in these contexts may be rendered as cognitive consciousness.

In relation to the wheel of dependent origination *viññāṇa* is seen as an unbroken stream directed by the rebirth-producing *kamma*. Here *viññāṇa* is the total consciousness, which includes the conscious as well as residual mental events of the individual.

The term *saṅkhāra* is also used in relation to the five aggregates as well as the wheel of dependent origination. Though it is not wise to artificially identify the meaning of *saṅkhāra* with any specific usage, we can broadly discern certain types of contexts in which it occurs. As one of the aggregate some scholars feel that the concept of will is central to its meaning,[45] and as a link in the wheel of dependent origination it is often rendered as *karmic* formation.

As acts of volition *saṅkhāra* and *viññāṇa* may be conscious or unconscious, and they include all reflexes and dispositions, these being of three kinds: *kāya* – bodily reflexes and such dispositions as breathing and walking; *vacī* – verbal reflexes and dispositions; *mano* – ideational reflexes and dispositions. Apart from these usages, *saṅkhāra* is also used to convey the idea that something is conditioned: for instance, that all phenomenal existence is conditioned. This meaning is found in the saying, 'all formations are impermanent' (*sabbe saṅkhāra aniccā*).

As has been said, the term *saṅkhāra* cannot be translated by a single term which will cover all its usages. However, the concept of volition forms a significant strand in its meaning, and in the suttas, the words *cetanā* and *saṅkhāra* are used synonymously.[46] Another interesting feature of the concept of *saṅkhāra* is that it combines the notion of deliberation concomitant with habit. As one of the *khandhas* some of the contexts emphasise the idea of deliberation and volition, whereas its use as a link in the wheel of dependent origination emphasises the factors of dynamism, habit and disposition. Finally it must again be said that both *viññāṇa* and *saṅkhāra* have varying contextual usages. They cannot be reduced to any single meaning, and only some of the psychologically interesting jobs performed by those concepts are being explored here.

2 The Psychology of Cognition

The senses are the channels through which we come into contact with the external world. But they are not merely the avenues through which we derive information as to what takes place in the outer world; they are also the avenues through which man's desires and passions may be excited. It is by the control of the sense organs (*indriyasaṁvara*) that a person can master his desires. When a person is able to control his sense organs, he will remain unaffected by sensory stimuli and indifferent to them, whether they be pleasant or unpleasant.[1]

It is also possible that the perception of objects in the external world is influenced by our desires and interests. If our 'perception' of objects is influenced by our desires it would be necessary to train our senses to see these objects as *they are* rather than project on to them what is really not there. If this is the case, sensory knowledge is shot through with our categories, concepts, constructs of the imagination, etc. The Buddha does not say like the idealist that the external world is a mere creation of the imagination. Rather, while accepting the reality of the sensory process, it is pointed out that to a great degree our perceptions are mixed with the non-sensory conceptual and imaginative components. The Buddha is making two significant points here: first, he is saying that we should not be excited by sensory stimuli and our passions and attachments should be restrained; he is also saying that even our perception of objects and our response to sensory stimuli are shot through with our psychological make-up. There is a clear link between the psychology of motivation and the psychology of perception in the narrow sense, or cognition in the broader sense.

The link between the sensory process and the enjoyment of the pleasures of the senses is presented in a number of contexts:

> if there were not this satisfaction that comes from the eye, beings

> would not lust after the eye. But in as much as there is satisfaction in the eye, therefore beings lust after it.
>
> If misery, brethren, pertained not to the eye beings would not be repelled by the eye. But in as much as there is misery in the eye, beings are repelled by it.[2]

Thus it may be said that there are certain types of contexts where the process of sense perception is discussed: contexts where people are admonished not to fall victim to sensual pleasures and those where the causal process of sense perception is described as it is; of the latter type of context, some describe the sensory process using the vocabulary of realism, of the perceptual given, others describe it as a composite and synthetic activity. A look at the nature of sense perception as a synthetic process will invariably take us to non-sensory cognitive factors. Finally, some of the limitations of the normal cognitive functions will take us to the role of extra-sensory perception in the psychology of Buddhism. We shall examine these facets of the psychology of cognition in relation to the material found in the discourses of the Buddha.

The *Middle Length Sayings* present the emergence of perception in this manner: when the eye that is internal is intact and external visible forms come within its range, and when there is an appropriate act of attention on the part of the mind, there is the emergence of perceptual consciousness.[3] Thus visual cognition is a causal process depending on three factors: an unimpaired sense organ, external visible forms and an act of attention. Here the term used for cognition is *viññāṇa*.[4] This process is not only true of the eye (*cakkhu*) but is similarly seen in the case of the ear (*sota*) nose (*ghāṇa*), tongue (*jivhā*) body (*kāya*) and mind (*mano*). In the psychology of Buddhism, the mind is a further sense-organ, in addition to the other five.

It is also said that the six forms of perception are grounded in the 'diversity of elements': The question is asked 'What brethren, is the diversity of elements?' To this question it is replied:

> The element of eye, of visible object, of eye awareness;
> the element of ear, of sound, of ear awareness;
> the element of nose, of odour, of nose awareness;
> element of tongue, of taste, of tongue awareness;
> element of body, of tangibles, of body awareness;

> the elements of mind, of ideas, of mind awareness;
> this brethren is called the diversity of elements.[5]

It is also said that the variety of sensory responses is due to the diversity of elements and the emergence of a diversity of feelings is due to the diversity of elements. It is also negatively said that the variety of sensory responses does not depend on the diversity of feelings nor the diversity of elements on the diversity of sensory responses. The elements here provide a relatively objective basis for the sensory process.

It is also said of the sense organs that they are different in range and pasture and do not react to the pasture and range of one another. However, in this context the mind is considered as the repository of the impressions obtained from the five other senses.[6]

There are other contexts where there is an emphasis on the synthetic nature of the perceptual activity. In these contexts the Buddha advocates that one should eliminate the biases and proclivities which underlie normal perception. Johansson presents this point of view well:

> Perception and thinking is in the ordinary person not altogether realistic and objective. There are usually some distortions from the needs (you exaggerate what you *want* to see) and defence mechanisms (a fact that is flattering to you is seen as more important).[7]

In the arahant these unrealistic influences are not present and it is said that he sees the world as it is: 'Then, Bahiya, thus must you train yourself: In the seen, there will be just the seen; in the heard, just the heard; in the sensed, just the sensed; in the cognized, just the cognized.'[8]

The classical context in which the synthetic nature of perceptual activity is presented is the *Madhupiṇḍikasutta*. This sutta avoids the usual stereotyped formula in which the emergence of perception is presented. The common form in which it is found can be seen in this passage:

> Because of sight and material objects visual consciousness arises, meeting of the three is contact; feeling is conditioned by contact, craving, by feeling; grasping is conditioned by craving and becoming by grasping.[9]

Here are the relevant lines from the *Madhupiṇḍikasutta*:

> Visual consciousness, your reverence, arises because of the eye and material shapes; the meeting of the three is sensory impingement; feelings are because of sensory impingement; what one feels one perceives; what one perceives one reasons about; what one reasons about obsesses one; what obsesses one is the origin of a number of concepts and obsessions which assail a man in regard to material shapes cognizable by the eye.[10]

Ñāṇananda in his *Concept and Reality* considers this passage as central to his interpretation of the process of perception: 'This passage indicates that "*papañca*" signifies the final stage in the process of sense-cognition. The term definitely concerns the grosser conceptual aspect of the process, since it is a consequent to "*vitakka*" (reasoning) and presupposes language.[11]

If the imagination of the ignorant 'runs riot', as Ñāṇananda says, the apparently simple sensory process results in distorted end-products. This may be an exaggerated way of saying that one's perception of material objects is shot through with one's psychological nature. But it must be mentioned that here the perceptions of the ordinary man are contrasted with those of the arahant, who 'sees the world as it is'.

This sort of concept is not alien to the west, for similar positions are found in the idealist philosophical traditions. However, as was mentioned earlier, there are contexts which fall within a relatively realistic framework of sense perception.

We feel that both 'realism' and 'idealism' as modes of emphasis and models of communication are found in the analysis of the psychology of perception. In moments of deep philosophical analysis the phenomenalistic mode, too, is used: the phenomenalistic mode discusses experience in terms of sensory phenomena (sense data) without raising questions about their reality or unreality.

In the end the sensory process has to be analysed not merely in terms of 'cognition', but also in relation to the 'passions' it excites:

> He meets with Ill, brethren, who hath not tamed
> The sixfold impact of the sphere of sense.
> They who have learned the mastery of these,
> With faith for comrade, – they dwell free from lust.
> Beholding with the eye delightful things

Or things unlovely, let him restrain his bent
To lust for loveliness, and let him not
Corrupt his heart with thoughts of 'O 'tis dear'.

And when, again, sounds sweet or harsh he hears,
Not led astray by sweetness, let him check
The error of his senses. Let him not
Corrupt his heart with thoughts of 'O 'tis sweet'.

If some delightful fragrance meet the nose,
And then again some foul malodrous stench,
Let him restrain repugnance for that stench,
Nor yet be led by lust for what is sweet.

Should he taste savours that are sweet and choice,
And then again what's bitter to the tongue,
He should not greedily devour the sweet,
Nor yet show loathing for the bitter taste.

By pleasure's impact not inebriate,
Nor yet distracted by the touch of pain,
To pain and pleasure both indifferent
Let him be free from likings and dislikes.

Obsessed (by lusts) are others: so obsessed
They know and so they fare. But he dispells
All the world's vulgar fashionings of mind,
And treads the path renunciation – bound.

By contact of these six, if mind be trained,
The heart is never shaken any more.
O'ercome these two, O brethren, lust and hate
Pass ye beyond the bounds of birth and death.[12]

THE VOCABULARY OF COGNITIVE TERMS

We have already presented the framework within which the psychology of perception is discussed by the Buddha. There are however some key terms which figure prominently in the analysis both of the process perception and of cognition in general. As the usage and the meanings given to these terms colour our understanding of the psychology of cognition, it will be necessary to have a brief look at some of these terms.

Viññāṅa and *saññā* are two terms that figure prominently in the analysis of the causal process that underlies the perception of material objects. Let us have a close look at a Pāli passage which describes the process of perception:

> *Ajjhattikañ ce āvuso cakkhuṃ aparibhinnaṃ hoti bāhirā ca rūpā na āpathaṃ āgacchanti no ca tajjo samannāhāro hoti, n'evatāva tajjaassa viññāṇabhāgassa pātubhāvo hoti.*[13]

Horner translates this passage to mean that even if the 'eye that is internal is intact but external material shapes do not come within its range and there is no appropriate impact, there is no appearance of the appropriate section of consciousness'.[14]

This passage really describes the conditions of cognition: (i) the eye as the organ of sight; (ii) external form that comes within the field of vision; (iii) an act of attention. It is when all these conditions are satisfied that we see the emergence of the cognitive process. The same may be said about the other sense organs. In this context the word *viññāṇa* has a cognitive import and is really a reference to the emergence of cognitive consciousness.

Attempts have been made to distinguish between the use of the word in contexts of this sort with that of the term *saññā*. It has been observed that in the context of the psychology of perception, *viññāṇa* be rendered as 'perception' and *saññā* as the conceptual activity which absorbs ideas, images and concepts.[15] Though an analysis of this sort helps us to place *viññāṇa* and *saññā* on the lines of the classical Humean distinction between sense-impressions and ideas,[16] a study of the wide variety of the contexts in the discourses of the Buddha suggests that it is difficult to abstract such a tidy distinction.

It appears that while it is difficult to give a translation of these terms to fit into all contexts, some of the meanings attached to these terms may be given: *viññāṇa* – acts of cognition, consciousness, total consciousness including conscious as well as residual mental events of the individual: *saññā* – ideas, mental images, impressions, etc.

VITAKKA

Apart from the knowledge gained through the avenue of the sense organs, the psychology of thinking deserves close study. It has to be discussed against the background of Buddhist epistemology, which examines questions pertaining to the valid means of knowledge. In discussing the methodological issues in the last chapter we mentioned that reasoning and sense and extra-sensory experience are the means of knowledge, and also that there are certain limits to the use of reasoning as well as of sense-experience. However much these two instruments of knowledge are sharpened, they have limitations. Some limitations are logical limitations; for instance just by pure reason you cannot prove the existence of a material object, and appeal to the sensory data will always be probable. Psychologically, as ordinary men, our powers of reasoning and experience are subject to varying levels of ignorance (*avijjā*).

Vitakka is the general term in the suttas for what we popularly mean by the word 'thinking'. Without the prefix (*vi*) the word *takka* means logical and dialectical reasoning. *Vicāra*, another term often used with *vitakka*, conveys the persistence of discursive thinking in man. As the role of such discursive thinking has limitations, it is superseded at the third stage of *samādhi* (concentration).

There are other cognitive terms closer to the dimension of meditative reflection, such as *pacchavekkhati*, *sati* and *sampajāna*. The word *pacchavekkhati* refers to continuous introspective reflection. The word stems from the vocabulary of vision and is compared to optical reflection. The Buddha's words of advice to Rahula describe the implications of the term: 'What is the use of a mirror?' 'To reflect, lord.' 'Even so must we reflect, and reflect in all our work of body, speech or thought, namely, This that I would do, will it be harmful to myself, or others'.[17] In the way that a mirror is used to look at the blemishes of the face, so should one look at one's psychological traits and qualities.

Words like *sati* (mindfulness) and *yoniso manasikāra* (wise attention) convey the development of one's powers of introspection and clarity, and lucidity of thought. Mrs Rhys Davids says:

> *Sati*, an important term in Buddhist ethical training, is not wholly covered by memory, and is on the whole, best rendered by mindfulness, inasmuch as it denotes rather the requisite condition for efficient remembrance, or thought of any kind, namely, lucidity and alertness of consciousness.[18]

Other compounds of this term, such as *anussati*, are used for reiterated recollection and *patissati* for vivid reinstatement.[19] *Sampajañña* is a word for clear consciousness (whereas *asampajañña* implies a lack of awareness). It is the development of these powers of introspection and methodical mental culture that provides the base for the development of higher cognitive powers.

HIGHER KNOWLEDGE

Verbal testimony, analogical reasoning, logical reasoning, etc., are not completely satisfactory as means of knowledge. Perceptions, both normal and paranormal, along with inferences based on them, are the valid means of knowledge in Buddhism.[20] *Dassana* is used to refer to visual as well as to extra-sensory perception. The term *ñāṇa-dassana* is used to denote the 'knowledge and insight of salvation' (*vimutti-ñāṇadassana*) as distinct from knowledge of things as they are (*yathābhūta-ñāṇadassana*).

Against the background of western psychology, where concepts are delineated in terms of experimental techniques, is it possible to give a meaningful rendering of the psychological bases of the concept of higher knowledge or paranormal cognitive powers?

The strongest arguments for the non-metaphysical nature of these concepts have been presented by K.N. Jayatilleke, who says: 'Early Buddhism should therefore be regarded not as a system of metaphysics but as a verifiable hypothesis discovered by the Buddha in the course of his "trial and error" experiment'.[21] Jayatilleke's argument is that the Buddha tried out various techniques which were current at the time – penance, self-mortification, avoidance and seclusion – and then evolved his own.[22] Jayatilleke also feels that the development of higher powers was not something mysterious but a natural development of certain potentials within man. It was also not a sudden emergence of a mysterious power but a gradual development. The gradual development is traced to the three stages of *sīla* (morality), *samādhi* (concentration) and *paññā* (spiritual knowledge). As an experiment this involves a person's whole life time, and the testing of the hypothesis involves a certain personal commitment. Western psychology with its own methodological framework will find it difficult to absorb a hypothesis of this sort.

The field of extra-sensory perception accepted by the Buddha has, of course, interested certain psychologists in the west and they are making attempts to clarify their position in the light of recent experimental work. The Buddha has accepted the following forms of knowledge in the suttas: psychokinesis, clairaudience, telepathic knowledge, retrocognitive knowledge, clairvoyance, and, finally, destruction of the defiling impulses.[23]

Anyone exploring the psychology of cognition in Buddhism cannot omit these higher reaches of the mind. But the psychology of cognition in relation to higher knowledge lacks an idiom through which it can be communicated to the West. Our discussion in this volume will therefore be directed more to the analysis of the psychology of behaviour as commonly encountered in every day life, and the study of motivation, emotion, personality development and therapy will be worked out within that dimension. Johansson's work on the psychology of the supra-mundane should prove to be a useful supplement to our work, especially for those who are anxious to understand the psychology of the transcendental.[24]

COGNITION AND MOTIVATION

The psychology of cognition cannot be separated from the study of motivation. It may be a good idea to remind ourselves again that the main objective of the Buddha in analysing the psychology of the human mind was to uncover the main springs of human suffering and search out ways in which to alleviate it. Delusion is one of the roots of human discontent and right beliefs are a very important part of the eightfold path. This requires one to sharpen and refine one's cognitive faculties, whether they relate to sensory cognition, thinking, memory, imagination or knowledge gained through insight.

Man's desires influence his cognitive powers and his cognitions have an impact on his desires. There is both a cognitive and emotional component to man's suffering, and these arise from his craving and ignorance:

> There are, in fact, two tap-roots from which existence and, with it, suffering spring: craving (*taṇhā*) and ignorance (*avijjā*). To weaken them first and finally eradicate them is the difficult task before us which, however, we can face courageously if guided by the methods of the Dhamma which are realistic as well as radical.[25]

Craving is related to the root causes *rāga* (passion) and *dosa* (hatred), whereas ignorance is related to the root cause *moha* (delusion).

In the therapeutic situation we get two character types, one dominated by a craving temperament (*rāga carita*) and the other by the deluded temperament (*diṭṭhicarita*). Therapeutically, 'quiet' is advocated for the man bound to craving and 'insight' for the man cloaked in 'ignorance'. Lack of control and restraint as well as lack of awareness and knowledge of one's motives are responsible for tensions and discontent. The emphasis on the unguarded senses and the need for restraint brings out the importance of the motivational aspect, and emphasis on insight and self-knowledge brings out the significance of cognition.

This analysis throws an interesting light on to the higher reaches of knowledge which we have discussed. The *Dīghanikāya*[26] makes a reference to seven types of person; and mention is made of the different ways in which people obtain freedom: Those freed both ways (*ubhatobhāga-vimutto*), those freed by insight (*paññā-vimutto*), and those freed by faith (*saddhā-vimutto*). 'Freed both ways' really refers to the combination of *paññāvimutti* and *cetovimutti*. *Cetovimutti* is derived from calm (*samatha*), which is the calming down of the passions, *paññāvimutti* is derived from *vipassanā* (insight) and is the ceasing of ignorance.

This would suggest a significant link between the psychology of cognition and that of motivation. Buddhism has been misunderstood as a system of psychology which advocates the 'cutting off' of the senses. In the *Discourse on the Development of the Senses* (*Indriyabhāvanāsutta*),[27] the Buddha says if he lays down the mere cutting down of the senses, then a blind man or a deaf man could achieve his ideal. Rather he advocates the training of the senses, so that external stimuli will not disturb them. The Buddha does not teach the atrophy of the senses, but their development and refinement. Here is a passage from the suttas which describes the control of the senses well:

> Eye, ear, nose, tongue and body, and also the mind, if a bhikku keep the gates guarded well, in eating with restraint and control, in the sense faculties he meets with ease, with ease of body and with ease of mind. With a body that does not burn, with a mind that does not burn, he lives at ease by day and night.[28]

COGNITION AND THERAPY

The analysis of the psychology of motivation, emotions and personality in this work will be concluded with a description of the therapeutic framework of the psychology of Buddhism, for this dominates and directly colours the role of man's cognitive functions.

Both our emotional and our intellectual lives are coloured by the limited perspectives from which we view phenomena. It is said that partiality, enmity, stupidity and fear are the causes of evil actions.[29] Both strong emotions and dogmatic adherence to a 'view' prevent a person from getting a clear enough picture of an object to be able to discern its true nature, whether that object be a material one, a psychological quality within oneself or in someone else, or a significant social or historical event which needs to be examined.

To *see* without prejudice, without partiality and uninfluenced by personal interest is a difficult task. Our minds are cloudy and disturbed, we are the slaves of strong dispositions which cannot be easily broken. To break completely through such limitations calls for the gradual elimination of the obstructing factors. The Buddha has clearly said that both the emergence of proper insight as well as the non-emergence of insight are causally conditioned. What are the factors responsible for the non-emergence of insight? According to the teachings of the Buddha there are two ways of achieving spiritual development: through tranquillity and through insight. There are five factors that disturb the development of tranquillity, and it is only when these are cleared away that the powers of meditation can be developed. According to the suttas, these five factors (sense desire, ill will, sloth and torpor, restlessness and worry, and sceptical doubt) condition our ability to see things as they are and in their wholeness. Along with the elimination of these impediments, the Buddha recommends the seven factors of enlightenment which foster knowledge and insight, namely: mindfullness (*sati*), investigation of the law (*dhamma*), energy (*vīriya*), rapture (*pīti*), tranquillity (*passaddhi*), concentration (*samādhi*) and equanimity (*upekkhā*).

In this connection, K. N. Jayatilleke observes:

> We note here the operation of a causal process. The elimination of the impediments makes the mind concentrated in meditation and this in turn makes it possible for it to have knowledge and insight of things as they are (*yathā-bhūtañāṇadassanaṃ*).[30]

He also points out a statement from the suttas: 'mental concentration is the cause of knowing and seeing things as they are'.[31]

Now it may be observed that while the psychology of Buddhism speaks of these higher reaches of mind, the term 'cognition' is used in a different way when it occurs in, for instance, a textbook on psychology; so that it becomes extremely difficult at this point to convey the Buddhist concepts of 'insight' and 'understanding' within the idiom and the technical vocabulary of western psychology. Johansson, too, who raises the same issue, finds an analogical resemblance in the Gestalt concept of intuition, which he sees as an act of understanding when the structure of things become clear:

> The Gestalt psychology of our time has recognized that the laws of thinking are very similar to the laws of perception and that they may perhaps be derived from the latter. In the same way, *paññā* is sometimes described as a process similar to visual perception, and indeed, *paññā* and *ñāna* are often combined with verbs like *passati* (see).[32]

There is a passage in the suttas which conveys the kind of analogical resemblance which he cites:

> Monks, it is like a pure, limpid, serene pool of water in which a man with vision standing on the bank might see oysters and shells, also gravel and pebbles, and shoals of fish are moving about and keeping still.[33]

It is in this manner that a monk comprehends the nature of anguish, 'as it is'.

However, in the final analysis, it is difficult to grasp the concept of higher knowledge in terms of the analysis of perception. The psychological processes that operate in the emergence of higher knowledge are different from those of visual perception.

The ability to transcend partial and biased viewpoints had a certain immediate significance to the Buddha, who attempted to make his way through the jungle of metaphysical theories that pervaded the intellectual horizons of his time. He condemned the dogmatic adherence to views of people who thought that only they had found the truth. This type of dogmatic adherence to partial intellectual standpoints, ideologies and life perspectives is not limited to individuals. There can be 'collectively oriented' groups who accept dogmatic viewpoints, and since such people sometimes feel that they are fighting for ends which transcend the individual, things can take a rather militant turn.

The futility of such ideological battles has been graphically presented in the *Alagaddūpama sutta* (The *Snake Simile*).[34] Here the man who does not have a correct grasp of the doctrine is compared to the man who does not hold the water-snake properly. If a man goes in search of a water-snake and after seeing it takes hold of it by the coil or the tail, the water-snake will turn round and bite him, thus bringing about his destruction. He who holds it properly is like the man who has an intuitive and correct grasp of the doctrine (*dhamma*). Thus, quite apart from wordy warfare with people who have rival doctrines, even within one's own doctrine dogmatism is to be discouraged. The man engulfed in purely intellectual battles is compared to the man who carries the raft on his head, when it was only meant for crossing the river.

The claim that the 'cognitions' of a group mind can be distorted is interesting, whether we are dealing with nations, small groups or mobs. Instead of falling prey to the stereotyped cognitive structures built up over the years, it is necessary to break through any forms of collective ignorance and prejudice.

The Buddha himself first cut himself away from the tangled network of interpersonal relations and the masks and mirrors of his own society, and in seclusion refined his powers of insight to 'see' things afresh and clearly. It was after he had cleared his own mind and found a technique of doing so, a technique which could be recommended to others, that he came back to society to present the *dhamma*. It was then that he described the man free of the tangle of partial viewpoints:

> There are no knots for him loosed from surmise,
> There are no errors for the wisdom freed:
> But they who both surmise and view accept,
> They wayfare in the world at odds with folk.[35]

The refinement of man's cognitive powers which we have discussed, whether of perception, thinking, introspection or para-normal insight, are in this manner presented within the framework of the psychology of a therapy. Their implications can be developed in relation to the external world, as well as in the area of self-knowledge, perception of others and understanding the workings of the group mind. The psychology of cognition has a central place in the system of therapy advocated by the Buddha.

3 Motivation and Emotions

The term 'motivation' is a general one that covers three aspects of behaviour: states that motivate behaviour, behaviour motivated by these states and the goals of such behaviour. All three aspects may be regarded as stages in a cycle. Hunger as a motivational state would impel a person to seek food, appropriate behaviour which is instigated by this need would be the seeking of means to attain the end, and the alleviation of hunger would be the final goal. The motivation cycle then terminates until the need for food emerges again.[1] Thus terms like need, want, motive, drive, etc., refer to some inner condition of the organism that initiates and directs its behaviour towards a goal. Some of the goals are of a positive nature, goals that individuals approach; others of a negative nature, which individuals try to avoid. Where the motivating states have a clear physiological base, the goals are relatively fixed – as in the need for sleep or food – whereas there will be a greater degree of flexibility and variation in the case of the desire for fame, status, position, etc.

In this chapter, we hope to examine and analyse the early Buddhist theory of motivation. Most of the significant theories of motivation are the result of a need to examine and explain a sense of puzzlement relating to some facet of human behaviour. The focus of the philosophical and psychological investigations of the Buddha being the predicament of human suffering (*dukkha*), Buddhist psychology of motivation is directly concerned with the factors that lead to human unrest, tension, anxiety and suffering in general. The psychological analysis found in the discourses of the Buddha, especially in relation to motivation, is deeply embedded in the desire to uncover the roots of unrest and to depict a positive path towards happiness. In this sense, the framework of the psychology of motivation in Buddhism is therapeutic. As has already been said in the west today, the word 'therapy' is used in a general sense to mean methods of treating mental sickness, while in the Buddhist context it refers to the deeper predicament of unrest and psychological conflict. The psychological ditch between the therapeutically 'wholesome' and 'unwholesome' cuts through the whole structure of motivational theory in Buddhism.

The unending nature of the motivation cycle is emphasised by the Buddha in a number of contexts. Desires find temporary satisfaction, but they surge up again and again, sometimes seeking new objects of exploration. In fact, the Pāli word *taṇhā* (craving) etymologically connotes 'thirst', and the metaphor of thirst can well be applied to the diverse manifestation of desires that spring from the root greed.

The basic springs of motivation are accordingly analysed into three wholesome roots (*kusala mūla*) and three unwholesome ones (*akusala mūla*); of the unwholesome roots, *lobha* rendered as greed or lust, generates the positive 'approach desires'; *dosa* generates the 'avoidance desires' in the form of hatred and resentment; and *moha*, rendered as delusion, creates confusion in the mind.[2] While the unwholesome springs of action generate unrest and conflict, their opposites charity (*alobha*), compassionate love (*adosa*) and wisdom (*amoha*) lead to inner happiness within the individual and harmony at the interpersonal level. Within this framework the Buddha focuses attention more on the drives with a clear psychological orientation and less on those with a clear physiological base. Even in the case of certain basic physiological needs, under certain circumstances a need could take the form of a greed. When basic needs go beyond their biological function and take possession of the whole personality, such obsessions and attachments overpower man and cripple his personality. However, the bulk of the discourses are devoted to analysing the psychologically oriented drives; for instance, man's acquisitive drive to amass wealth, hoard and possess it, his inordinate ambition for power and desire to outdo others, sexual infatuation, and in general all those pseudo-life-styles which in the long run create human misery and discontent. The Buddha does not analyse the needs and desires of man for its own sake, but rather in terms of the valuational structure which generates and directs the satisfaction of human drives.

According to the psychology of motivation in Buddism, the approach desires generated by greed take a dual form – the drive for self-preservation (*bhava-taṇhā*) and the drive for sensuous gratification (*kāma-taṇhā*) — while the avoidance desires like hatred generate the drive for annihilation and aggressive tendencies (*vibhava-taṇhā*). Though needs like thirst, hunger and sleep can be explained in terms of self-preservation, *bhava-taṇhā* is also linked with the need for self-assertion, power, fame, wealth, recognition, etc. The drive for sensuous gratification goes beyond genital or sexual pleasure, and explains the need for excitement, diversion, exposure to novel stimuli and a wide variety of other pleasures. The drive for annihilation involves aggressive behaviour, suicide and violent short-cuts to remove painful stimuli. Needs like affection, love and sympathy have to be analysed in the light of situation and context. There are clear cases of altruistic loving kindness, compassion and sympathetic joy, but they have to be differentiated from quasi-sexual love, expressions of worldly sorrow, attachment and possessive love, and tender emotions with an ambivalent affective tone. A certain degree of semantic study and persistent self-analysis is necessary to differentiate between 'love' and 'lust'.

The arousal of these drives to activity is due to stimuli in the sensory field or at the ideational level. Such a stimulus excites a person's feelings. Pleasant feelings (*sukhavedanā*)and painful feelings (*dukhavedanā*) are affective reactions to sensations. Thus, due to the stimulation of the five sense organs and the mind organ, there result six kinds of feelings based on eye-impressions, ear-impressions, body-impressions, nose-impressions, mouth-impressions and mind-impressions. These feelings have a certain hedonic tone which differentiates them into pleasant (*sukha*), painful (*dukkha*) or indifferent (*adukkhayasukha*) experiences. Pleasant feelings stimulate the impulse towards pleasure-giving objects, and thus the drive for sensuous gratification is kindled. Pleasurable experiences also stabilise the yearning for continued existence and thus feed the desire for self-preservation. Painful feelings can arouse a sense of resentment (*paṭigha*) and thus feed the drive for aggression and annihilation. Thus we see that feeling is conditioned by contact and craving is conditioned by feeling.

The objects of pleasure are referred to as, 'delightful, dear, passion-fraught and inciting to lust'.[3] When a person's passions are roused by oncoming stimuli, clinging (*upādanā*), which is conditioned by craving, emerges and the object of pleasure is held on to tenaciously. Unless clinging persists, excitation of the sense organs is not sufficient to rouse the individual to activity. In the context of painful sensations, *upādānā* may be more correctly rendered as 'entanglement' rather than 'clinging', referring to an obsession with what we like as well as what we dislike.

Apart from the notion of 'entanglement', there are other concepts which account for the persistence of certain patterns of behaviour.

Our attitudes and beliefs which have been formed in the past influence our present reactions to oncoming stimuli, and these attitudes are often rooted in dynamic personality traits. According to the Buddha, these attitudes are not the result of deliberation at a conscious level, but emerge on deep-rooted and dormant proclivities referred to as *anusaya*.

Pleasurable feelings induce an attachment to pleasant objects, for they rouse latent sensuous greed (*rāgānusaya*); painful feelings rouse latent anger and hatred (*paṭighānusaya*). The 'approach desires' emerge on the root greed and excite the *rāgānusaya*; the 'avoidance desires' emerge on the root hate and excite the *paṭighānusaya*. The root 'delusion' is related to leaning and to attachment to one's ego, which finds direct expression in the latent proclivity towards conceit and ignorance (*diṭṭhi-mānānusaya*). It is only when the three roots of unwholesome behaviour are properly comprehended and the addiction to these latent manifestations of attachment, hatred, conceit and ignorance eliminated, that a person is regarded as an 'end-maker of anguish'.[4]

While we have discussed some of the psychological mechanisms with reference to the *arousal* and *persistence* of motivational states in relation to springs of motivation such as greed, hatred and delusion, the diverse forms of activity in relation to the *direction* of behaviour are also of significance. These are often discussed in the context of morals and ethical reflections. Facets of ideational (*mano*), vocal (*vacī*) and bodily (*kāya*) behaviour rooted in greed, hatred and delusion are discussed in ethical contexts, as what a person should not do; and forms of behaviour rooted in non-greed, non-hatred and non-delusion are prescribed as what a person ought to do. For instance, assaults on others, stealing, sexual misconduct, harsh speech, covetousness and wrath are forms of behaviour which are unwholesome, while kindness to animals, nursing the sick, charity, self-restraint, truthfulness, etc., are the kinds of activities recommended for the man bent on leading a virtuous life.

In general, if we take a bird's-eye view of the discussion of the ramifications of human behaviour, the Buddha at times analyses actual situations, at others possible situations, and sometimes specifies which actions are suitable and which unsuitable. This link between the ethical and the psychological cuts across the analysis of psychological phenomena in Buddhism.

Apart from the specific forms of behaviour which can be traced to the six motivational roots, there are life-perspectives and character types that can be analysed against the background of motivational theory. The way of sensuality and the way of self-mortification are both life-perspectives condemned by the Buddha, for they emerge on unwholesome roots and are a manifestation of craving; while the way of sensuality is a clear manifestation of craving, the way of self-mortification is a subtle manifestation of displaced craving. Since the way of sensuality has been condemned by the Buddha as leading to unrest, tension and boredom, some people go to the opposite extreme and follow the way of self-mortification. The deliberate attempt to live through painful experiences and the technique for burning up the effects of *karma*[5] has been criticised by the Buddha in his discourses on the philosophy of the Jains. The way of the Buddha goes beyond the opposites of pleasure-pain, attraction-repulsion, attachment-shunning and greed-hatred. What has been discussed in terms of life-perspective can also be discussed in terms of character type – *rāga carita* (the personality type whose conduct is dominated by greed) and *dosa carita* (the personality type whose conduct is dominated by hatred). The middle way of the Buddha is not within the reach of those who 'walk in greed' and those who 'walk in hate'.

The preceding analysis will have shown the close link between the Buddhist psychology of motivation and the therapeutic framework within which it is cast. Now we shall examine in detail some of the significant facets of its theory of motivation.

FEELINGS

Facets of the psychological process we have briefly outlined may be summarised in the following manner: eye and objects give rise to eye-consciousness; the coming together of the three is contact; dependent on contact is feeling; dependent on feeling is craving; dependent on craving is grasping; dependent on grasping is coming to be.[6]

What is said of the eye may also be said of the ear and sounds, the nose and scents, the tongue and savours, the body and tangibles and the mind and mental states. Certain sensory stimulations would be associated with pleasantness: the fragrance of a perfume, the taste of a chocolate or the sound of music may be pleasant, whereas a bad odour, a vegetable that tastes stale or an irritating sound may be painful. The stimulus could also emerge from the internal organism in the form of hunger pangs, a parched throat, fatigue, etc., and there will be corresponding pleasant organic sensations when they are alleviated.

While 'contact' is merely a reaction to stimuli, the emergence of the hedonic tone only appears at the level of feeling. With the emergence of craving and grasping we discern the transition from the state of a feeling into the experience of an emotion. While feeling (*vedanā*) comes under the standard psychological categories of Buddhism, there is no generic term for emotion. Specific emotions are discussed in a variety of contexts, and the integration of the material on the psychology of emotions in the discourses of the Buddha is an important task. We shall deal with the nature of emotions in the next section.

Vedanā as one of the five *khandhas* (groups) comprises five types of possible feelings: bodily agreeable feelings, bodily painful feelings, mentally agreeable feelings, mentally painful feelings and feelings of indifference. Though this is one of the most central classifications of feeling, the Buddha says that different types of classifications are possible depending on the context: there is a twofold classification in which the reference is to bodily and mental feelings; the threefold classification makes reference to pleasant, painful and neutral; the fivefold one makes reference to the five sense organs; and the sixfold one is based on sensory impingements by way of the doors of the senses. Feelings are also put into an eighteenfold group which is again divided into three sub-groups – six ways of attending to material shapes based on happiness, six founded on grief and six on equanimity; the thirty-sixfold classification refers to six forms of happiness connected with domestic life, six with renunciation, six forms of misery connected with domestic life, six with renunciation, the six indifferences of a householder and the six indifferences of renunciation; finally, the hundred-and-eightfold grouping refers to the same thirty-six feelings as manifest in the past, present and future.

These classifications of feelings are found in the *Bahuvedanīya Sutta*[7], a sutta which compares the kind of pleasure derived from the sensory organs with the higher pleasures attained at various stages in the development of meditational experience. For instance, the *Middle Length Sayings* describe the first stage of mediation in the following way

Here, Ananda, a monk, aloof from pleasures of the senses, aloof

> from unskilled states of mind, enters and abides in the first meditation that is accompanied by initial thought and discursive thought, is born of aloofness and is rapturous and joyful. This Ananda, is the other happiness that is more excellent and exquisite than that happiness.[8]

In this context, the gross pleasures derived from the sense organs and the experience of joy derived from the meditational exercises are differentiated by the Buddha, the grosser pleasures containing a latency to attachment, repugnance and ignorance. The grosser pleasures excite the dormant drive to engage in lustful and aggressive activity. The question is raised of whether there is a tendency to attachment in every pleasant feeling, a tendency to repugnance in every painful feeling and whether all neutral feelings are rooted in a tendency to ignorance.[9] To this question it is replied that a state aloof from the pleasures of the senses does not have such latencies. This ethical and spiritual dimension that cuts across the analysis of feeling, making subtle distinctions between different qualitative levels of pleasure, is of course something alien to modern western psychology.

In the context of the ethico-psychological teachings of Buddhism, it is this potential to rouse attachment and obsession or repugnance and animosity that is important. When a person has eliminated the tendencies to attachment and repugnance, 'he does not delight in that feeling, he does not welcome it or persist in cleaving to it'.[10] Sorrow, lamentation and despair do not necessarily follow the end of the process of attachment and clinging. For example, Assaji, who was striken with a sore disease, said that both pleasant and painful feelings have to be experienced without any attachment: 'If he feels a pleasant feeling, he knows it as impermanent, he knows it as not clung to, he knows it has no lure for him.'[11]

The implications of the pleasure-pain dichotomy are not limited to the emergence of unhealthy mental states, but even whole life-perspectives such as the way of sensuality and the way of asceticism, and broad character types like the lustful and the hateful have to be understood against the psychological category of hedonic tones (*vedanā*).

EMOTIONS

A deeper understanding of the psychology of feeling in Buddhism can only be arrived at by studying the related concept of emotions. One reason perhaps why this facet of the psychology of Buddhism has been neglected is that there is no generic term for emotions within the discourses. In this section we shall put together the material on specific emotions discussed by the Buddha, in the hope of working out a Buddhist theory of emotions.

In the English language, the word emotion, as accepted by most psychologists, is the term used to describe basic affective processes, feelings being generally restricted to pleasantness or unpleasantness. In line with a recent psychological analysis, feelings may be considered as 'affective reactions to sensations'; it is also said that in feeling the reference is to the reaction on the subject, whereas in emotion, there are diverse types of relation to an object.[12]

Emotion or an affect can be considered as a 'felt tendency towards an object judged suitable, or away from an object judged unsuitable, reinforced by specific bodily changes according to the type of emotion'.[13] That emotions involve dispositions to act by way of approach or withdrawal is a quality of emotional phenomena that fits in well with the Buddhist analysis. There is a felt tendency impelling people towards suitable objects and impelling them to move away from unsuitable or harmful objects. The individual also perceives and judges the situation in relation to himself as attractive or repellent. While a person feels attraction (*sārajjati*) for agreeable material shapes, he feels repugnance (*byāpajjati*) for disagreeable ones. An individual thus possessed of like (*anurodha*) and dislike (*virodha*) approaches pleasure-giving objects or avoids painful objects.[14]

Pleasant feelings (*sukha vedanā*) and painful feelings (*dukkha vedanā*) are affective reactions to sensations. When we make a judgement in terms of the hedonic tone of these affective reactions, there are excited in us certain dispositions to possess the object (greed), to destroy it (hatred), flee from it (fear), get obsessed and worried over it (anxiety), and so on. An emotional response occurs when a situation has been perceived and evaluated in relation to its effect on the individual. The emergence of emotions depends on the evaluation of the situation and its meaning for the individual. Estimation of the situation brings about somatic expressions and organic changes.

Buddhism accepts the position that there are emotions drawing people to suitable objects and emotions tending to draw them away from harmful objects. But these can occur under favourable conditions' or 'under unfavourable conditions'. Under favourable conditions, desire will be generated to obtain the pleasure-giving object, and there will be pleasure and delight in the attainment of the object. If unsuitable objects intrude into a person's sensory or ideational field there will be aversion, dislike and unhappiness.

However, when conditions are not favourable, our normal emotions emerge not as 'impulse emotions', but as 'contending emotions'. In spite of obstructions, if we feel that the objects are attainable we have 'hope', but if we feel that the objects are not attainable we succumb to 'despair'. In the case of negative objects (which we do not want), courage, anger and fear will emerge depending on the context.[15] Though the depicting of impulse emotions is given a central place in the psychology of Buddhism, contending emotions are also discussed in a number of contexts.

In this manner certain emotions are interlocked with other emotions. Emotions are also dynamically fed by our drives and dispositions. The attitudes that we have formed in the past will influence our response to the stimuli of the present, and these attitudes will be rooted in dynamic personality traits. According to the Buddha, these attitudes are not always the result of conscious decision, but emerge on deep-rooted proclivities (referred to as *anusaya*). Pleasant feelings induce an attachment to pleasant objects, for they rouse latent sensuous greed (*rāgānusaya*), and painful feelings will rouse latent anger and hatred (*paṭighānusaya*). States like pride, jealousy, envy, etc., can be explained in terms of similar (*anusaya*).

We have already referred to the six motivational roots which are related to emotions. An interesting feature in this analysis is the impact of beliefs on the affective life of man: delusion as a root generates the wrong beliefs that colour our emotional life and non-delusion provides the base for wholesome emotions. Wrong beliefs exist at the level of dormant dispositions (*diṭṭhānusaya*) and account for the unconscious roots of prejudices and strong biases which colour our emotional life. The most persistent ideological component that stands behind the impact of beliefs on emotion is the false concept of a pure ego, which gives rise to a variety of ego-illusions. In a deeper sense man is prone to some form of basic anxiety: anxiety is caused by an attachment to the belief in 'I' and 'me', which instead of giving us a feeling of security, creates worry and anxiety (*paritassana*). Though the ego psychology of Buddhism savours of meta-empirical theorising, a deep understanding of the sources and manifestations of the ego-illusions provides a fascinating study for psychologists. Some of our observations on the therapeutic value of the Buddhist doctrine of 'egolessness' will be taken up in the concluding chapter. In general the link between emotion and beliefs in Buddhism is significant, a point that has entered into some of the recent writings in the area of philosophical psychology.[16]

Before we examine some of the specific emotions, there is one more facet of the concept of emotions to be discussed. In the religious and ethical context, emotions are often regarded as states that interfere with the spiritual development of a person. Good reasoning is considered to be thinking which is not coloured by emotion. In psychological contexts, emotions are regarded as states of 'imbalance' and 'agitation'.

But emotions need not always be considered as the source of irrationalities. Emotions are forms of appraisal and there is a cognitive component in them. This means that we can have good reasons for certain emotions - to feel fear when we see a situation as dangerous or to feel envious when someone else possesses what I wish to have, etc. If emotions have a logic of their own, then education of the emotions is possible. When we speak of education of the emotions in the Buddhist context, we have to look for emotions which are 'ethically wholesome'.

An interesting comment made in this context by Spinoza is that 'it takes an emotion to control another emotion'.[17] R. S. Peters observes that love, respect, a sense of justice and a concern for truth, which are 'self-transcending emotions' rather than 'self-referential emotions', are of this positive kind.[18] Thus it may be said that though there are emotions that distort reasoning, feed one's prejudices and darken the vision, there are others which break through one's egotism and expand one's mental horizons. In the Buddhist context there are emotions that sharpen a healthy sense of the tragic and others that evoke the ennobling emotions of sympathy and compassion for one's fellow-men.

In keeping with the search for positive and creative emotions in the psychology of Buddhism, non-greed, non-hatred and non-delusion may be regarded as the roots of wholesome emotions. Regarding the impact of the wholesome roots on the forms of wholesome consciousness, the following observations have been made by the Venerable Nyanaponika:

> Non-greed and non-hate may, according to the particular case, have either a mainly negative meaning signifying absence of greed and hate, or they may possess a distinctive positive character, for example: non-greed as renunciation, liberality; non-hate as amity, kindness, forbearance. Non-delusion has always a positive meaning: for it represents the knowledge which motivates the respective state of consciousness. In their positive aspects, non-greed and non-hate are likewise strong motives of good actions. They supply the non-rational, volitional or emotional motives, while non-delusion represents the rational motive of a good thought or action.[19]

In the light of these observations non-greed and non-hatred may be regarded as the springs of healthy, positive and creative emotions. In fact non-delusion may be considered as a basis for forming affective dispositions arising from well-grounded beliefs and sound reasoning. The psychology of Buddhism accepts that actions may be based on rational motives as well as on rationalizations influenced by desires. Because of desire there is clinging (*taṇhā-paccayā diṭṭhi-upādānaṃ*), and clinging is said to be of four forms, one of which is clinging to metaphysical beliefs. If both good reasons as well as rationalisations are features of our emotional life, there should be a basis for healthy and creative emotions grounded in good reasons, and good reasons fed by healthy emotions.

It must be emphasized in this context that feelings *need* not be followed by unwholesome emotions (greed, hate) but can be followed by wholesome (*kusala*) emotions or neutral feeling; a pleasant feeling may evoke the wish to share the pleasure-giving object with others (*alobha*), an unpleasant feeling may evoke patience and compassion (*adosa*).

The claim that Buddhist psychology provides a basis for a creative emotional response is a significant claim with interesting implications for the development of a Buddhist ethics, social theory and even art and aesthetics. While we shall take up the role of the creative emotions as we proceed, it is now necessary to examine in detail some of the specific emotions discussed by the Buddha.

Fear

If we glance through the discourses of the Buddha as preserved in the Pāli canon, the available material on the nature of emotions appears to be dispersed, as well as coloured by the nature of the diverse contextual situations where emotions are discussed. However, in general discussion centres on four groups of emotions: those which obstruct the ideal of the virtuous life sought by the layman, emotions that interfere with the recluse seeking the path of perfection, emotions enhancing the layman's ideal of the virtuous life and emotions developed by the recluse seeking the path of perfection. The grouping of emotions in this manner brings an ethical and spiritual dimension to the psychology of emotions in Buddhism. In the context of the psychology of the west, the undesirable emotions are those that create adjustive problems and impair our mental health, and the desirable ones are valuable as an adaptive resource. The delineation of mental health merely in terms of adjustment is being questioned in some psychological groups in the west, and new horizons have emerged, a trend which might help to bridge the gap between the psychology of Buddhism and the currently dominant psychology of the west.

Fear generally arises as a response to a specific danger, whereas anxiety arises as a reaction to a danger which is not clearly seen. In anxiety, both the nature of the object and one's attitude to it are obscured. However, these states fade off into each other in certain contexts. *Bhaya* in Pāli can be rendered as fear, fright or dread.

Regarding the genesis of the emotion of fear, there are at least two clear types of situation which cause fear. Fear is often caused by strong desires (*taṇhāya jāyati bhayaṃ*).[20] Strong desires and attachment to either persons or things cause fear because if we cling to some precious and valuable object, we have to defend it against loss or theft; thieves can even be a threat to one's life. If one is deeply attached to a person, and if the person is struck by a serious sickness, concern for his well-being turns into fear. The possibility of death causes anguish and anxiety. It is the same with the attachment to one's own self, a threat to one's life, sickness, the threat of losing one's job or reputation – all situations leading up to the emergence of fear. It is because of the strong drive towards self-preservation (*bhavataṇhā*) which in turn is fed by the *bhavarāgānusaya* (the lurking tendency to crave for existence) that fear becomes such an agitating condition. In addition to the instinct for self-preservation, the desire for power, lust, jealousy and pride is intimately related to the emergence of fear. As we mentioned earlier, some emotions are interlocked with other emotions, as is the case, for instance, with jealousy, pride and fear.

The second type of fear is the consequence of leading an undesirable life. Here the emotion of fear is related to the emotion of guilt. In this context the emotion of fear has an unhealthy destructive aspect and a positive healthy aspect. If a person is burdened with a heavy sense of pathological remorse, it has a bad effect, for it creates worry and restlessness. On the other hand a lively sense of moral dread and shame (*hiri-ottappa*) prevents man from taking to an evil life and forms the basis of responsibility and a civic sense.

The damaging aspect of a bad conscience in respect to morals has been the subject of discussion since the work of Sigmund Freud. In admonishing both the layman and the recluse regarding the bad effects of a pathological sense of guilt, the Buddha refers to a person who is subject to anxiety, fear and dejection: a person who has done the wrong thing fears that other people talk about him, and if he is in a place where people congregate, he fears that that is what they are doing. When he sees others being punished by the king, he thinks that the same will happen to him and is disturbed by this possibility. Finally, when he is resting on a chair or the bed, thoughts of this kind come to him and he fears that he will be born in a bad place. 'Monks, as at eventide the shadows of the great mountain peaks rest, lie and settle on the earth, so, monks, do these evil deeds . . . lie and settle on him.'[21] The kind of fear and guilt that disturbs the man here is different from a healthy, productive sense of shame and fear (*hiri-ottappa*). In the *Anguttara Nikāya* there is a reference to four types of fear: of self-reproach (*attānuvādabhaya*), fear of others' reproach (*parānuvādabhaya*), fear of punishment (*daṇdabhaya*) and fear of lower worlds (*duggatibhaya*). Fears of this kind will have a good effect on the person: 'he abandons evil', and 'develops the practice of good'.

Fear is often found mixed with hatred (even self-hate) and discontent, and this is often so in the emergence of pathological guilt. *Kukkucca*, which can be rendered as uneasiness of conscience, remorse or worry, is considered a hindrance to spiritual development. It is associated with a hateful and discontented consciousness, similar to the Freudian super-ego and consisting of aggressive elements. Among people who are disappointed with the way that they have lived in the past, some can become better more productive men; but others take a more unrewarding line and display a complex admixture of fear, hatred and guilt.[22] The religious melancholy, the self-punishing ascetic, and similar types have an unproductive sense of fear and dread. Restlessness and worry are described in the Nikayas with an apt analogy: if a pot of water were shaken by the wind so that the water trembles, eddies and ripples, and a man were to look there for his own reflection, he would not see it. Thus restlessness and worry obscure one's vision of oneself, and form an obstruction to the development of tranquillity and insight.[23]

Hiri-ottappa (shame and dread), however, is a positive and healthy sense which must be cultivated and developed. In the words of Mrs Rhys Davids, 'taken together they give us the emotional and conative aspects of the modern notion of conscience, just as *sati* represents it on its intellectual side'.[24] He who lacks these positive emotions lacks a conscience.

In a recent study, under the title 'Morality and Emotions',[25] Bernard Williams says that if we grasp the distinction made in Kleinian psychoanalytical work between 'persecutary guilt' and 'reparative guilt' we do not neglect the possibility for a creative aspect for remorse or guilt:

> He who thinks he has done wrong may not just torment himself, he may seek to put things together again. In this rather evident possibility, we not only have in general a connexion between the emotions and the moral life, we also have something that illustrates the point about the interpretation of a set of actions in terms of an emotional structure.

It is also of interest to note that a student of Buddhism in the west has made an analysis of the 'Dynamics of Confession in Early Buddhism'.[26] Teresina Havens, too, says that in place of the external rites of purification like bathing in the river, and so on, which are advocated by existing religions, the Buddha advocated a radical inner transformation of the affective side of man. According to Havens, the Buddha was as realistic as Freud or St Paul in accepting and 'recognising the egocentric, lustful, hostile and grasping proclivities in unawakened man'.[27] While advocating a method to uproot these traits, the Buddha 'condemned worry over past offences as a hindrance to concentration and founded a religion which in general seems to have produced far fewer neurotic guilt feelings than has Judaism or Christianity'.[28] The principle of catharsis of emotions has certainly caught the eyes of contemporary students of Buddhism in the west.

Fear and Anxiety

As has been said, we often make a distinction between fear and anxiety, fear being response to a specific situation or a particular object, and as such both specific and demonstrable, whereas dread is objectless, diffuse and vague, since in anxiety both the nature of the object and one's attitude to it are not clearly recognised.

Anxiety is generally born out of ego-centred desires of one kind or another. Some forms of anxiety or vague apprehension under clear analysis can be seen to be specific fears. For instance, a person approaching the possibility of marriage may feel some anxiety regarding financial problems, or a sense of apprehension as to whether the marriage will be a success, but when analysed such vague apprehensions can be explained as arising from specific causes. The Buddha says that a more basic type of anxiety arises from our deep-rooted attachment to the ego. In the words of Conze, a 'concealed suffering'[29] lies behind many everyday apprehensions. These emerge from the nature of the basic human condition. Something can be both pleasant and yet tied up with anxiety, since one is afraid to lose it. Here anxiety is inseparable from attachment, in which something pleasant, like the possession of a body, binds us to conditions which will inevitably entail a great deal of suffering. And, finally, the five aggregates (*khandha*) have their own form of built-in anxiety.

Inability to face the inner vacuity of the so-called ego results in flight from anxiety. Compulsive gregariousness, frantic club-joining, filling one's leisure hours with feverish activity – all these are facets of covert anxiety, all help people to avoid being alone.[30] The love of solitude and the way of silence advocated by the Buddha is anathema to large numbers of people who live in the 'lonely crowd'!

The Buddha traces this predilection of the 'anxious man' to his inability to grasp the basic truth of egolessness, which is the key to understanding any form of anxiety. The belief in 'I' and 'mine', though it gives a superficial feeling of security, is the cause of anxiety, fear and worry. The discourse on *The Snake Simile* refers to anxiety (*paritassana*) about unrealities that are external and those that are internal; external unrealities refer to houses, gold and other possessions, or to children and friends; the internal to the non-existing 'I'.

The *Bhaya Bherava Sutta* (Discourse on Fear and Dread) says that purely subjective conditions can cause fear in a recluse who has gone off to live alone in the forest. If a recluse who has gone to the forest has not mastered such emotions as lust and covetousness, is corrupt in heart, etc., the rustling of fallen leaves by the wind or the breaking of a twig by an animal can cause fear and dread. Thus, whether we are dealing with the fears of a man attached to his possessions, the anxieties of one torn between conflicting desires, the fear and dread of a recluse living in the wilderness, or the fears consequent on leading a bad life – in all these senses the Buddha is for us a 'dispeller of fear, dread and panic'.[31] Now the most natural question is, Is there no creative, existential stirring that awakens man to his real predicament? There are references to authentic religious emotions caused by the contemplation of the miseries of the world. The emotion of *saṃvega*, translated as 'stirring' or 'deeply moving', can be an invigorating experience which enhances one's faith and understanding of the *dhamma*[32] – a concept which must of course be distinguished from *paritassana*, which is a kind of anxiety.

The doctrine of the Buddha is compared to a lion's roar. In the forest, when the lesser creatures hear the roar of the king of the beasts, they tremble. In the same way, when the devas, who are long-lived and blissful, hear the doctrine of conditioned origination they tremble, but they yet understand the Buddha's doctrine of impermanence. This should be compared with the state of *paritassana*, where a person finds his eternalism challenged, but sees the doctrine of the Buddha through the eyes of an annihilationist, and laments, '"I" will be annihilated.' When *saṃvega* is kindled in a person, he sticks to the doctrine with more earnestness.

Fear and Emotional Ambivalence

Fear is something which by its very nature entails 'avoidance', but there is a strange phenomenon which may be described as 'flirting with fear'. There are people who search for forms of entertainment and sports which excite a mild degree of fear, like participating in hazardous mountain climbing, motor sports, fire walking etc. There are others who like to read, see and talk about gruesome incidents, and many of those who go on wild-life safaris are looking for a little excitement rather than just wanting to look at animals from a distance. This kind of ambivalent nature is reflected in behaviour where a mild degree of fear created by situations helps to break through monotomy and boredom. Also, disgust with their lives and their own selves can make people court situations which are potentially dangerous to them. Freud's study of the death instinct (which we have elsewhere compared with *vibhava taṇhā*) might shed some light on this rather dark facet of human nature. Even in ancient Rome it was said that people wanted both bread and circuses. It is possible that situations of disorder, turmoil and violence, etc., are fed by this ambivalent nature.

Another facet of this compulsion to 'flirt with fear' is found in the strange delight people find in violating taboos, laws and commands. When desires are curbed through fear, they are repressed and emerge through other channels. The co-existence of states which are condemned at the conscious level and approved at the unconscious level partly explains this compulsion to violate taboos. Other types of irrational fears are presently being unearthed in the field of abnormal psychology[33] which stress that an undesirable situation has to be avoided on the basis of understanding rather than by an irrational fear or a process of drilling oneself.

The Control and Expression of Fear

This brings us to the final aspect of the emotion of fear. The Buddha was not often directly concerned with the question of whether the spontaneous expression of an emotion is good or whether it should be inhibited. He held, rather, that by a process of self-understanding, diligent self-analysis and insight one can come to the point where emotions will not overwhelm one.

A recent study which attempts to work out a technique of living based on Buddhist principles has something significant to say on this problem.[34] Leonard Bullen says that there are three aspects to the disciplining of emotions: first, the development of a habit of self-observation with regard to one's own emotional condition (a detailed observation of the mental state); second, the control of emotional manifestations as they arise; and, finally, the development of a new set of values, so that the situations which earlier elicited responses of fear or anger will fail to do so. As Bullen himself points out, the disciplining of emotions at the level of the individual has social implications.

If we begin with ourselves, we do not excite emotions of fear, hatred, jealousy and pride in others. If others do not excite them in us, we are not impelled to see the shadows of our own fears and jealousies in their hearts. Self-analysis and understanding when practised within a community has a reciprocal effect. The emotion of fear when it is generated at the social level creates mutual mistrust, suspicion and hatred. The roots of racial prejudice, for instance, can be understood in the light of this phenomenon of mutual fear.

Hatred

Emotions often create a kind of fog between the subject and the object. In 'approach desires', like greed, there is an infatuation due to which the person is blind to the undesirable aspects of the object which he longs to possess. In the case of 'avoidance desires', generated by fear, and more so by hatred, the subject projects his hatred in perceiving the object; in extreme anger his vision is blinded, like the fury of a serpent. Thus there is a positive attitude towards things we like and a negative aversion for those we dislike. If we wish to avoid a situation or a person that we dislike, and we cannot do so, there is excited in us an urge to destroy, harm, fight, etc. In the case of response to people, the situation is a little more complicated, for sometimes one attribute will attract us, while another aspect of the same person repels us, and when this is so, under certain conditions what is lovable will turn out to be repellent. The kind of emotional ambivalence that exists between parents and children is a case in point. Then there are things that we consciously like but unconsciously detest.

In the ethico-psychological analysis of emotions that we find in Buddhism, a number of terms are used to describe the existence and expression of anger and hatred: *dosa* (hate), *vyāpāda* (ill will), *paṭigha* (aversion), *kodha* (anger), and so on. Hatred is also related to states such as *issā* (envy), *macchariya* (jealousy) and *hīnamāna* (sense of inferiority).

Dosa (hate) is one of the basic roots of immoral action, along with greed and delusion. Sometimes in a particular situation all the roots of immoral action may be excited: a person is longing to obtain object B, but A stands on his way. Thus greed for B is followed by a hatred for A, and the desire for B is in turn nourished by the root delusion. Hatred can manifest itself in various ways: by thoughts (wishing the person dead), by harsh words, by aggressive behaviour. In fact, hatred is an emotion which has been so generally condemned by the Buddha, that it is difficult for the Buddhist to think of any positive form that it may take, such as 'righteous indignation' or a 'just war'.

Due to certain forms of development that the human being has undergone, often people do not speak out and express their feelings, but by a process of repression and concealment accumulate them. Accumulated anger of this sort can explode in very many subtle forms, for such anger exists at a subterranean level in the form of *paṭighānusaya*. A baby who is angry with the mother will direct this on to a doll – this is called 'displacement'. If a person takes pleasure in beating a child, he will say it will do the child good – a form of rationalisation. A person who unconsciously hates a person can be over-solicitous about his health – this is reaction formation. If someone suspects, without grounds, that another person is harbouring a grievance against him, he is merely projecting his own hatred on to someone else. If a person starves himself to death because of a social grievance it may be a way of directing the accumulated hatred on to himself. We have elsewhere discussed this concept of self-deception, but it is relevant directly to the emotion of hatred, too.

Then there is a classic case of the child who refused to take medicine, and finally through compulsion, drank it with a vengeance. It is in the understanding of the deceptive spell of the aggressive urges in man that the Buddha condemned both suicide and the path of self-mortification (*attakilamathānuyoga*). It is a way of life that generates suffering (*dukkha*), annoyance (*upaghāta*), trouble (*upāyāsa*) and fret (*parilāha*). The Buddha advocated a middle path that will dry up the roots of both greed and hatred, and of delusion also.

In an era closer to ours Sigmund Freud, too, remarked that the voice of agression is sometimes subtle, invisible and difficult to unravel. With deep appreciation of the psychological mechanisms in Buddhism, Mrs Rhys Davids says that 'compared with the ascetic excesses of the times, the Buddhist standpoint was markedly hygienic'.[35] Not only does the Buddha grasp the subtle mechanism through which the aggressive urge manifests itself, but he presents the finest antidote to the springs of hatred in man in the form of the doctrine of the four Sublime States. If the genius for both good and evil rests within ourselves the Buddha has given us a sense of optimism to deal with the turmoil both within and around us.

Though the Buddha attempted to deal with the emergence of hatred both at the social and individual level, it is through the inner transformation of the individual that the urge to aggression can be tamed. Thus in working out the different levels of spiritual development, there are references to the forms of anger, hatred and ill will that obstruct man. Hatred in the form of *vyāpāda* (ill will) is referred to as one of the hindrances (*nīvaraṇa*), along with sensuality, sloth and torpor, restlessness and remorse and doubt. It is one of the fetters that bind beings to the wheel of existence, and with *kodha* (anger) and *upanāha* (malice), *issā* (envy) and *macchariya* is considered as one of the sixteen defilements (*upakkilesā*). These defilements have to be eliminated before insight can be developed. These states work in significant combinations; for instance, in contempt there is a combination of aversion and conceit, and denigration is a stronger form of this contempt.[36] Envy is fed by greed and aversion. If we succumb to the last defilement of negligence, then these defilements will form into a layer which is hard to break through, when it has hardened into habit. It is in this way that we can account for the emergence of certain personality types, and the type referred to as the *dosa carita* will be the very embodiment of hatred.

There is a graphic description of the angry man in the *Anguttara Nikāya*, some of which we shall reproduce here:

When anger does possess a man;
He looks ugly; he lies in pain:
What benefit he may come by
He misconstrues as a mischance;
He loses property (through fines)
Because he has been working harm
Through acts of body and of speech
By angry passion overwhelmed:
The wrath and rage that madden him
Gain him a name of ill repute;
His fellows, relatives and kin
Will seek to shun him from afar;
And anger fathers misery:
Thus fury does so cloud the mind
Of man that he cannot discern
This fearful inner danger.
An angry man no meaning knows,
No angry man sees an idea,
So wrapped in darkness, as if blind,

Is he whom anger dogs.
Someone a man in anger hurts;
But, when his anger is later spent
With difficulty or with ease,
He suffers as if scared by fire
His look betrays the sulkiness
Of some dim smoky smouldering glow,
Whence may flare up an anger-blaze
That sets the world of man aflame
He has no shame or conscience curb
No kindly words come forth from him,
There is no island refuge for
The man whom anger dogs.
Such acts as will ensure remorse
Such as are far from True Ideals:
It is of these that I would tell,
So harken to my words
Anger makes man a patricide
Anger makes him a matricide
Anger can make him slay the saint
As he would kill the common man
Nursed and reared by a mother's care
He comes to look upon the world,
Yet the common man in anger kills
The being who gave him life.
No being but seeks his own self's good
None dearer to him than himself
Yet men in anger kill themselves,
Distraught for reasons manifold:
For crazed they stab themselves with daggers,
In desperation swallow poison,
Perish hanged by ropes, or fling
Themselves over a precipice.
Yet how their life-destroying acts
Bring death into themselves as well,
That they cannot discern, and that
Is the ruin anger breeds.
This secret place, with anger's aid
Is where Mortality sets the snare,
To blot it out with discipline
With vision, strength, and understanding,

To blot each fault out one by one,
The wise man should apply himself,
Training likewise in True Ideals:
'Let smouldering be far from us'.
Then rid of wrath and free from anger,
And rid of lust and free from envy,
Tamed, and with anger left behind,
  Taintless, they reach Nibbāna.[37]

On the therapeutic side there are many contexts where the Buddha offers us advice to help us to face situations in such a way that our anger, wrath and ill will will not be excited; and if we become agitated there are techniques to get rid of this. This is not a process of repression by which one pushes hostile feelings down into a lower level of consciousness, but one which uses understanding, insight, and mindfulness to control and restrain them. While the Buddhist analysis of the genesis of emotional states helps one to understand their emergence, positive techniques are advocated to deal with them, and this is done in the case of anger, fear, greed, jealousy or other unwholesome emotional states. The *Vitakkasaṇṭhāna* sutta recommends five such techniques.[38]

Grief and Sorrow

Grief is a universal phenomenon. It is basically a reaction to bereavement, but it is also consequent on other types of losses. If there has been a close identification with the person or the thing lost, the person concerned feels as if a part of himself has been lost. The most significant observations on the nature of 'mourning and melancholy' were made by Sigmund Freud.[39]

When an object is charged with a strong emotional cathexis, or in Buddhist terminology 'clinging' (*upādāna*), a sudden loss or separation creates a disturbing vacuum. Feelings of guilt, depression and self-pity may colour the emotion of grief in various situations. It is said that sometimes people will not be able to distinguish between sorrow and compassion; but while the distant enemy of compassion is cruelty, the close enemy is a kind of self-pity filled with worldly sorrow.[40] While a deep sense of compassion has a power to transform a person spiritually, worldly sorrow binds him more insidiously to the wheel of *saṃsāra*.

Sorrow, grief and lamentation are all facets of *dukkha* and in Buddhism can be overcome only by grasping the philosophy of the 'tragic'.[41] Mourning and weeping are not effective ways of dealing with the tragic. We should understand the causes and conditions of suffering and work out a therapy to remove the causes of suffering. The Buddhist attitude demands a sense of reality; this is different from either excessive mourning or the use of diversions to drown one's sorrow. *Dukkha* is a universal feature of *samsaric* existence, along with impermanence and egolessness. The Buddha has said: 'What is impermanent, that is suffering. What is suffering, that is void of an ego.' To think that there is an ego where there is only a changing psycho-physical complex is to create the conditions that generate sorrow, grief and dejection.

The Buddhist philosophy of tragedy is contained in the four noble truths: the truth of suffering, the origin of suffering, the extinction of suffering, and the eightfold path leading to the extinction of suffering. Birth, decay, disease, death, sorrow, lamentation, pain, grief and despair are suffering, says the Buddha. To be joined with the unpleasant and to be separated from the pleasant is suffering, the failure to get what one wants is suffering. In short, clinging to the five groups of mental and physical qualities that go to make up the individual constitutes suffering. It is the last part of the formula that gives a sense of depth to the meaning of tragedy in Buddhism.

If the nature of the Buddhist analysis of *dukkha* is understood, within that setting the confrontation of genuine tragic situations in life may have a positive role to play: it could break through natural slumber and complacency and create a sense of urgency in the mind of the Buddhist. Authentic tragic experience (*saṃvega*) should be a spur to the religious life and strengthen one's faith in the doctrine.

The way in which the impact of genuine tragic situations may bring about a spiritual alertness without falling into the unwholesome extreme of morbidity is brought out clearly in the *Aṅguttara Nikāya*.[42] A certain person hears that in a village or town someone is afflicted or dead, and stirred in this way he realises the truth; another beholds with his own eyes . . . and realises the truth; the third person sees a kinsman afflicted and realises the truth; and finally the person himself is stricken with pain and suffering and this situation stirs him to a realisation of the truth of suffering. This is by analogy compared to a steed that is stirred when the stick is seen, one stirred when the stick touches the skin, a third when the flesh is pierced and a fourth when the very bone is pierced by a stick. There is an element of stirring (which the translator renders as agitation) which awakens a person to the tragic sense of life and the emergence of faith in the doctrine. Even if we call this a state of 'agitation', it is different from that of a person whose fear, anger or grief has been aroused. Even the sense of the tragic in life can turn out to be a creative emotional response.

Love and Compassion

So far we have discussed three negative emotions: fear, hatred and sorrow. However, we found that unlike the case of hatred, both fear and sorrow have a positive aspect. Now we shall focus attention on the positive emotions of love and compassion.

Love and compassion in the Buddhist context fall within a continuum of emotions some of which shade off into each other: erotic love, sexual love, attachment, fondness, affection, motherly love, sympathy, concern for one's fellow-beings, compassion, etc. An ethical stance cuts across this analysis, recommending the wholesome emotional states only.

In the Greek language, the word *eros* refers to the sensual aspect of love and *agape* to the spiritual aspect of love. In English, we use the one word 'love', which if not qualified by a prefix would remain vague.

Sexual pleasure has to be viewed from two standpoints: the standpoint of the layman and that of the monk.[43] Those who take to the holy life (*brahmacariya*) cannot enjoy sexual pleasures, whereas the householder (*gahapati*) is permitted to enjoy pleasures of a sensual or sexual nature within a legitimate limit. The five precepts to which the layman adheres emphasise chastity, while the eight religious vows of the holy life aim at celibacy. While the Buddha condemns the unchaste life of the married man, the sanctity of family life and the value of conjugal love are upheld in Buddhism. Negatively, Buddhist laymen are expected to refrain from unlawful sexual relations, and positively the homily to Sigāla lays down the basic duties of people that will ensure domestic happiness.[44] The homily gives a charming code of domestic relations, and describes the mutual duties between husband and wife as well as those between parents and children, servants and masters, teachers and pupils, friends and companions, laymen and recluses. It is within such an ethical framework and spiritual quest that conjugal love finds its due place within the Buddhist theory of human relations. Immoral lust (*adhammarāga*), inordinate craving (*visamalobha*) and perversion of the moral sense (*micchādhamma*) are evils that lead to the degeneration of society, whereas filial and religious piety form the basis of a healthy society.[45] In a society where adultery and other forms of sexual misbehaviour (*Kamesu micchācāra*) become rampant, society will relapse into a barbaric state. Thus the very base of a healthy social ethics gives a vital role to conjugal love, filial piety and parental respect.

While what we have discussed is an ethical argument for conjugal love, there is also a significant psychological argument. If someone seeks the satisfaction of sexual greed as an end in itself, the dialectic of desire points out that it is bound to flounder on the very basis of its foundation. If a person cannot visualise a higher level of existence which goes beyond the level of immediacy and novelty, he is bound to become enmeshed by the very distressing experience of boredom and ennui. This type of self-indulgence may give some temporary satisfaction, but the law of diminishing returns soon sets in. The behaviour patterns of sex addicts merely mirror the destructive life-styles of the many who attempt to satisfy a spiral of needs which they have artificially created to stave off boredom. We have elsewhere discussed the Buddhist concept of emotional maturity when examining the 'critique of pleasure' in Buddhism and Soren Kierkegaard.[46]

From the standpoint of the 'homeless life' even healthy family relations have to be given up for the sake of the spiritual quest. Companionship (*samsagga*), fondness for children (*sineha*) and love (*pema*) have to be given up, for they are 'ties' which will lead a person to neglect his spiritual quest. It is also said that love and affection bring about anxieties and sorrow. The *Dhammapada* describes this in an often quoted stanza:

> From affection springs grief
> From affection springs fear
> For him who is wholly free from affection
> There is neither grief nor fear.[47]

The four sublime states provide a stronger dimension for a creative emotional response. Not only does compassion form the basis for a wholesome dimension of emotional warmth and positive concern for others, but it is specifically advocated as a corrective to the presence of hatred, fear and allied states. But it has its own alluring disguises and, as stated earlier, it must be saved from its near enemies: worldly sorrow, pseudo-love and superficial attachments.

The four sublime states (the Brahmavihārā) are *mettā* (loving kindness), *Karuṇa* (compassion), *muditā* (sympathetic joy) and *upekkhā* (equanimity). Their potential to deal with conflicts, jealousies, prejudice and hatred is immense. They have been referred to as removers of tension and builders of harmonious communities.[48] These states are considered boundless, since they are not limited and narrowed down by being directed towards particular individuals. These are not merely principles of conduct, but subjects of methodical meditation. It is through meditative practice that they sink deeply into the heart and later emerge as spontaneous emotions. In these four sublime states we see the finest base for a creative emotional response, and a response related to the emotion of natural sympathy and concern for one's fellow-beings. It has even been pointed out that one type of moral justification used by the Buddha was the appeal to sympathetic feelings.[49] Again, at this point we see the relevance of the psychology of emotions for moral assessment. Whether we concentrate on the negative or the positive emotions, it seems that the study of psychological phenomena in Buddhism cannot be completely separated from the ethical dimension which cuts through it.

THE PSYCHOLOGY OF CRAVING

In discussing feelings and emotions it was mentioned that feelings can be discussed under the category of *vedanā* (hedonic tone). It was also mentioned that there is no generic term for emotions, but that specific emotions are discussed in the discourses of the Buddha. Closely tied to these feelings and emotions is the Buddhist concept of craving. The psychology of emotions has to be understood against the background of the three forms of craving: craving for sensuous gratification, craving for self-preservation and craving for annihilation.

The concept of craving (*taṇhā*) is hard to translate into the terminology of western psychology for a number of reasons. Western psychologists have used theoretical constructs like 'instinct', 'drive', 'motives' etc., as aids to explain behaviour, and the use of these terms in different systems of psychology is not uniform. A 'drive' or an 'instinct' is not something concrete like a pen or a pencil: they are concepts associated with certain theories which attempt to explain visible forms of behaviour. Bearing this qualification in mind, it may be mentioned that a number of psychologists in the west have searched for some primary determinants of behaviour or fundamental bases of behaviour. Independent of semantic battles (as to whether we should use the word 'drive', 'instinct', etc.,) the search for the primary bases of behaviour is also found in the psychology of Buddhism.

In the psychology of the west, some, like McDougal, have introduced a large number of different instincts to account for diverse types of activity. Others, like Freud, suggest two or three basic instincts to explain the varied manifestations of behaviour. In this respect, the three forms of craving in Buddhism – for sensuality, self-preservation and annihilation – offer significant similarities to the libido, ego instinct and death instinct of Freud.[50] In this section, we shall discuss the nature of sexuality and sensuality, the manifestations of the instinct of self-preservation and the nature of aggression as found in the psychology of Buddhism.

Sexuality

The concept of *Kāma-taṇhā* has a very broad usage which goes beyond mere 'sexuality' as such; it is basically the craving for 'sensuous gratification' rather than 'sexual gratification'. The suttas refer to two significant terms, *pañcakāmaguṇa* and *kāma-rāga*: *pañcakāmaguṇa* refers to the five types of pleasure objects obtained by the eye, ear, nose, tongue and body, *kāma-rāga* refers to the desires and passions of a sensual nature. Thus the term *pañcakāmagunika-rāga* refers to the fact that in a human being there is a deep-seated proclivity for the enjoyment of the five senses. In a still broader sense, *kāma-taṇhā* may be regarded as the 'pleasure principle', as the term used in, for instance, the work of Freud: the natural proneness in man to seek pleasure and be repelled by pain.[51] It is important to emphasise that the drive for sensuous gratification goes beyond genital or otherwise specifically sexual pleasure and accounts for such manifestations as the need for diversion, the craving for excitement and the search for novelty.

Kāma in the context of Buddhism is the enjoyment of the five senses, and 'sexuality' is only one of the expressions of man's sensuous nature. The lure of the senses is constantly discussed by the Buddba and on numerous occasions he emphasises the need to restrain and control the senses.

Apart from the specific manner in which the word *kāma* is used, the ethico-religious dimension that cuts across the critique of pleasure is important. There are two basic standpoints to the enjoyment of pleasure in Buddhism. From one standpoint, the Buddha describes the ills besetting the pursuit of pleasure in general, but from another standpoint he distinguishes pleasures obtained by legitimate means and those obtained by illegitimate means, pleasures obtained within the legitimate restraints of a limit and the excessive craving for them, between harmless pleasures and perverted lust, and so on.[52]

For the layman, an attempt is made to work out a *via media* between complete suppression of sexuality and complete permissiveness. Sexual control in the sense of perfect celibacy and abstinence is limited to the monks. There is, however, one thing common to both standpoints – the search for pleasure as the only ideal in life is not possible within either standpoint. A life of pure sensuality without any ethical consideration is what the Buddha condemns as *kāmasukhallikānuyoga* (the way of sensuality). This is referred to as low, pagan practice and is compared with an equally pagan extreme, the way of self-mortification. The Buddha recommends the eightfold path as the middle way.

In the beginning of this chapter, it was stated that the main focus of Buddhist psychological analysis was human suffering and that the Buddha was directly concerned with the factors that lead to human unrest, tension and anxiety. It is in this context that the deep-rooted instinct for sensuous gratification has to be analysed. Sensuality as an expression of craving is the very base and source of suffering (*dukkha*). The origin of suffering (*dukkha-samudaya*) is traced to craving (*taṇhā*). Craving is a factor leading to rebirth (*ponobhavika*), it is accompanied by lust and self-indulgence (*nandi-rāga*), it seeks for temporary satisfaction 'now here, now there' (*tatra tatrābhinandanī*).[53] In the *Dialogues of the Buddha*, there is a detailed analysis of the factors in which craving is rooted.[54] The question is raised as to where 'craving takes its rise' and where it 'has a dwelling'. First it is said that craving has its rise and dwelling in the material things which are pleasant and dear to us: the sense of sight, sense of hearing, sense of smell, taste, touch and imagination; things seen, heard, smelt, tasted, touched and recalled in memory are dear and pleasant. This discussion of the excitation of the senses made in terms of *rūpa* (material things) is continued in terms of consciousness, sensory stimuli, feeling, perception, intentions, conceptual and discursive thinking.[55] This analysis is not limited to sensuous gratification but holds true of the other forms of craving.

However, in the final analysis, it is not the existence of the sense-organs or the impact of sense impressions that is emphasised, but the persistence of desire and lust. The eye is not the bond of objects, nor are objects the bond of eye, but desire and lust that arise owing to these two. The concepts of *kāma-rāga* (sensuous passion), *kāma upādāna* (sense clinging) and *kāma-āsava* (the canker of sensuous desire) refer to the persistence and upsurge of the craving for sense-gratification. Man's craving may be excited by stimuli either in the form of somatic factors or sensory stimuli, but its roots are of a deep-rooted psychological nature.

When a person's passions are roused, there emerges a kind of tenacity to hold on to these pleasures. This is the emergence of clinging (*upādāna*). Unless there is the persistence of clinging, excitation of the sense organs is not sufficient to rouse the individual to activity. Though clinging emerges always with craving as a condition, clinging as such works on a far deeper level and once a person clings to pleasure-giving objects, some latent tendencies (*anusaya*) will already have been excited. The pursuit of pleasure is fed by such undercurrents.

When one is under the spell of the drive for sensuous gratification, one can never get out of the vicious circle of 'want, tension and satisfaction'. The word '*taṇhā*', as implied by the metaphor of 'thirst', with which it is often associated, implies a constant state of striving. In spite of intermittent states of satisfaction, the unquenchable thirst re-emerges. When obstruction sets in there is frustration and anger, and if society lays down taboos there is retreat into the realms of phantasy. But deeper than all these ramifications of the pleasure drive is the sense of boredom and ennui that overcomes the man who has succumbed to the search for pleasure as his one dominating goal. Pleasures also contain within them the seeds of decay and loss, and thus within the incessant search for pleasure, delight turns into melancholy. The deeper psychological aspects of boredom, melancholy, dissatisfaction and restlessness are all contained within the Buddhist concept of *dukkha*. The psychology of *taṇhā* cannot be separated from the concept of *dukkha* (suffering).

We have referred to the meaning of *kāma* as sensuality, then to the ethico-religious dimension regarding acceptable and unacceptable pleasures, then to the deeper dynamics of the psychology of pleasure and finally to the predicament of the pure pleasure lover in the form of boredom, ennui and emptiness. Now we turn to another facet of craving, the instinct of self-preservation.

Self-preservation

The second aspect of craving – the instinct for self-preservation – involves greed (*lobha*), generates the desire to gratify the senses through *kāma-rāga* and *kāma-taṇhā*, and also the egoistic drives of *bhava-rāga* and *bhava-taṇhā*. The egoistic drives we discuss here are fed by false beliefs and illusions referred to as *diṭṭhi*, and these false beliefs are fed in their turn by the egoistic desires, so that they emerge as rationalisations.

The ego desires can be analysed in terms of the craving for self-preservation (*bhava-taṇhā*). The craving for diverse selfish pursuits is deeply rooted in the beliefs and ideological components referred to under the blanket heading of the dogma of personal immortality (*sassata-diṭṭhi*). We tend to believe in a pure ego existing independently of the psycho-physiological processes that constitute life. This 'pure ego' is believed to exist as an entity which continues even after the decay of the body.

The 'bias towards egocentricity'[56] (rooted in wrong belief in an abiding ego-entity) manifests itself at various levels – linguistic, emotional, intellectual, ethical, and so on. The acquisitive and possessive personality structure of the egocentric person has a threefold base in craving (*taṇhā*), conceit (*māna*) and false views (*diṭṭhi*). This erroneous concept of the self is induced by craving manifesting itself in the linguistic form, 'This is mine', conceit manifesting itself in the linguistic form 'This I am' and false views in the form of 'This is my self'. Such false views, craving and conceit can emerge in relation to body, feeling, perception, dispositions and consciousness. From this process of the mutual nourishment of the intellecutual and the affective roots of egocentricity emerge the diverse manifestations of egoistic behaviour – the desire for self-preservation, self-continuity, self-assertion (power), fame, self-display, etc. These egoistic drives are often woven into the daily run of life, so that they become clearly manifest only in dramatic situations such as a threat to one's life. Dormant traits, like the disposition to cling to existence (*bhavarāgānusaya*), will be excited on such occasions. The dividing line between a healthy self-regarding attitude and violent self-aggrandisement, quiet egoistic pursuits and spiritually enhancing self-transcending activities, etc., is an issue relevant to the Buddhist dimensions of personality study.[57] In what follows we shall discuss three facets of man's egoistic nature – his craving, his conceit and his ego illusions.

We have already referred to three aspects of craving in discussing sexuality: that it is a factor leading to rebirth, that it is accompanied by lust and self-indulgence, and that it seeks for temporary satisfaction, 'now here', 'now there'. It must clearly be mentioned that the drive for self-preservation has both physiological and psychological elements; some basic needs like the need for fresh air, water, food and sleep are necessary for survival. To remain alive a person needs water, food and rest and these are not considered by the Buddha as an expression of craving. Even in the perfected arahat (saint) the need for food is recognised. In condemning the way of asceticism, the Buddha was striking a middle path according to which basic human needs should not be neglected. On the whole, the recommendations for the monk are more stringent than for the layman, but even for the monk the value of physical well-being as a prerequisite for the development of the mind was accepted by the Buddha.

However, the need for food may be converted into an excessive greed for it, and gluttony can be both bodily and psychologically harmful. Functions like eating and drinking are natural biological functions, but if they are abstracted from their basic biological functions and pursued as sole ends, man becomes a slave to them. Today, in the world in which we live, the satisfaction of such basic desires is vitiated by false and destructive patterns of consumption – the factor of ever-increasing consumption intensifies man's need for a never-ending spiral of desires. Artificial and pseudo desires are not in keeping with a healthy life-style according to the Buddha. The Buddha does not discuss in detail biological drives like hunger, thirst and sleep, but makes a persistent attempt to bring out the roots of inordinate greed, pseudo desires and acquisitiveness that tarnish our ability to distinguish between needs and greeds.

The concept of *bhava-taṇhā* is also linked with other strong desires like the drive for power, status and prestige. The dividing lines between a healthy achievement motive and the goals of compensation, inferiority feelings and self-conceit can be worked out on the classification of psychological states made by the Buddha.

Self-conceit according to the Buddha can take three forms: 'I am superior to others' (*seyyo 'ham asmītimāna*), 'I am equal to others' (*sadiso 'ham asmitimāna*), 'I am inferior to others' (*hīno 'ham asmītimāna*). *Māna* is one of the fetters that bind man to the ills of existence, and it varies from a crude feeling of pride to a subtle feeling of distinctiveness that prevails until the attainment of arahatship (sainthood).

A person can be proud of his physical appearance or his attainments. He might also feel infuriated when someone laughs at his appearance or looks down on his position and status. If a person underestimates his attainments or becomes disgusted with his own 'image of himself', feelings of inferiority are excited. The phenomenon referred to in clinical situations as 'depression' is also related to a feeling of 'lack of worth' on the part of a person. The ego is also like an easily tipped canoe and an egoistic person is highly sensitive to remarks or actions calculated to belittle him. In fact 'wounded narcissism' has the potential to rouse a person's aggressive and hostile nature. In general the disturbance of a person's vanity can give way to either ego collapse and depression or anger and fury. When one's anger cannot be vented on an object or person in the external world, it can be directed against oneself and emerge in some of the subtle manifestations of self-hatred.

The roots of conceit exist at a subterranean level in the form of a dormant proclivity: we are subject to the latent conceit described in the linguistic form 'I am the doer' and 'this is my doing' (*ahaṃkāramamaṃkāra mānānusaya*). This insidious tendency to vain conceits can take five forms: in relation to the body, feelings, perceptions, dispositions and consciousness. Pride and conceit arise from a false valuation of oneself based on measuring oneself with others. Both superiority and inferiority conceits are a dual manifestation of the same root, an inflated sense of vanity (*māna-mada*).

A person subject to constant feelings of vanity and pride may be described in the terminology of Freud as a 'narcissistic person'. As Horney points out, the root of the narcissistic character-structure is a sense of self-inflation rather than self-love, with a need not for love but for the admiration of others. In the final analysis the potential for sensory, verbal and ideational stimuli to excite a sense of 'ego-injury' or 'ego-elation' will be there as long as the dormant proclivity to vain conceits and pride (*manānusaya*) exists.

The false views pertaining to the ego are referred to as *sakkāya diṭṭhi* (twenty forms of erroneous personality beliefs). Where there is a mere complex of corporeality, feeling, perception, dispositions and consciousness, the individual being subject to the ego-illusion assumes the existence of an ego: 1–5 ego is identified with corporeality, feeling, perceptions, disposition and consciousness, the individual being subject to the ego-illusion assuming the existence of an ego in terms of these five by a process of identification.

6–10 ego the individual is contained in them
11–15 ego the individual is independent of them
16–20 ego the individual is their owner

The breakdown of ego-illusion into twenty components does not mean that the ego is merely an intellectual construction. The roots of ego-illusion are strong and it is fed by deep affective processes. Most of the varieties of ego-identifications (if not all) found in the writings of philosophical and psychological reflections may be explained on the basis of these twenty manifestations of the ego-illusion. A materialist view of the self would identify the self with corporeality, a hedonist view of life would identify the self with feeling, a 'sensationist' view would identify the self with the perceptions, a vitalist would identify the self with will and some idealists would identify the self with consciousness, and so on. It is not merely the false view itself that matters, but a strong attachment to it. Thus the instinct for self-assertion, power and self-aggrandisement as well as self-perpetuation would feed the eternalist view of the self.

To cite an example from psychological writings, an identification of the body with self can be illustrated with the myth of Narcissus, a beautiful youth in mythology who loved no one till he saw his own body reflected in water. This concept of 'narcissism' developed by Freud was originally the idea of Paul Nacke, who used the term to describe a perversion, where an adult individual lavishes upon his own body all the caresses expended only upon a sexual object other than himself'.[58] A more subtle identification with the body would be seen in the opposite case of inflicting torture on the body. This would be understood in the light of the craving for annihilation.[59]

The corporeal overtones of the ego-illusion are described thus in the suttas: those people who are untrained in the doctrine of the Buddha, 'regard body as the self (*attā*, Sankrit: *ātman*), they regard the self as having a body, body as being in the self, the self as being in the body. "I am the body", say they, "body is mine", and are possessed by this idea.'[60] The Buddha also says that due to excessive attachment to the body, when it alters and changes, sorrow and grief set in, thus bringing out a link between the doctrines of egolessness and suffering. What has been said about the body can be said about the feelings, perceptions, disposition and consciousness.

Here is another passage from the suttas relevant to our discussion:

'What must exist, and what must be the condition, that such views may arise as "This is my Ego, this is the world. After death I shall continue, be everlasting, eternal, not subject to any change"?'

'The five groups of existence must exist . . . that such views may arise.'

'What do you think: Are these five groups permanent or are they impermanent?'

'Impermanent, Venerable Sir.'

'But what is impermanent, is that joyful or woeful?'

'Woeful, Venerable Sir.'

'But based on that which is impermanent, woeful, and subject to change, may (rightly) arise such views as: "This is my Ego, this is the world. After death I shall continue, be everlasting, eternal, not subject to any change."'

'No, Venerable Sir.'[61]

This passage discusses how ego-illusion emerges in relation to eternity views and in the next section we discuss this in relation to the annihilationist view.

Self-annihilation and aggression

While *bhava-taṇhā* arises with a false conception of personality based on the dogma of personal immortality, *vibhava-taṇhā* emerges from the view that the physical and mental processes identified with the ego will be annihilated at death (*uccheda diṭṭhi*). Though on a superficial examination these two attitudes appear to be diametrically opposed, against the larger setting of the law of dependent origination they are merely considered as the contrasting attitudes of a man bound to craving.

We have already referred to the existence and expression of hatred as an emotional state. In this section it would be necessary to probe further and examine whether Buddhism accepts the existence of a basic destructive urge.

Though Buddhist psychology does not uphold a kind of Freudian 'death-wish', it does trace the destructive urges to the root hatred (*dosa*). When this root hate is excited the individual is disposed to exhibit behaviour of an aggressive sort. At the initial stage, there is a desire to avoid situations we dislike, and when this is not possible there is excited in us an urge to destroy objects and persons we do not like. Painful sensations excite dormant hatred (*paṭighānusaya*).

Unlike Freud, the Buddha would consider self-destruction and suicidal tendencies as 'reactive' rather than 'appetitive'. It is when one fails to vent one's anger on objects or persons in the external world that it is deflected towards oneself, as in diverse forms of self-inflicted torture and suicide. The ignorant person when attracted by pleasant objects hankers after them and is flattered by success, but when touched by painful stimuli and failure he becomes infuriated and aggressive or dejected and depressed. When violent methods of getting rid of unpleasant stimuli fail, the venom is directed towards oneself:

> For crazed they stab themselves with daggers,
> In desperation swallow poison,
> Perish hanged by rope, or fling
> Themselves over a precipice.[62]

The word *vibhava-taṇhā* needs careful analysis, for its meaning is more complex than the other two forms of *taṇhā* (craving), *kāma-taṇhā* and *bhava-taṇhā*. The word *vibhava* as found in the discourses of the Buddha has two meanings: (i) power, health, prosperity; (ii) non-existence, cessation of life, annihilation. The meaning of the phrase *vibhava-taṇhā* is coloured by which central meaning we give to the word *vibhava*. If we take the first meaning, *vibhava-taṇhā* may be rendered as a craving for power and success based on the belief that there is no future state. This meaning does not fit in with some of the crucial contexts given in the suttas. According to the second meaning, which fits in with most of the contexts, the desire for annihilation and the belief that there is a self-entity that is annihilated at death are two psychological states that nourish each other.

The desire for annihilation can of course rest on two kinds of base – a carefree pleasure-lover or a Don Juan without any respect for ethics who sees death as the end of life; and a man full of anxieties and worries wishing for the end of life and attempting suicide. The second base is the one which is psychologically closer to *vibhava-taṇha*, for a pleasure lover would wish for self-continuity and prolongation of life. If life is unbearable and disgusting, and if there is no life after death, suicide is a logical solution to one's emotional predicament.

The concept of a 'death-wish' is something that baffled the very originator of the theory in western psychology:

> So immense is the ego's self-love, which we have come to recognize as the primal state from which instinctual life proceeds, and so vast is the amount of narcissistic libido which we see liberated in the fear that emerges at a threat to life, that we cannot conceive how the ego can consent to its own distruction.[63]

Though the psychology of Buddhism does not accept a death-wish in the Freudian sense, it does accommodate the existence of aggressive and hostile tendencies in man.[64] Destructive and hostile impulses emerge from the root hate (*dosa*), as has already been said, and the existence of dormant hatred at a subterranean level is suggested by the concept of *paṭighānusaya*. Such states as ill will, anger, malice and envy are regarded as defilements of the mind.

The most significant context in relation to the concept of *vibhava-taṇhā* is found in the Middle Length Sayings:

> Those worthy recluses and brahmans who lay down the cutting off (*ucchedaṃ*), the destruction (*vināsaṃ*), the disappearance (*vibhavaṃ*) of the essential being, these afraid of their own body, loathing their own body, simply keep running and circling round their own body. Just as the dog that is tied by a leash to a strong post or stake keeps running and circling round that post or stake, so do these worthy recluses and brahmans, afraid of their own body, simply keep running and circling round their own body.[65]

The three terms *uccheda*, *vināsa* and *vibhava* are used as synonyms, and the word *vibhava* clearly connotes the idea of destruction. Even those who attempt to 'destroy' the 'essential being' are assuming an ego which does not exist.

This context is significant for another reason. This passage shows how apparently contradictory attitudes like the craving for self-preservation and the craving for annihilation are merely the two sides of the same coin. That such contradictory attitudes like narcissistic self-love and co-existing self-hatred and ambivalent desires like the urge to live and the urge to die stem from a basic ego-illusion is one of the most subtle psychological discoveries of the Buddha. He who inflicts torture on his body with the aim of destroying it as well as the one who adorns and beautifies it are both running in the same vicious circle as the dog tied to the post. It has been observed of both the eternalist and the annihilationist that the 'former ran after his shadow', while 'the latter try in vain to outstrip it, both being equally obsessed to take it to be real'.[66]

The analysis of the roots of hatred, aggression and the destructive urge is also linked to the ethical and spiritual goals of the doctrine. In fact, the Buddhist goal of *nibbāna* was wrongly labelled as annihilationism, and the Buddha makes a specific attempt to differentiate the two. The wanderers who misunderstood the doctrine of the Buddha described him as a nihilist (*venayika*)[67] and a destroyer of growth (*bhunahu*).[68]

The role of aggression turned against the self, self-torture, asceticism, suicide, etc., in religious contexts has been studied by western psychologists.[69] If the Buddha was critical of the 'narcissistic' character he was equally critical of the 'nemesistic' type where aggression is turned against the self, and his doctrine steers clear of such extremes as self-punishing ascetism.

Those who attempt suicide as an escape from suffering are subject to the annihilationist delusion. Destruction of one's body does not put an end to one's suffering, for a person is liable to be born again. And heightened and impatient forms of self-torture do not offer release from suffering; in the very anxiety to put an end to suffering a person becomes subject to the craving for annihilation. The Buddha's analysis of some of the techniques and doctrines of contemporary religious groups exhibits a deep understanding of the inroads of aggression into the behaviour of religious teachers.

During the time of the Buddha there were some religious teachers who upheld that the mortification of the body would result in the purification of the soul. The path of self-mortification was one of the methods tried by Gotama for eight long years and rejected, and his way offers a striking contrast to the methods of self-mortification practised by the Jains. The deliberate attempt to live through painful experiences and the technique of burning the past effects of *kamma* were condemned by the Buddha, who saw some of these methods as the expression of craving and deflected aggression. He also condemned forms of punitive asceticism which required self-inflicted punishments for guilt in the form of penances, considering all violent attempts to deal with the problem of human suffering as lacking in insight and being subject to the delusion of the ego in a subtle form.

UNCONSCIOUS MOTIVATION

The question whether motives, desires and drives always operate at the conscious level is a significant problem for students of human motivation. Since the work of Freud became popular in the field of psychoanalytic theory, the realm of 'unconscious motivation' has been considered to be even more important than the realm of conscious desires. Though this is also a central issue in the Buddhist psychology of motivation, it would be necessary to find out in what sense or senses the term 'unconscious' may be used in the context of Buddhist analysis.

When we speak about unconscious motives we imply that a person is not aware of the *real motives* that impel him to perform some action. At least three explanations may be given for the existence of unconscious motives. Since our daily activities exhibit bits of behaviour into which several goals and desires are intertwined, it is difficult to isolate the motive for a specific action. Another explanation is that since motives are to a large extent habits, we acquire habits of which we are to a very great extent unaware. Third, in the special sense in which Freud used the term, 'motives are often fashioned under unpleasant circumstances that we would like to forget'.[70] In this sense the unconscious is the realm of repressed memories and emotions.

The tangle of human desires, the unreflective habits which have eaten into our daily routine and the 'defence mechanisms' which have become a part of our personalities without our conscious awareness[71] – all these facets of unconscious motivation can be accomodated within the concept of the unconscious in Buddhism. In making a diagnostic study of the human predicament the Buddha probed deeply into the roots of human motivation. The practice of diligent self-analysis, the techniques of concentration and mindfulness and the development of insight were all combined in a system of therapy. In this process of mind development, the dark interior regions of the mind, the patterns of compulsive behaviour and the irrational biases had all to be laid bare and brought to the surface of clear consciousness, mindfulness and wakefulness.

There are at least four polarities in the Buddhist context that run through the 'conscious-unconscious' dichotomy: calm and quiet as contrasted with turmoil and agitation; clarity and lucidity as contrasted with confusion and obscurity; mastery and control of desires as contrasted with domination by involuntary impulses; insight and knowledge as contrasted with delusion and ignorance.

The concept of unconscious motivation becomes important in the Buddhist context in the evaluation of actions based on ethical criteria. A 'significant action' on which praise or blame can be bestowed is an action done with an intention (*cetanā*). Even if an action is done impulsively or automatically, it can be an intentional activity and evaluated in ethical terms either as wholesome (*kusala*) or unwholesome (*akusala*). Though intention is the minimal necessity for the evaluation of an action, a 'wholesome action' in the full sense of the word has other facets – its appropriateness, its consequences, the manner in which it is done and the grades and types of consciousness that generate it or contribute to its emergence. Take, for instance, a driver who kills a person without any intention to do so; lack of vigilance on his part would have been a contributory factor, nevertheless. For a complete evaluation of an action in this manner the concept of unconscious motivation is important. We have already mentioned that turmoil, obscurity, impulsiveness and delusion have to be broken through if actions based on calm, lucidity, self-restraint and knowledge are to emerge. Let us examine some of the concepts used in connection with unconscious motivation which will help us to grasp the meanings of the word unconscious in the psychology of Buddhism.

ANALYSIS OF CONCEPTS RELATED TO UNCONSCIOUS MOTIVATION

We have already referred to the fact that attitudes and beliefs formed in the past influence our reactions to oncoming stimuli. According to the Buddha these attitudes are not always the result of deliberation at a conscious level, but are fed by deep-rooted dormant proclivities referred to in the suttas as *anusaya*.

The Pāli-English dictionary defines *anusaya* thus: 'Bent, bias, proclivity, the persistence of a dormant or latent disposition, predisposition, tendency.'[72] The word 'dormant' or 'latent' describes the psychological status of the *anusaya*. They are basically dormant passions which become excited into activity by suitable stimuli (*pariyuṭṭhāna*); because of their strong pertinacity they provide the base for the emergence of greed, anger and pride.

In the *Greater Discourse to Mālunkya*, the heretics say that as passions cannot arise in the mind of an infant, the concept of 'dormant passions' is not feasible. The Buddha replies that even in a baby boy a view regarding 'own body' is latent. A number of other latent 'leanings' in the infant are mentioned in the same context: a leaning to attachment towards sense pleasure (*kāmarāgānusaya*), a leaning to malevolence (*byāpādānusaya*), a leaning to cling to rites and rituals (*sīlabhataparāmāsa*), a leaning to perplexity (*vicikichānusaya*) and a leaning to the view of 'own body' (*sakkāyadiṭṭhānusaya*).[73] The Buddha would consider dormant leanings as persistent traits coming down innumerable lives. The idea of character traits which extend to more than one life-span is something that is alien to most systems of western psychology, though a rather distant echo of it may be found in the notion of a 'collective unconscious', mentioned by Freud and developed by Jung.[74]

The *anusaya* differ from passing mental states: they are states which have eaten into one's nature and found a habitat. People are not aware of their existence and power. Continuous self-analysis and the development of insight are necessary in order to be able to do so, and they can only be eliminated by the achievement of different levels of spiritual development. The relative strength and power of these dormant leanings can be worked out, since some of them are eliminated at an early state of development, while the potency of others will not be eliminated till one attains the state of the perfect one (*arahat*).

Seven *anusayas* are in the *Dialogues of the Buddha*:

(1) Sensuous craving – (*kamarāga*)
(2) Anger – (*paṭigha*)
(3) Conceit – (*māna*)
(4) Erroneous opinion – (*diṭṭhi*)
(5) Scepticism – (*vicikicchā*)
(6) Craving for existence – (*bhavarāga*)
(7) Ignorance – (*avijjā*)

The 'stream winner' (*sotāpanna*) and the once-returners (*sakadāgāmi*) still have five *anusayas*: 1, 2, 3, 6 and 7. The never-returners (*anāgāmi*) are subject to three *anusayas*: 3, 6 and 7. This shows that conceit, craving for existence and ignorance are the most powerful of the seven.

The concept of *anusaya* may be linked with the three aspects of craving we discussed: *kāmarāgānusaya* with the craving for sensual pleasures, *paṭighānusaya* with the destructive and annihilationist urges, *māna*, *diṭṭhi* and *bhavarāganusaya* with the ego instinct.

As the *anusayas* lie dormant in the deeper recesses of our personality and may be excited by appropriate stimuli, and as these processes can occur without conscious awareness, this psychological process may be considered as a facet of unconscious motivation in the psychology of Buddhism.

Āsava

Some of the psychological terms we find in the suttas are described by imagery, and even their meanings are often charged with metaphorical associations. In this connection the word '*āsava*' is clarified by the use of metaphors and two such metaphors are used in the Buddhist writings: intoxicating extract of a flower or tree; discharge from a sore or wound.

Like liquor which is kept for a long time, the psychological states referred to as *āsava* have been simmering in the deeper recesses of a person's mind. A close equivalent of this concept in western psychology would be the Freudian notion of the Id, which again has been described in metaphorical terms – 'a cauldron of seething excitations'. Both concepts seem to depict in a metaphorical way the archaic roots of the irrational in man. Some scholars feel that this idea of overwelming intoxication is the central meaning of the word *āsava*, compared with other meanings like 'taint' or oozing from a wound. However, the comparison of the mind to a festering sore is also found in the suttas.[75]

The *āsavas* which are mentioned frequently are *kāmāsava, bhavāsava, diṭṭhāsava* and *avijjāsava*. Horner translates these as the cankers of sense-pleasure, becoming, false views and ignorance.[76] The word canker suggests something that corrodes or corrupts slowly. These figurative meanings perhaps describe facets of the concept of *āsava*: kept in long storage, oozing out, taint, corroding, etc.

There is a sutta called the *Sabbāsavasutta* (*Discourse on All the Cankers*) in which it is said that *āsavas* can be got rid of by insight, restraint of the senses, avoidance, wise use of life's necessities, eliminating unclear thoughts, the development of the mind, and so on. The development of the mind is specially effective in stabilising the 'links in awakening' that will keep out corroding and consuming passions.[77]

The Stream of Consciousness (viññāṇa-sota)

Consciousness (*viññāṇa*) in one of the senses in which it is used refers to the survival factor which links one life and another.[78] A special term, (*saṃvattanika viññāṇa*) is used to convey this idea of the relinking consciousness. Some critics feel that the Buddha considered consciousness to be a permanent entity and as a substance which moves from one life to another. The Buddha rejected the notion of consciousness as a permanent entity and pointed out that consciousness is the product of conditions, in the absence of which, there will be no origination of consciousness.[79]

In the suttas it is pointed out that consciousness is one of the four sustenances (*āhāra*) for the maintanence of beings. The Buddha also says that if someone raises the question, 'Who now is it, lord, who feeds on the consciousness?' this is not a proper question; but if someone were to ask, 'Of what, lord, is the consciousness a sustenance?' that *is* a proper question. The answer is that consciousness-sustenance is the cause of renewed becoming, of rebirth in the future.[80]

Consciousness is the influx conditioned by a causal pattern and it is a dynamic continuum. It is also referred to as a stream of consciousness (*viññāṇa sota*), and a stream of becoming (*bhavasota*). The evolving consciousness which continues after death maintains its dynamism because it is nourished by the manifestations of craving. There is a residuum from the psychological dispositions of the individual which by its dynamic nature nourishes the continuation of the individual or of phenomenal existence in general.

It is also said of the 'stream of consciousness' of a living person, that a part of it is present in this world (*idhaloke patiṭṭhitam*) and a part in the world beyond (*paraloke patiṭṭhitam*); this stream of consciousness has two components, a conscious and an unconscious facet. The part of the stream of consciousness of which the individual is not aware may be the dynamic unconscious comprised of the dispositions (*saṅkhāra*) that determine the character of the next birth.[81] Knowledge of this stream of consciousness with a conscious and unconscious component is only within the reach of those who develop the practice of meditation, and in the context in which this is discussed in the *Dialogues of the Buddha* it is said that when a person enters into the third stage of meditation such knowledge is accessible. This direct knowledge of unconscious processes would be superior to whatever inferences we make on reasoning, the behaviour of others and the limited introspective study of our own minds.

The concept of *saṇkhāra* (disposition) is important here. Because such dispositions function both at a conscious and an unconscious level, it is said in the *Gradual Sayings*, in a context which discusses four methods of knowing the mind of another, that a yogin is able to discern the mind of another person and develop an insight into the mental dispositions of another person. According to the mental dispositions of another person, he is able to predict that the person will at a certain time have 'such and such a thought'.[82] As the person is not conscious of the mental dispositions (*mano-saṅkhāra*) which subsequently influence his process of thought, they are not present in his consciousness when they are discerned by others. The suttas also make specific reference to *asampajā-mano-saṅkhāra* (mental dispositions of the mind of which we are not aware).[83]

In the concepts of the dormant proclivities (*anusayas*), corroding cankers or intoxicants (*āsavas*), the dynamic dispositions (*saṅkhāra*) connecting two lives, mental dispositions of which we are not aware *asampajāna-mano-saṅkhāra*), etc., we have an authentic base for the development of a notion of unconscious activity. Two other concepts often referred to in Buddhist writings, those of *ālayavijñāna* (storehouse consciousness) and *bhavaṅga sota* (stream of existence), do not belong to the psychology of the suttas. The former is a concept found in Mahāyana works and the latter belongs to the Abhidhamma literature.[84]

Conative Activity (*Saṅkhāra*)

There are two significant facets to the psychology of motivation: the affective and the conative facets of human behaviour. Contemporary psychologists do not accept the tripartite psychological divisions of conative, affective and cognitive, but would rather consider them as facets of integrated activity which may be found in a particular action. As we have already mentioned, for the purposes of study and analysis, by a process of abstraction *vedanā* may be considered as the basic concept for affective experience, while conative action and volition are centred on the concept of *saṅkhāra*.

It has been maintained that there has been a paucity of studies pertaining to the psychology of will in Buddhism.[85] It has also been mentioned that some of the early western scholars of Buddhism associated 'will' with 'thirst' (*taṇha*), and such strong desires were considered as bad and deleterious. Thus the possibility of developing a positive psychology of will (as a factor to be developed rather than repressed) was neglected by Buddhist scholars.

This certainly is an important area to be explored. But the word 'will' is semantically troublesome. In keeping with the psychology of Buddhism we may speak of a broad conative dimension of behaviour, under which we could study specific concepts like effort, volition, aspiration, etc. The semantic position here is important: the term 'will' is so vague that it cannot be identical with the more diversified, specific and analytical Buddhist terms. Thus without using the broad term 'will', we shall examine specific facets of effort, volition, aspiration, etc., against the background of the concept of *saṅkhāra*.

Saṅkhāra may be described as 'motivated and purposeful activity' which also has moral consequences.[86] However, as was mentioned in Chapter 1, there are two psychological aspects to *saṅkhāra*: deliberation and volition on the one hand, and dynamism, persistence and habit on the other. The word '*cetanā*', with which the word *saṅkhāra* is often used synonymously, suggests the idea of volition. The concept of *abhisaṅkhāra* brings out the element of dynamism which emphasises the meaning of *saṅkhāra* as karma formation: 'The wheel kept rolling so long as the impulse that set it moving lasted (*abhisaṅkhārassa gati*). Then it circled round and fell to the ground.'[87] This graphic image from the *Aṅguttara Nikāya* refers to the idea of momentum and dynamism that the concept of *saṅkhāra* indicates as a link in the wheel of dependant origination.

The fusing of concepts like deliberation and habit-behaviour is not foreign to western psychology. Flugel, for instance, cites the concept of 'orexis' which brings together the conative and affective elements. Thus 'conative dispositions' appears to be a fitting translation of the world *saṅkhāra*.[88]

These conative dispositions may be divided into wholesome and unwholesome dispositions, as well as conscious and unconscious dispositions. The elimination of passions and the control of the senses rest on the development of wholesome conative dispositions. As the passions and the defiling elements are strong, a great deal of effort is necessary to go against the current (*paṭisotagāmi*). Right intention, effort, energy and persistence are the qualities that help people to withstand the strength of defiling impulses, as well as to develop more positive aspirations towards the paths of spiritual growth.

In the *Anguttara Nikāya* it is said that there are four kinds of efforts:

the effort to restrain, the effort to abandon, the effort to make become and the effort to watch over.[89] The effort to restrain implies that a person guards his senses without letting either convetousness or dejection disturb his mind. In the effort to abandon, if an evil thought emerges in a person's mind, either a sensual thought or a cruel and malign one, it is expelled and eliminated. The effort to make become is the attempt to let positive spiritual skills emerge, such as mindfulness, investigation of the *dhamma*, zest, tranquillity, equanimity, etc. The effort to watch over concentrates on repulsive objects and signs that will destroy any emerging lust and greed.

Cetanā *and the Vocabulary of Conation*

Cetanā is a key term that gives special significance to the actions of people. But it cannot in all contexts be adequately rendered by the English words 'will' or 'volition'. It is a mental factor (*cetasika*) common to all states of consciousness, karmically neutral ones and even the weakest among them. Its function, valid for all states of consciousness, is said to be the co-ordinating, organising and directing the other conjoined mental properties. It is the presence of some of these co-nascent factors that determines the specific and 'developed' functions of *cetanā*. For instance, if *kusala* or *akusala* thoughts are present, *cetanā* becomes moral or immoral karmic volition, and may even produce rebirth. It becomes intensifed by the presence of *vīriya* (energic effort); when *vitakka-vicāra* is present its 'thought organising' function becomes intensifed; etc.

This analysis of the nature of *cetanā* may be concluded by mentioning that in the psychology of Buddhism representations of all four mental *khandhas* are present in all states of consciousness. Thus mental factors like volition are not separate entities, but are inseparably associated with other factors. They are just functions in a dynamic unit of consciousness. They are as inseparable as the shape, colour and flavour of a mango. Thus, though we have for the sake of analysis spoken of the cognitive, conative and affective dimensions of behaviour, the psychology of Buddhism cannot strictly uphold traditional tripartite faculty psychology. They are really aspects found in all states of consciousness and behaviour.

4 Personality

PSYCHOLOGICAL PERSPECTIVES OF PERSONALITY STUDY AND THE BUDDHIST CONCEPT OF THE HUMAN PERSON

In the discourses of the Buddha the philosophical and psychological aspects of the 'person' concept are often intermingled and even interwoven, and it is only by a process of dissection and abstraction that the material can be separated for purposes of study.

Let us first take a look at the psychological perspectives of personality study. The term 'personality' has a distinctive meaning within the field of psychology: for the psychologist the term implies

> the study of the characteristic and distinctive traits of an individual, the stable and shifting patterns of relationships between these traits, the origin of the traits, and the ways the traits interact to help or hinder the adjustment of a person to other people and situations.[1]

Such a study has two facets: a structural aspect that deals with the description of traits and their relationship, and a dynamic aspect that deals with the motivational influence of traits upon adjustment. Thus the analysis of emotions and motivation which we have made in the preceding chapter is directly related to the study of personality. In fact, out of the many areas of study in contemporary psychology, the triad of motivation, emotion and personality takes a central place in the psychology of Buddhism.

In dealing with personality characteristics, one does not get at occasional events like 'A was angry yesterday morning', but whether A is characteristically a hostile person or a person with a calm disposition. It can be said of a person with a calm disposition that even if you pass irritating comments or abuse him, it is not easy to excite him. Also, the aspects of personality that we choose from must be distinctive. To say that a certain person works for a living may not be very significant (as there are large numbers who do so), compared with statements like 'A is industrious', 'B is lazy' or 'C is self-assertive', etc., which pinpoint distinguishing personality characteristics. Thus the psychology of personality study directs attention on to aspects which are *characteristic* and *distinctive*. A trait is an aspect of personality that is both characteristic and distinctive of a person. Because of the large variety of traits found in people, some have tried to put the traits together by finding clusters of related traits.

There have also been attempts to focus attention on the more dramatic and outstanding qualities of people and group them according to 'personality types'. But such typologies might lead to excessive generalisation and simplification. Personality typologies might be used for a specific purpose tied to a limited context.

The psychology of Buddhism offers material for the study of both *traits* and *types* of personality. However, in keeping with the framework within which Buddhist psychological analysis emerged, both trait and type analysis are rooted in a basic ethical and spiritual concern about man. This means that the discourses of the Buddha focus attention on psychological qualities which are of ethical and spiritual concern. There is a reference to personality types in *Aṅguttara Nikāya*[2] and the *Saṅgīti-sutta* of the *Dīgha-Nikāya*,[3] and a more systematic analysis in the *Puggala-Paññatti* (Human Types). The subject is also given stimulating discussion in the *Visuddhimagga*. Since the material in the suttas is dispersed, the other works may be consulted with a certain amount of caution.[4] The classification of the types of people discussed there centres on ethically wholesome and unwholesome psychological traits, as well as on levels of spiritual development. The personality types are linked up with aspects of therapy and techniques of meditation.

Due to the strong ethical flavour in the psychology of human personality in Buddhism the 'psychology of conflict' takes a significant place. Conflicts between specific desires as well as the more general conflict between 'the flesh and spirit' need discussion. Thus the world of turbulent passions on one side and their control, restraint, elimination, redirection, etc., on the other side are of central importance in the dynamics of personality study within the doctrine. The primitive desires (*āsava*), which we have already referred to as being similar to the Freudian Id, are regulated by the strength of one's own conscience (*attādhipateyya*), concern for what the world says (*lokādhipateyya*) and respect for the *dhamma* (*dhammādhipateyya*). This picture has a certain resemblance to the

Freudian notions of Id, Ego and the Super-ego, the difference being that Buddhism brings out both the damaging as well as the healthy facets of the Super-ego. In the study of emotions we have already mentioned that the Buddha requires man to develop a healthy and productive sense of shame and fear (*hiri-ottappa*), as distinct from pathological guilt and worry, which can be a hindrance to one's spiritual development. In this manner the psychology of conflict would form a significant problem for the study of personality.

Finally, in the suttas problems relating to individuality, uniqueness of personality, self and continuity are given an analysis which is more philosophical than psychological. But the philosophical perspectives throw a considerable amount of light on the texture of the concepts and terminology of Buddhist psychology.

PHILOSOPHICAL PERSPECTIVES

Philosophers use the term 'persons' to specify an area of study, and the psychologists use the word 'personality' to deal with a parallel problem area, although, in the work of humanistic psychologists like Maslow and Rogers and existentially oriented psychologists like Rollo May, the word 'person' is used. In fact, today problems such as the 'crisis in identity' and a basic concern with the human person have paved the way for refreshing interdisciplinary discussion among philosophers, psychologists and sociologists. In some of the emerging inter-disciplinary as well as cross-cultural studies, there is a cutting across through 'well-fenced' problem areas and methodological stances. This trend has not taken place in a chaotic manner, but rather is a persistent yet cautious attempt to search for new horizons in humanistic as well as social science studies.

In the context of Buddhism, the psychological perspectives on personality study cannot be *completely* separated from the more philosophically oriented (or 'meta-psychological') analysis of the person concept. On the one hand, there is a significant analysis of the psychology of motivational factors and personality traits in Buddhism, but on the other there is a highly critical and sustained analysis of such philosophical problem-creators as 'soul', 'consciousness', 'mind', 'self', etc.

The question of how a religion which denies a permanent self can make provision for personality study has often been put in an almost polemical form. In this context, it may be mentioned that very early in the history of human thought Buddhism began to 'psychologise without a soul' and the doctrine's view of human experience as a process falls in line with accepted dynamic psychology in the west.

The Buddha rejected an eternally abiding pure ego (*attā*) and described the universe in terms of the arising, decay and dissolution of all things. He maintained that all things, including both mind and body, are subject to change and transient. The doctrines of egolessness (*anattā*) and of transcience (*anicca*), along with that of suffering (*dukkha*), form the central base of the philosophy of the human person in Buddhism. Within the psychological analysis of Buddhism, it will be seen that there is no substance, but a continuous flux of material and mental processes arising from particular conditions. The mind is a dynamic continuum which is described by the Buddha by means of a number of analogies. Sometimes, it is compared to a flame, whose existence depends upon a number of factors: i.e. the wick, oil, etc.; sometimes it is compared to a stream (*sota*), and again the movements of a monkey jumping from branch to branch, letting go of one branch only after it clings to another, etc., are used. One significant point on which the Buddhist analysis may differ from western psychology is that this dynamic continuum is not limited to one life-span; it consists of a conscious mind as well as an unconscious in which is stored the residue of emotionally charged memories going back not only to childhood, but also to past lives. A personality study within such a dynamic psychology sounds plausible and interesting, and what we can do in this chapter is to do some clearing of the ground regarding the possibility of such a project.

The more philosophically oriented questions have centred on the question of 'personal identity'. The ethics of Buddhism has a concept of responsibility, which calls for a sense of 'continuity' as far as the person is concerned. If I am to be responsible for my acts, 'I must continue to exist and be capable of acknowledging that I am the same individual who performed them . . . '[5]

Thus in philosophical discussions, the central question is, What are the necessary and sufficient logical criteria for identifying persons? Attempts have been made to present logically adequate criteria for re-identifying persons in terms of consciousness, memory and body.[6] Strawson's position on this is very instructive: persons are distinct from material bodies, though this does not imply that they are therefore immaterial bodies. A person has states of consciousness as well as physical attributes and it is not merely to be identified with one or the other. This concept of the human person as a psycho-physical being fits in well with the Buddhist analysis.

The contention that in rejecting the existence of a permanent soul, the Buddha is not also rejecting the existence of a continuous person is important.[7] The Buddhist doctrine requires some sense of a 'continuing person' as an agent of moral action and responsibility. The same requirement would be needed for a study of the psychology of personality.

In some recent studies on the human person there are few relevant observations made in this connection. Buddhism accepts that there is a continuous person and that the person consists of organic factors which are causally interdependent and subject to change.[8] Though the Buddha does not accept a persisting substratum, the word 'person' is used in a conventional sense to 'distinguish one serial process from another'.[9]

Against the background of this analysis persons will have purposes of their own, and they are the sources of the values they generate; they are capable of taking decisions and accepting responsibility for their acts. They will have rights and duties and are capable of being punished. In general, they are agents who can be both rational and irrational, but basically always responsible for their actions. Psychologically, it is of significance to say that persons have memories, thought, feeling and communicate with others.

In a psychological sense, the word 'personality' has merely conventional usage, referring to a certain unity of functions – for example, walking, standing, perceiving, thinking, deciding, a proneness to get annoyed, etc. As the parts of a chariot work together, so do the body, feeling, consciousness and dispositions combine.[10]

Rune Johansson feels that in this analogy we find a functional concept of personality:

> Here the functional unity of personality is really what contemporary psychologists call 'personality'. The car has clearly some sort of primitive personality, an individual constellation of parts; it is capable of functioning only when all the parts are there. None of the parts can be called 'car', not even all the parts together, if they are not combined in a very special way . . . A personality is also not the body, not the perceptual function, not the feeling etc., but the proper combination of them.[11]

Johansson feels that this concept of personality is something that 'modern psychology can only applaud.'[12]

Now that we have clarified the important aspects of the logical, ethical and psychological framework of the concepts of 'person' and 'personality', it should be possible to work out in detail the material in the discourses of the Buddha pertaining to the psychology of personality.

PERSONALITY TRAITS AND TYPES

There is a discussion in the *Aṅguttara nikāya* regarding the ways of knowing a person's character.[13] It is said that a person's qualities cannot be found out casually but require continuous contact. The four qualities of character discussed are virtue, integrity, fortitude and wisdom. It is said that to find out whether a person is virtuous living with that person is necessary:

> Living together with a person, one comes to know him thus: For a long time the actions of this worthy have shown weakness, defects, taints and blemishes as to his morals; and he was, morally, not consistent in his actions and conduct. This worthy is an immoral person, he is not virtuous.
>
> For a long time the actions of this worthy have shown no weaknesses, defects, taints or blemishes as to his morals; he is morally consistent in his actions and conduct. This worthy is virtuous, he is not an immoral person.

In this manner qualities of character may be discovered over a long period. Of course, what has been said about the virtuous and the immoral at a very high level of generality, may be done with more specific aspects of virtue or its opposite like lying, stealing, etc.

In the same manner it is said that a man's integrity can be checked by having dealings with him. You have to check whether his early behaviour falls in line with his later behaviour and whether the way he deals with one person is similar to or dissimilar from the way he deals with others.

It is then said that at times of crises or when misfortune falls, it is possible to test one's fortitude. If one has to face situations like the loss of someone dear to him, loss of wealth or falling a prey to sickness – a man of fortitude will not be perturbed in facing such situations. He will understand that 'gain and loss, fame and disrepute, praise and blame, happiness and unhappiness' are a part of natural worldly vicissitudes (*aṭṭha-lokadhammā*). The opposite of this type of person is the one who will be disturbed by such situations and will lament, grieve and be worried about them – the anxiety-prone person.

Finally, it is said that through conversation it is possible to find out whether a man has wisdom. From the way he examines, formulates and presents a problem, it is possible to discuss whether he is a wise man; the words that he utters may be shallow and superficial or loaded with subtle and profound meaning.

This discussion is significant for two reasons: it examines four ways of discovering the true nature of people, and at the same time indicates the kind of personality traits which are central to the psychology of Buddhism, revealing that it is basically qualities of character which are important within the ethical scaffolding of Buddhism. These are somewhat different from the kind of 'personality traits' studied by modern psychologists, and even traits which are psychological in nature are presented within the same ethical framework. What is more, some of the qualities are so general in nature that they may have to be further split into components with more specific meanings if they are to be capable of empirical delineation. However this shows that apart from the use of introspection, which holds a central place as a way of obtaining self-knowledge, the Buddha recognises the value of certain behavioural tests to find out the qualities of people and their dispositions.

Another significant aspect of these 'character traits' is that they cut across the dispositions of people over a number of births and thus go beyond the limits of childhood experience. This, too, is a concept that has not been absorbed by contemporary psychology in the west. Consider the following:

> . . . a certain woman is ill-tempered, of a very irritable nature. On very little provocation she becomes cross and agitated. She is upset and becomes stubborn, she shows temper and ill-will and displeasure. She is no giver of charity to recluse or brahmin, nor gives food, drink, clothing, vehicle, flowers, scent, ointment, bed, lodging or light. Moreover, she is jealous minded, she is jealous of other folk's gain, of the honour, respect, reverence, homage and worship paid to them. She is revengeful and harbours a grudge. . . .[14]

This person who bears the traits of being ill-tempered, jealous, revengeful and not-generous will carry these traits with her to the next life:

> Such a one, if deceasing from that life, she comes back to this state of things, wherever she is reborn, is ill-favoured, ill-formed, of a mean appearance and poor, having little of her own, of small possessions, and is of small account.[15]

Such a conception of personality or character traits cutting across a number of births has not even come under serious consideration by the clinical psychology of the west.

The question whether it is possible to give a systematic breakdown of the 'character traits' is an important one. The character traits are discussed mainly in terms of the ethical and spiritual development of the person and there are specific enumerations of traits that obstruct development. For instance in the sutta called the *Simile of the Cloth*, there are sixteen qualities which are enumerated as defilements of the mind: covetousness, ill will, anger, hostility, denigration, overbearingness, envy, jealousy, hypocrisy, fraud, obstinacy, presumption, conceit, arrogance, vanity and negligence.[16]

Psychological traits that obstruct one's spiritual development are listed in the suttas under, for instance, the dormant proclivities (*anusaya*), hindrances (*nīvaraṇa*), cankers (*āsava*), etc. No purpose is served by listing all the many different groupings – they simply manifest the ethical and spiritual scaffolding within which the psychologically significant traits are presented.

In the psychology of Buddhism there is a close connection between psychological traits and personality types. As the discussion in the sutta on this issue is somewhat dispersed, it may be helpful to read the analysis found in the *Visuddhimagga*. This material has already been neatly arranged and presented by Edward Conze.[17] This analysis in the *Visuddhimagga* represents six types of persons: in the six types there are six dominating qualities: greed, hate, delusion, faith, intelligence and discursiveness, greed, hate and delusion being, of course, directly related to the unwholesome roots of motivation.[18]

CONFLICT AND FRUSTRATION

A significant way of characterising people is to examine their modes of adjustment to situations, especially the satisfaction of needs under varying circumstances. The satisfaction of some of the needs and basic drives that we discussed in the previous chapter creates conflicts, disappointment, frustration and anxiety. The individual finds his own way of coping with frustrations, tensions and conflict, and these modes of adjustment, too, colour the personality of the person.

The Buddha says that the condition of the average man is basically one that generates conflicts and disturbances. In the *Araṇavibhaṅga Sutta* an ideal state of peace and absence of conflict (*araṇa*) is compared with the condition of the ordinary man.[19] The word *santi* refers to absence of conflict or peace in a more positive sense. A peculiarity of the psychology of Buddhism is that the notions of 'conflict' and 'peace' have to be examined at two levels. On the one hand, there is the absolute state of peace, quietude and harmony signified by the concept of *nibbāna*, which is compared to the state of the man subject to *dukkha*, filled with unrest, tension, anxiety and conflict. There is also the difference in concept between the harmony which is the ideal for the householder, and that which the recluse in search of absolute peace seeks to achieve. The psychology of conflict and anxiety has to be understood at two levels, and so do the ideals of personality development.

For the person who does not commit himself to the life of renunciation, the Buddha recommends the life of the righteous householder. The righteous householder seeks wealth by lawful means, without greed and longing, gets ease and pleasure for himself and does meritorious deeds.[20] While the recluse seeking ultimate release from suffering will obtain inner peace (*ajjhatta-santi*), the righteous householder aims at harmonious living (*dhammacariyā*, *samacariyā*).[21] This is the concept of the well-adjusted and balanced person, who, while he seeks pleasure, exercises a degree of restraint and limits his wants. Thus, while the enjoyment of pleasure as such is not condemned, excessive and illegitimate pleasures are.[22]

Keeping in mind these two ideals of peace and harmony, the psychology of conflict, also, will take two forms. This is a significant point, since the personalities of the householder and the recluse are coloured by the kind of goals and ideals they seek. Their motivation, conflicts and even anxieties have to be examined from this dual standpoint.

Let us first analyse the nature of conflicts encountered by the householder following the ideal of a righteous, balanced and harmonious life. He will be subjected to both personal and social conflicts. If a person's desires are strong and he is subject to excessive craving, then in his pursuit for pleasure and the achievement of his ambitions he will come into conflict with other people. It is said in the *Dīghanikāya* that when a man is subjected to strong craving, he clings to the objects of his desire with a tenacity and avarice which will ultimately issue in violent interpersonal relations: 'blows and wounds, strife, contradiction and retort, quarrelling, slander and lies'.[23] Also, if a person is blind to the accepted legal and moral order, for example committing adultery or trespassing on others' property, he will come into conflict with the law. That is why the righteous householder is expected to achieve his aims by 'lawful means' and 'without greed and longing'.

At a deeper psychological level such an individual will be subject to inner psychological conflicts: as a person who has made a compromise with life and lives the life of a householder, he will be subject to conflicts within the accepted limits of his wants and desires – between two pleasure-giving objects of equal attractiveness neither of which can be had, between the desire for security and the risks involved in making a livelihood, between the need to control his temper against one who has been mean and his wish to respond in kind, etc.

'Conflict' in the psychological sense emerges in a situation where a person is impelled to engage in two or more mutually exclusive activities, as the satisfaction of one implies the frustration of the other. The alternatives which are present to the individual may be of an equal degree of attractiveness or unattractiveness. The proverbial donkey who was torn between two equally attractive bales of hay starved to death. And a man may find himself faced with having to choose between two equally repulsive alternatives, like the man poised between the devil and the deep blue sea. But the more complex situation very relevant to the psychology of Buddhism is the situation where the same object has both a 'positive valence' and 'negative valence' – pleasures are manifold and sweet (*kamā citrā madhurā*), but yet they cause little delight (*appassādā*), much suffering (*bahudukkhā*) and much turbulence (*bahūpāyasā*).[24]

The roots of these conflicts can be understood against the

psychology of motivation we outlined in the last chapter. *Lobha* rendered as greed or lust generates the positive desires and the conflicts dependent on such desires; *dosa* generates the avoidance desires in the form of anger, and hate; it is *moha* rendered as delusion that makes a conflict into a complex state, since a lack of understanding regarding the genesis of one's motives converts a simple conflict into an incessant tangle, a state of confused consciousness.

While these immoral roots of action bring about conflicts within the individual as well as between individuals, their opposites bring about inner happiness (*ajjhattāsukha*) and peace (*santi*) within the individual as well as a group of individuals.

The psychology of conflicts has to be analysed in terms of the powerful expressions of craving that we discussed in the last chapter. The strong drive for sensuous pursuits, with the search for novelty, excitement and possessiveness, is a generator of conflicts. With the limited means at his disposal, and within the framework of existing taboos, morality and law, man has to decide between competing desires related to the satisfaction of his drives. Though people develop strong attachments to pleasures and pleasure-giving objects, there is also, as the Buddha points out, an equally strong proclivity to search for variety. Man searches for variety, finds delight in the ever-changing panorama of stimuli that titillates his senses: he finds delight 'in this and that, here and there' (*tatra tatrābhinandinī*).

The temporary satisfaction that every change of sensations brings conceals whatever dissatisfaction emerges in this restless craving for novelty. A deep appreciation of this psychology is seen in the image of the person in tremendous pain, who will drown even this by contact with fire:

> It is both now, good Gotama, that contact with the fire is painful, exceedingly hot and afflicting and also before that contact with that fire was painful, exceedingly hot and afflicting. Yet good Gotama, this leper, a man with his limbs all ravaged and festering, being eaten by vermin . . . might from the painful contact with the fire, receive *a change of sensation* and think it pleasant.[25]

This image of the leper in pain is further developed by the Buddha in the light of the reply he elicited from Magandiya, who answered his query. If a person has a painful wound it must be cured and healed by medicine, and not by the process of drowning one pain by another. The man who is struck by the disease, 'burning with the fever of sense pleasures', cannot find happiness by rushing after a never-ending succession of pleasures.[26]

The man who is drowned in this 'fever of sense pleasures' sees no other way of proceeding, except to seek a 'change of sensations'. It is against this background that the Buddha presents the psychology of conflict. Thus the man will be beset with what the psychologist calls an 'approach-approach conflict' – the strength of mutually attractive alternatives. Sometimes we are forcefully tied to painful situations, and the only alternative would be between two painful situations which have to be equally avoided, again like the man poised between the devil and the deep blue sea. This is described by the psychologist as an 'avoidance-avoidance conflict'. Pleasure-giving objects also have both a positive aspect that attracts and a negative aspect that repels – *kāmānam assādo* (satisfaction in pleasures of the senses) and *kāmānam ādīnavo* (the peril in sense pleasures).[27] Thus conflicting desires emerge between two equally attractive objects, equally painful objects and facets of the same object partly pleasant and partly unpleasant. The Buddha, of course, says that in a deeper sense and in the final analysis, all those pleasures that emerge from greed, hatred and delusion lead to discontent.

As we do not always get what we want, we are liable to frustration. It is really the threat of frustration rather than actual frustration as such that intensifies the stress in a conflict situation. Powerful and strong wishes are as capable of creating anxiety as actual disappointments. Also, the things that we obtain are liable to decay or to become stale and boring, and the resultant inner discontent will be deeper than merely not getting what one wants. This deep sense of frustration emerges when the pleasures and excitement that you run after turn out to be empty ones. This deeper sense of 'frustration' does not emerge into full awareness in the same way as simpler forms of frustration like missing a specific target. In the accepted terminology of western psychology, it may not be proper to use the term 'frustration' to describe inner discontent, for 'frustration' is the thwarting of goal-directed behaviour. The Buddha, of course, says that below these simple situations of frustration are the deeper roots of staleness and boredom.

Apart from the craving for sensuous gratification, another source of psychological conflict is the craving for self-preservation (*bhava-taṇhā*). The personality that is described as the lustful type (*rāgacarita*) broadly falls into two sub-types, the one in whom the lust for sensuality dominates and the other in whom the lust for power, ambition, status, fame and various forms of aggressive self-assertion overpower other facets of his personality. In this latter sub-type the drive for self-preservation is more dominant than the drive for sensuality, and the person's conflicts are coloured by this personality make-up. When an ambition for power, status and fame is excited in a person, he gets pushed from one object of desire to another, all of which cannot be had. The man with a strong power drive will have strong psychological conflicts and will be equally prone to a sense of frustration when he is obstructed. He is also liable to the deeper sense of staleness and boredom. Achievement of certain goals may enhance a personality, but those directed by a strong lust for power will not enrich one's personality; rather they will eat parasitically into one's personality and cripple one's potential for creative work.

This type of personality is also liable to the three kinds of conflict that we discussed earlier in relation to sensuality. The aggression consequent on frustration is also of equal significance. When objects of one's ambitions cannot be achieved due to obstruction, one's proneness to aggression (*paṭighānusaya*) is excited. When frustration reaches an unbearable point, we come across an apparently rare phenomenon, the conflict between the desire to live (*bhava-taṇhā*) and the craving for annihilation (*vibhava-taṇhā*) which emerges in attempted suicide.

The craving for annihilation triggered off by states of frustration is first directed against repulsive objects and then deflected against oneself. Certain types of self-mortification, too, are a disguised manifestation of the craving for annihilation. Such contradictory attitudes like the desire to live and the desire to destroy oneself can co-exist below the level of conscious awareness, and account for the patterns of emotional ambivalence displayed by people in conflict situations.

In this manner, the psychology of conflict may be analysed in terms of the desires for sensuous gratification, self-preservation and self-annihilation, and the motivational roots of greed and hatred. But the psychology of conflict and frustration in Buddhism goes deeper than this to the roots of delusion, in terms of which the subtler manifestations of anxiety can be comprehended.

ANXIETY

Anxiety and vexation (*kodhaupāyāsa*) may be generated by one's attempt to obtain specific objects in the external world or by some haunting inner disquiet. While analysing the specific fears and anxieties, the Buddha always takes us into the level of a basic anxiety fed by the various forms of ego-illusion. Thus the root delusion is as important as the roots of greed and hatred in understanding the psychology of conflict, frustration and anxiety in Buddhism.

Some psychologists feel that frustrations produced by 'avoidance-avoidance' conflicts and 'approach-avoidance' conflicts are likely to produce anxiety as a general reaction.[28] In the former people vaccilate between two negative or fear-producing situations. Fear is produced as a person gets close to one such situation and moves away from it; but as he moves away he gets closer to the other fear-producing situation. To take the second type of conflict (approach-avoidance), a person is tempted to strike at a person whom he hates intensely, but fears that the other person will retaliate.

When such fears are repressed and pushed beyond awareness the seeds of anxiety develop. After repression, the person feels afraid, but does not know exactly what he is afraid of. What is called objectless anxiety is such a diffuse state of uneasiness. Fears which had a specific object take such a form after repression.

The psychology of Buddhism also deals with anxieties which can by analysis be reduced to specific fears, but it points as well towards a more basic anxiety that lies behind both everyday unhappiness and hysterical uneasiness. There are anxieties about externalities like the possession of a house, property or money and the internal anxieties caused by one's attachment to the ego. In this deeper sense, man is incessantly tied to conflict situations and prone to anxiety, and this is caused by the attachment to the belief in 'I' and 'me', which instead of giving us a feeling of security, creates worry and anxiety (*paritassana*).[28]

In general, conflicts and anxieties emerge in three types of situations: the relationship between the self and the outer world, between the self and other selves, and finally between the discordant aspects of one's own self. The difficulty in seeing through the conflicting welter of ego-attitudes and ambiguities in these relationships is due to the condition of half-obscurity and ignorance that colours the emotional conflicts of people.[29] It is the root delusion that explains this phenomenon, by way of the diverse forms of ego-illusion, which the Buddha presents as the twenty forms of wrong personality-belief (*sakkāya-diṭṭhi*).[30] The link between the ego and forms of anxiety is central to the teaching of the Buddha.

CONFLICTS AND THE RELIGIOUS LIFE

The recluse in search of inner peace will be liable to temptations that he has to master, which in general may be described as the conflict between 'flesh and spirit'. A recluse should not be subject to conflicts generated by an unhealthy conscience or pathological sense of guilt. He should develop a healthy and vigorous sense of shame of evil (*hiri*) and dread of evil (*ottappa*). This should not be confused with restlessness and worry (*uddhacca-kukucca*), which obstructs the development of the mind.

Specific advice is given to the recluse regarding ways of handling conflicts, fears and anxieties. If a recluse goes to the forest in search of inner peace, but is yet disturbed by emerging passions, he should remain calm, unshaken and strive to control his turbulent emotions.[31] This can be done by the strength of his own conscience (*attādhipateyya*). If thoughts of sensuality and malice arise in him, the concern for what the world will think will act as a spur to vigilance; this is *lokādhipateyya*. If, however, he cannot be energetic and is subject to negligence and sloth, the respect for the *dhamma* should be an aid; this is *dhammādhipateyya*.

Thus, in discussing the psychology of conflict, the dialogues of the Buddha examine this issue from the standpoint of both the layman and the recluse.

DEFENCE MECHANISMS

Though both layman and the recluse have been advised to deal with conflicts and anxieties in a rational and healthy manner with full awareness, sometimes certain defence mechanisms push these conflicts into the level of the unconscious.

A 'defence mechanism' is a device the individual 'uses unconsciously to protect himself against ego-involving frustration.[32] It is also thus considered as a way in which the individual fools himself, without seeing clearly the nature of his conflicts. Though there is no systematic presentation of the defence mechanisms in the discourses of the Buddha, the harm done by *some* of the defence mechanisms is implicitly hinted at in the material pertaining to the psychology of Buddhism.

First let us take the Buddhist attitude to 'repression'. If a person by his own efforts generates a train of wholesome thoughts which conflict with some of his unwholesome habits, there emerges a healthy conflict which may result in the building up of wholesome activity. Even if such conflicts persist, if they come within the range of one's conscious awareness, they can be handled in a rational manner. But repressed conflicts cannot be handled in this way. Repression is a process by which one's cravings and attachments are relegated to the unconscious level. Such repressed conflicts, existing at the subterranean level, are fed by the *anusayas*, and are causally related to the emergence of unconscious anxieties and fears. If a person 'feels anxious but does not know why', it is necessary to lay bare these repressed conflicts by a constant introspective understanding of one's mental states. Thus, while an ordinary conflict which comes within conscious awareness might even be a spur to the development of personality, repressed conflicts are damaging. According to Buddhist psychology it is by methodical mental culture that one can reach these dark and hidden facets of the mind.

Pathological behaviour is often fed by these repressed conflicts. In this context the practice of meditation should help us to scrutinise our thoughts carefully so that no room is left for the operation of psychological mechanisms like repression. In fact, the five techniques for dealing with the removal of distracting thoughts in the *Vitakkasaṇṭhāna Sutta* (*Discourse on the Forms of Thought*) are of special interest here.[33]

The first is the method of *aññanimitta* ('different object'): ideational activity (*vitakka*) associated with desire (*chanda*), aversion (*dosa*) and confusion (*moha*) can be eliminated by reflection on a different object connected with the wholesome. This method is analogically compared to a carpenter driving out a large peg with a small one. The second method, that of *ādīnava*, aims at scrutinising the peril of these evil thoughts. This is compared to a man in the prime of life who is fond of adornment and beautifying the body and who suddenly sees the disgusting sight of a carcass round his neck. The sense of shock brings out the peril of the unwholesome thoughts that disturbed him. The third is that of *asati amanasikāra* (not paying attention and not attending), where unwholesome thoughts are eliminated by not paying attention to them. This is compared to the man who closes his eyes when he sees an object before him. The fourth method is the method of *mūla bheda*, where a search is made for the cause and source of unwholesome thoughts.

If these techniques fail and if the person is still disturbed by unwholesome thoughts, it is said that by the method of *abhiniggaha* he should restrain these thoughts – with 'his teeth clenched, his tongue pressed against his palate, should by his mind subdue, restrain and dominate the mind'.[34] By the use of these methods, the mind becomes steady, calm and fixed on one point. By repeated practice, one can become, 'a master of the paths taken by the turns of thought' (*vasī vitakkavarapathesu*).[35]

As all these methods are used with full conscious awareness and understanding, they can be clearly distinguished from the operation of unconscious repression. The psychological sophistication betrayed in this sutta by implication rules out any unconscious defence mechanism as a technique for handling conflict.

The mechanism of 'reaction formation' is seen in the development of the way of asceticism (*attakilamathānuyoga*) as an alternative to the way of pure sensuality (*kāmasukhallikānuyoga*). The technique of self-mortification was condemned by the Buddha as a jump into an equally profitless extreme. It is merely an expression of displaced craving. The notion of 'rationalisation' receives more general treatment, it being said here that strong desires are often given justification by a process of reasoning of a metaphysical nature: on account of desire there is clinging (*taṇhā-paccayā diṭṭhi-upādānam*), and clinging is of four forms, one of which is clinging to metaphysical beliefs. The four kinds of clinging referred to are: sensuous clinging, clinging to views, clinging to rules and rituals and clinging to personality beliefs. The clinging to rules and rituals echoes Freud's concept of religious fetishes, and the Buddha criticised those religious rites which attracted people by exciting a feeling of compulsion within them rather than by appealing to a judicious understanding of their function. Here is a description of the religious fetishes that he criticised:

> Such ways as fastings, crouching on the ground, bathing at dawn, reciting of the three, wearing rough hides, and matted hair . . . Chantings and empty rites and penances . . . washings, ablutions, rinsing of the mouth.[36]

While most of the defence mechanisms do not accord with the kind of therapy recommended by the Buddha, there is definitely one context in which the Buddha recommends some form of sublimation. It is said that the self-centred desires that impel men towards egoistic pursuits can be eliminated by another desire – the desire for *nirvāna* (*taṇhaṃ nissāya taṇhaṃ pahātabhaṃ*).[37] This master desire is of a higher order than the first-order desires – and it is not the kind of feverish longing for *nirvāna* which is condemned in another context that he is referring to here, but the development of right aspirations.[38] Since the function of this master desire is to eliminate first-order desires, it may be considered as a form of sublimation.

PERSONALITY AND SOCIETY

The study of drives and emotions cannot be separated from the 'social values' in terms of which they are satisfied and restrained. Drives also involve a process of thwarting and frustration calling for a process of adjustment in a social setting. When we focus attention on the purely internal dynamics of the satisfaction of drives, the triggering events are within the biological make-up of the individual. But there is a process of interaction with the environment during which external stimuli excite the individual to activity. Some of the basic drives with a hard physiological core like thirst and hunger emerge as reactions to internal stimuli; while the sexual drive has both a strong physiological base as well as a socio-psychological orientation, others, like the drive for power, desire for fame, prestige and status, emerge within a process of interaction with the social environment.

In dealing with the basic drives of man which we have already discussed, the Buddha recommends a way of life and a code of ethics in terms of which they *ought* to be satisfied. Thus here we find an analysis of interpersonal relations shot through a normative rather than a descriptive framework. The Buddha accepts that the most significant conditions to which man as a social being is subject are not the physical and the economic ones but the psychological factors. For instance in the *Cakkavattisīhanāda sutta*,[39] which presents in the form of a myth the evolution of a society, and its gradual degeneration and then renewal, the psychological factors of inordinate lust, sexual misbehaviour and craving cause its degeneration; and the resurgent society which emerges from the ruins of the lost society has its base in healthy socio-psychological virtues.

The psychology of Buddhism is not based on an *ideographic* study of the individual case; rather, the approach is *nomothetic*, seeking to uncover general laws of human behaviour; and very few insights are derived from specific groups, a very wide range of generality embracing the human mind as such being drawn upon instead. This special quality in the psychology of Buddhism should provide an interesting approach to understanding group behaviour.

The Buddha recommends a social ethic which will help people to establish healthy interpersonal relations and the ideals of social harmony. In the light of this aim, an interesting analysis of the roots of social disharmony is found in the suttas. The therapy of the Buddha is aimed at changing the psychological dispositions of individuals rather than established social structures. He traces the roots of social conflicts to greed, hatred and the ego-illusion emerging on delusion.

In fact, on certain occasions the Buddha cuts across the somewhat exaggerated dichotomy between the individual and society. It is said, 'Protecting others one protects oneself' (*attānaṃ rakkhanto paraṃ rakkhati, paraṃ rakkhanto attānaṃ rakkhati*).[40] Emotions like greed, hatred, pride, jealousy and envy derive meaning in an interpersonal context, but if we begin with ourselves and try to restrain them, we do not spread the seeds of disharmony to others. If others do not excite our sense of greed or hatred by their own greed and hatred, then greed and hatred lose meaning as forms of social encounter. Thus if each of us begins with himself to eliminate the potential seeds of social discord, the ground clearing for a good society has already been done. But if we leave untouched the sources of social conflicts within ourselves, no social institution can create the conditions for peace and harmony.

A close analysis of the roots of social conflicts shows that the idea of protecting others by protecting oneself can be applied to all three roots of motivation, and in terms of these to three personality types. The lustful type (*rāgacarita*) excites the acquisitive instinct of man and kindles the flames of passion; the hateful type (*dosacarita*) calls for vengeance and sows the seeds of violence; the deluded type (*diṭṭhi carita*) builds up the barriers of prejudice. This would be the Buddhist diagnosis of social disharmony in terms of personality types.

5 Buddhist Psychology and the West: An Encounter between Therapeutic Systems

During ancient times, when people were confronted with what we refer to as 'behaviour disorders' today, they sought assistance through witchcraft, demonology and diverse means of exorcising evil spirits and demons. Some of the developing religious systems absorbed a part of the rites and ceremonies connected with these healing rituals. There were others who rejected the theory of demonic possession and put forward the counter-theory that mental illness was due to the malfunction of the brain. But there was no clear scientific analysis of behaviour disorders until the beginning of the twentieth century.

There were two competing hypotheses which replaced the notion of 'demonic possession'. One was the 'somatogenic hypothesis', which claimed that mental illness could be traced to destruction of nervous tissue, metabolic disorders, improper bodily economy, etc.; the other backed the 'psychogenic hypothesis' that mental illness could be explained in terms of disordered psychological processes.[1] While the former hypothesis was put forward by people like Kraepline, the latter was developed gradually by the cumulative impact of the work of Mesmer, Charcot, Janet, Breuer and Freud. With the assistance of Breuer, Freud realised that hysterical symptoms were not the result of accidental factors like a damaged nervous system, but produced by psychological conflicts.[2] Freud was the most celebrated exponent of the psychogenic hypothesis, though he recognised its limits and accepted structural defects of the nervous system as being of significance in explaining schizophrenia. While accepting the importance of somatogenic factors, we shall in this chapter focus attention mainly on the psychogenic factors related to mental sickness. Regarding the techniques of therapy, our interest will again be in the use of psychological techniques to deal with human suffering rather than the use of physical, electrical or chemical agents.

The first significant attempt to build a comprehensive system of therapy and a theory of mental illness was made by Sigmund Freud. Freud was the founder of psychoanalysis and, since his work spread into the centres of clinical work, other systems of therapy developed – some in opposition to his work, others as critical developments of it. In this chapter, we have selected four theoretical frameworks of therapy: the Freudian one; that of the humanistic psychology of Maslow and Rogers; and the behaviourist and existential forms. Some of these present not just a system of therapy, but also a model of man, and nearly all of them are concerned not merely with treating a limited number of maladjusted people, but extend their work to the normal person as well. In fact, the rigid gap between the normal and the abnormal is not always significant; terms like, for instance, 'sick society' and 'pathology of normalcy', used by Fromm, betray the dimension in which the concepts of the 'normal' and 'abnormal' are used today. According to Fromm the pathology of contemporary society includes such features as alienation, anxiety, alienation, the fear of feeling deeply, passivity, lack of joy, etc. Symptoms of this nature have made it necessary that the psychologist deal not only with the sick patient, but with the deeper diagnosis of a sick society also.

While we have elsewhere made a comparative study in depth of the Freudian and the Buddhist systems of therapy, here we shall take a number of systems in the west and present them in brief outline against the background of Buddhist therapy.[3]

FREUDIAN PSYCHOANALYSIS

The clinical data that Freud collected over the years were continuously welded together, so as to give him some insight into the working of the human mind. He also supplemented his work with studies of the abnormal, by studying the pathology of the normal mind in such phenomena as slips of the tongue, forgetting, mistakes in writing, dreams, etc. He also made a study of art, literature and mythology. On the basis of all the insights he gathered, he worked out his final theory in simple terms, in a book called, *An Outline of Psychoanalysis*, one of the last books he wrote.

According to the final picture of mind which he worked out, he says that man is impelled by three basic instincts, the sexual instinct, the ego instinct and a self-destructive urge. Freud used the word 'libido' (which conceptualised the sex drive) in a very broad sense: on the one hand, it included all bodily pleasure inclusive of genital contact, and on the other hand feelings of tenderness and affection. The word 'libido' comes from the Latin word for 'lust' which, as pointed out by Carl Jung, has etymological affinities with the Buddhist concept of *lobha* (greed). Later Freud came to accept that even self-love (referred to by him as 'narcissism') was a libidinal complement of the egoistic part of the self-preservative instinct. These libidinal drives could be gratified, repressed or handled by such defence mechanisms as reaction-formation, displacement, identification, etc. The repressed impulses remain active at the unconscious level. Repressed conflicts, though pushed out of awareness, remain active at a deeper level and create the conditions for the emergence of tensions and anxiety. For Freud, a pathological symptom is a disguised gratification of an unacceptable impulse.

The drive for self-preservation expresses itself in many ways as the desire for fame, power, status, admiration by others, narcissism, etc. The 'death-instinct' is basically directed against the self and secondarily turned outwards towards people and objects of an unpleasant nature. It has also been said by Freud that the entire psychical activity is bent on procuring pleasure and avoiding pain. However, immediate gratification of the senses is not always possible and often detrimental. The individual has to learn to postpone gratification, renounce a certain amount of pleasure and respect society, law and morality. Thus the 'reality principle' cannot be completely violated in this search for pleasure.

Later, in a work entitled *Beyond the Pleasure Principle*, Freud said that in spite of the strong urge towards pleasurable gratification, there are ways and means of making what is in itself disagreeable the object of psychic pre-occupation. The factor of sadism, where a person inflicts torture on another, and of masochism, where a person inflicts torture on himself, were features which were introduced in support of the notion of a 'death-instinct'. Very many psychologists were prepared to admit a basic aggressiveness in man but not a self-destructive urge, while others went further and said that aggression was merely a defence reaction. Freud also analysed the personality into three components: the Id, a reservoir of impulses; the Ego, which controls the impulses in the light of realities; and the Super-ego, which represents the demands of morality, religion and man's inner conscience.

This picture of man emerged out of his encounter with patients. The patient was encouraged by the analyst to 'talk about himself' using a technique known as 'free association'. In ordinary conversation we leave out the irrelevant, but here the patient is encouraged to bring out whatever trivialities pass through his mind; and, in fact, the apparent trivialities will prove to have significant antecedents in the patient's experiences which have been repressed.

Though the Freudian theory underwent modifications in the work of his followers, its therapeutic context offers some significant insights that will for all time remain as the lasting contribution of Freud: the concept of accepting those parts of oneself which have hitherto been denied as unacceptable; the encouragement to give up façade-building and defence-mechanisms and change one's habitual modes of perception of oneself, the world and other people; the technique of having an interested person, in the form of the analyst, who will listen and enhance one's sense of hope and dignity.[4] This regaining of one's own sense of the self is a concept that was developed by the humanistic school of Maslow, Rogers and later by the existentially oriented work of Laing. While the neo-Freudians like Horney, Sullivan and Fromm developed on Freudian lines (in spite of the criticism they made of Freud), a number of alternative systems of therapy emerged, some of which we will now discuss.

THE HUMANISTIC MODEL

In the work of Freud there was a conflict between the 'humanistic' and the 'mechanistic' models of man. Freudian therapy focused attention on human discontent and misery, but there was an emphasis on such concepts as energy, mechanisms, psychic determinism, and so on. This theoretical stance was in need of revision and the task was attempted by Rogers and Maslow. The outlook of humanistic psychology has been described as one which goes beyond the models of man in psychoanalysis as well as behaviourism:

> They view the behaviouristic model, with its emphasis upon the stimulus situation, as an over simplification: they feel that it needs to be balanced by a consideration of the internal psychological make-up of the individual. At the same time, they do not concur with the negative and pessimistic psychological dynamics of the psychoanalytical model. Rather they emphasize the essentially positive and rational propensities of man and view him as having some measure of freedom and self-direction.[5]

Unlike the behaviourists they do not make an excessive use of animal studies, but they have made studies of normal and exceptional individuals, as well as the maladjusted. It has been claimed that Freudian theory had two setbacks: the domination of the mechanistic model of mind as a reservoir of psychic energy was one feature to which the humanistic tradition reacted; and as a scientist Freud kept meanings and values out of his system. It was necessary for Rogers, Maslow and others to accept the claim that the search for values, meaning and personal growth was basic to the human predicament. It is really the negative aspect of this that caught the eye of the existential therapist – alienation, boredom and lack of meaning. Though there is a degree of conditioning, man can resist environmental influences, and he is self-aware and future-oriented. The system of therapy evolved by Rogers was described as 'client-centred therapy'. Psychotherapists came to realise that patients will not always change by being given instructions or by changing their environment. It is also necessary for the patient to learn how to solve his own problems. The system of Rogers is thus sometimes referred to as a non-directive system of therapy. The individual becomes more important than a specific problem, the present more significant than the past and the ideal of a therapeutic situation is emotional growth. The basic thread that runs through Rogers's client-centred therapy is that people are responsible for their own destinies, and the goal of his therapy is to *get* the client to change his perception of himself. Client-centred therapy has worked well with normal people who have adjustive problems, but not with dependent ones or those who have complex emotional problems.

BEHAVIOUR THERAPY

Behaviour therapy offers a significant contrast to the other systems of therapy discussed here. The general framework of behaviour therapy is rooted in the psychology initiated by John Watson and the later modifications made by B. F. Skinner. Watson considered psychology strictly as the 'science of behaviour', and rejected the technique of introspection, the study of internal mental states and the use of mentalistic concepts in psychology. The behaviourists emphasised objective techniques of observation ('visibles, audibles, tangibles'). Their main speciality was the psychology of learning, and they focused their studies on the stimulus-response relation and the process of psychological conditioning.

Behaviour therapists believe that pathological behaviour is due to undesirable responses to environmental stimuli, and these can be replaced by more effective ones. As a therapeutic technique, they use the methods of conditioning: Wolpe uses the techniques of classical conditioning and Skinner that of operant conditioning. The therapist sees a specific and precise problem, and it is handled in a well-controlled manner. The therapist takes the responsibility for the patient's recovery, and the patient co-operates in doing what he is asked to do. The basis of this therapy is that the symptoms of disorders were learned, and with the appropriate learning techniques, they can be unlearnt and extinguished.

EXISTENTIAL THERAPY

It will be seen from what we said about behaviour therapy that it has a limited purpose – the elimination of a neurotic symptom. It does not concern itself with the patient's style of life. Existential therapy, which emerged within the philosophical dimensions of existentialism, offers a radical contrast to behaviour therapy. Existentialism emerged as a philosophical school based on the work of Soren Kierkegaard, Martin Heidegger, Jean-Paul Sartre and Karl Jaspers. Sartre had himself, while making a critique of Freud, hinted at the possibility of developing a theory of existential psychoanalysis, Jaspers has written a book on psychopathology, and what is called phenomenological psychiatry owes its inspiration to Heidegger. The most prominent phenomenological psychiatrists are Minowski, Erwin Straus and Gebsattel. Existential psychoanalysis was originated by Ludwig Binswanger. The most stimulating work in psychology influenced by existentialism has come from Rollo May.[6]

While there were significant differences between Freud and Binswanger or Freud and philosophers like Sartre and psychologists like Rollo May, they had a common focus of interest. In fact, it has been observed by Peter Lomas in 'Psychoanalysis Freudian or Existential' that it would certainly be a pity if the two systems grew apart rather than together.[7] However, the differences between the behaviour therapist and the existential therapist are more radical. The humanistic therapy of Rogers and Maslow had significant parallels with existential therapy.

In a sense existential therapists were not interested like other psychologies in developing a highly systematised scheme of techniques and a theory; rather they were re-examining the concept of man that underlies therapy. Thus they were attempting to widen the horizons of psychotherapy regarding the application of new ideas to the therapeutic situation.

> It was not with specific techniques of therapy that these psychiatrists and psychologists took issue. They recognize for example, that psychoanalysis is valid for certain types of cases, and some of them, bona fide members of the Freudian movement, employ it themselves. But they all had grave doubts about its theory of man. And they believed these difficulties and limitations in the concept of man not only seriously blocked research but would in the long run also seriously limit the effectiveness and development of therapeutic techniques.[8]

The existential psychologists were attempting to understand the assumptions behind all situations of human beings in crises. In fact, they say that they are not merely concerned with the *ill man*, but with *man as such*. They do not accept the great use made of drives, energy systems, unconscious mechanisms or stimulus response relations. Their focus of interest is on concepts like decision, responsibility, autonomy and identity – all of which may be summarised as the search for the 'authentic person'. Maslow, commenting on existentialism, says that he considers the concept of *identity* as a more basic concept than *existence*. Existentialists like Rollo May believe that 'the loss of illusions and the discovery of identity' though at first sight painful can turn out to be an exhilarating experience. Though both the philosophy of existentialism and existential therapy has come under criticism for the metaphysical temper that pervades them and the lack of specificity of the latter's search, their advocates insist that they are more interested in the wider framework of the images of man and theories of human nature than the development of specific theories.

Though there are other significant therapeutic traditions like Gestalt therapy and group therapy, we have concentrated on therapies with a basic model of man that offer interesting similarities to and differences from the psychology and therapy in Buddhism.

THE THERAPEUTIC AIMS OF BUDDHISM

There are two significant points which make the presentation of the Buddhist standpoint here interesting. A glance at the selected therapies cited above will show that all of them have something significant to offer, and in a comprehensive framework of therapy most of their significant contributions should be absorbed. It appears that a Buddhist perspective on therapy may also be able to absorb some of the valuable insights of all these systems, and thus offer a point of convergence and integration.

Another point of interest is that both in its philosophy and psychology, Buddhism is basically 'therapy oriented'. While its philosophy offers a message for the ideologically dazed and the intellectually bewildered (*diṭṭhi carita*), the psychology offers a message for those who suffer from lust-bound anxieties (*rāgacarita*) and those liable to aggression-prone ones (*dosacarita*). While we are here focusing attention on the psychology of Buddhism, its philosophical underpinning cannot be separated. Perhaps in Buddhism we find a therapy integrated with an image of man which would interest those who are making a plea for widening the horizons of psychotherapy.

The Buddha did not pursue theoretical questions unless they had a bearing on the suffering human being and the psychology of Buddhism is linked to this central therapeutic role, as has been said several times already. Buddhism addresses itself mainly to the question of human suffering and the form in which this is presented corresponds to the structure of traditional Indian medicine: malady – suffering; cause of suffering according to diagnosis – craving and ignorance; treatment – eightfold path; goal of treatment (health) – *nibbāna*.

Suffering has emotional roots in craving (*taṇhā*) and intellectual roots in ignorance (*avijjā*). Craving is derived from the root causes of passion (*rāga*) and hatred (*dosa*) and ignorance from delusion (*moha*). In the therapeutic setting tranquillity is advocated for the man of the 'craving temperament' and insight for the man who is intellectually confused. This falls in line with two forms of meditation found in Buddhism: development of tranquillity (*samatha*) and development of insight (*vipassanā*).

Though there is a dominating therapeutic stance in the philosophy and psychology of Buddhism, there are, when it is compared with the other systems of therapy presented here, significant differences of emphasis and goals of therapy. The Buddha was not directly concerned with a limited number of maladjusted individuals but with the basic human predicament. The Buddha remarked that diseases could be divided into bodily disease (*kāyikarogo*) and mental disease (*cetasikarogo*). We suffer from bodily diseases from time to time, but mental disease will not be extinguished until the attainment of sainthood. Continuous unrest, discontent, tension and anxieties are caused by the roots of craving and ignorance. However, the Buddha offered two ideals of happiness and concepts of anxiety. There is the path of renunciation of the monk in search of complete peace and quietude, and there is that of the layman who has made a compromise with life.

In the dialogues of the Buddha, the higher ideal of *nibbāna*, signifying calm and quietude, is compared with the human predicament of suffering (*dukkha*). The other ideal is that of the righteous householder. While the recluse seeking ultimate release from suffering will obtain inner peace (*ajjhattasanti*) the righteous householder's aim is harmonious living (*samacariyā*). The latter is the concept of the well-adjusted man, who seeks a balanced life, avoids excess, exercises a degree of restraint and is content with the satisfaction of limited wants. He practices regular self-analysis, helps other people and generates the seeds of peace and harmony necessary for healthy community life. The development of a therapy based on the psychology of Buddhism has to recognise these two ideals of mental health, but the dichotomy need not be radical since the eradication of lust, hatred and delusion are common to both. The difference is that while the recluse takes an immediate plunge and hopes to make swift progress, the layman aims at a more gradual progress.

In the final analysis the development of a spiritual dimension, where meditational practice aims at a higher level of consciousness, has not been absorbed by western psychologists. Though some of them are interested in measuring the impact of meditation on man's bodily processes as well as the psychological condition, no significant impact has yet been seen in the field of psychotherapy.

Buddhism makes a distinction between normal consciousness (*saññasaññī*) and the consciousness of a neurotic (*khitta-citta*), of a psychotic (*unmattaka*), and of one who has an abnormal 'disjointed consciousness' (*Visañña-saññī*). But the Buddha also speaks of a developed consciousness (*vibhūta-saññī*).[9] This mystical dimension regarding the development of higher consciousness is foreign to the psychology of the west.

BUDDHISM AND THE THERAPEUTIC SYSTEMS OF THE WEST

In general, Buddhism offers significant points of convergence with psychoanalysis, humanistic psychology and existential therapy, whereas the model of behaviourism offers some significant points of difference.

The gap between Buddhism and behaviour therapy rests on a number of factors: Buddhism accepts 'introspection' as a technique for self-understanding; it is also not a piecemeal therapy attacking specific symptoms but focuses attention on the general conditions which lie below all specific symptoms. While accepting the claim that conditioning is a powerful factor in the growth of habit-bound behaviour, Buddhism prefers insight and self-understanding to processes like counter-conditioning and desensitisation. However, in the philosophy of Buddhism there is a significant empiricist stance, emphasising observation and verification. Buddhism also criticises metaphysical theories of mind which uphold pure-ego theories. The stimulus response relation is one of the avenues that according to the Buddha excites man's animosity and conceit. Nevertheless, he felt that the stimulus response works on deep-seated proclivities in man which extend beyond one life-span, to innumerable births.

Freudian psychoanalysis, which has not been understood completely by men of religion, offers interesting insights. The psychology of Buddhism holds that there are three significant manifestations of craving: the craving for sense gratification, the desire for selfish pursuits and the desire for destruction. These have some amazing similarities to the Freudian libido, ego instinct and death-instinct. Of course, in the case of the destructive urge, Buddhism considers destruction of unpleasant objects as a basic drive and self-destruction as a reactive instinct. The Freudian concept of self-love described in the concept of narcissism offers a significant point of convergence between the two theories.[10]

There is also a concept of unconscious motivation in Buddhism which we discussed in a previous chapter.[11] It was seen that the craving for pleasurable excitement is fed by deeper undercurrents. Pleasurable feelings induce an attachment to pleasant objects, for they rouse latent sensuous greed; painful feelings rouse latent anger; false compliments can excite latent conceit; a threat to life will excite a dormant proclivity to cling to existence; and so on. These dormant undercurrents provide the base for ever-recurring greed, anger, pride, jealousy and varying types of anxiety. The mind is not an unchanging soul, but a dynamic continuum in which is stored the residue of emotionally charged memories going back to childhood as well as past births. The Buddha considers the ego as the seat of anxiety and the attachment to a false sense of the ego nourished by unconscious proclivities as a base for the generation of tensions and unrest. This ego-anxiety linkage offers an interesting point of intersection, not merely for the Buddhist and Freudian therapies, but also for the humanistic and existential systems.

Buddhism offers a more positive path for growth based on a spiritual and ethical ideal. It also offers the ideal of harmonious living for the householder and the elimination of all conflicts to the recluse. Freud sought only a limited and attainable ideal of happiness. In fact, he even says that his aim was to 'transform hysterical misery into common unhappiness', and also says that he was not devising a scheme to rub away all conflicts and passions from a person's mind. Analysis, according to Freud, does not make pathological reactions impossible but stimulates the freedom to develop personal autonomy which will make the emergence of pathological reactions unlikely.

Rogers's claim that people are responsible for their destiny, make their own future and have a sense of choice and responsibility are premises that accord with the psychological and ethical outlook of Buddhism. The Buddha rejected various forms of determinism which existed at his time – natural determinism (*svabhāva-vada*), theistic determinism (*issara-kāraṇa-vāda*) and karmic determinism (*pubba-kamma-vāda*). While a person's psychological past, heredity and the social environment may condition a man's actions, they do not determine them. Thus the element of 'psychic determinism' in Freud will not fall in line with Buddhism. Though the Buddha offered a systematic path for liberation from anxieties, it is not imposed on individuals as in client-centred therapy. Unlike client-centred therapy there are more positive guidelines and a way of life in Buddhism. The term 'client-centred' therapy would remain somewhat ambiguous in this context, as the Buddha was not a therapist in the full sense of the word. Also, there is no Buddhist therapy as a competing technique, as is the case with the other systems we have mentioned. The psychology of Buddhism in its therapeutic outlook emphasises the world of decisions and responsibility as the humanistic school does, but also looks at the dynamic, deeply rooted character traits emerging from the past as Freud does – it is both past and future oriented.

There are significant resemblances between the Buddhist and the existential dimensions of therapy.[12] The 'Tragic Sense of Life', which is the focus of existential therapy is basically an expression of the Buddhist concept of *dukkha*. The basic dissonance, emptiness and boredom which emerge out of a life of pure pleasure-seeking form an extremely significant point of convergence between the Buddha and Kierkegaard. Without falling into the extremes of mere sensuality or pure melancholy, the confrontation of genuine tragedy is a highly cathartic experience. At a time when the realities of life are submerged by petty diversions, existential analysis offers a serious encounter with life.

Apart from the 'tragic', the other focus of interest common to both is what may be called 'basic anxiety'. Anxiety is generally caused by ego-centred desires of various types. There are some anxieties and apprehensions which under the sharp eye of the therapist may be reduced to specific fears. But both the existentialist and the Buddhist say that there is a deeper 'basic anxiety', and in the view of Buddhism this is due to our deep-rooted attachment to the ego. The Buddha traces the predilection of the anxious man to his inability to grasp the truth of egoism, which is the key to understanding any form of anxiety. The belief in 'I' and 'me', though it gives a superficial feeling of security, is the cause of anxiety and worry. It is on the analysis of the 'tragic' and 'basic anxiety' that there is room for a stimulating dialogue between Buddhism and existentialism.

Death of a loved one disturbs the relationships that sustain a person's sense of 'identity' and the high level of binding and cathexis concentrated on the person who is lost is suddenly disrupted. The Buddha's therapy for facing the unbearable suffering caused by the disruption of strong attachments is a central part of the doctrine. In Buddhism there is a close link between the doctrines of egolessness (*anattā*) and suffering (*dukkha*). The word *dukkha* etymologically suggests the existence of an 'evil hollow'. If this interpretation is correct, the empty hollow around which human anxieties are woven is the non-existent ego. The Buddha said, 'What is impermanent, that is suffering, what is suffering, that is void of an ego.' To think that there is an ego, where there is only a changing psycho-physical complex, and to cling to this, is to create the conditions for the emergence of anxiety, mourning, grief and boredom. Even the strong 'existential anguish' found in the writings of the existentialist might be a subtle manifestation of the ego. The dialectic of the ego-identity analysis in Buddhism is so subtle that a Buddhist can discern the shadows of the ego even in the bosom of existential anguish.

Thus while both the Buddhist and the existentialist focus attention on tragedy and anxiety, the Buddhist analysis goes beyond the existentialist and would even consider existentialism as a symptom of a deeper spiritual anguish calling for systematic diagnosis and therapy. The existentialist is useful in awakening man from his slumber, but the questions that he has raised need an answer. An answer of a sort is given by the Buddha.

The resemblance between the existentialist and the Buddhist in raising similar questions has been pointed out by certain Buddhist scholars. Ñāṇavīra Thero says:

> There is no suggestion, of course, that it is necessary to become an existentialist philosopher before one can understand the Buddha . . . Nonetheless many people, on first coming across the *suttas*, are puzzled to know what their relevance is in the elaborate context of modern thought: and for them an indication that the existential philosophies (in their general methods, that is to say, rather than their individual conclusions) afford a way of approach to the *suttas* may be helpful.[13]

Thero also observes that he who has *understood* the Buddha's teaching has gone beyond the range of existential philosophers, 'but he would never have reached the point of listening to the Buddha's teaching had he not been disquieted by existential questions about himself and the world'. The same point of view has been put across by Edward Conze in relation to the origin and diagnosis of human suffering, which in effect is the basic therapeutic concern of Buddhism:

> In terms of the Four Truths the existentialists have only the first, which teaches that everything is ill. Of the second, which assigns the origin of ill to craving, they have only a very imperfect grasp. As for the third and the fourth, they are quite unheard of.[14]

In the final analysis, the Buddha would say that human suffering is due to the contradictions issuing out of the temporary identifications made by one's ego, and the attempt to repress or cover these contradictions by temporary palliatives. The existentialist tries to force open some of these contradictions by an honest encounter with oneself, but by way of diagnosis and specific remedies the psychology of Buddhism offers an answer to existential anguish.

In the light of the brief sketch of selected therapies in western psychology and the points of comparison we made, it may be concluded that the basic themes that run through the psychoanalysis of Freud, the neo-Freudians, humanistic psychology and existential analysis offer stimulating points of convergence. Though the mainstream of behaviour therapy presents some significant differences from Buddhism, some of the similarities which deserve careful consideration may be absorbed by a system of therapy inspired by the teachings of the Buddha. It may also be said that, while we have only examined the therapeutic stances, a deeper study of specific techniques in a comparative setting would prove to be a worthwhile venture.

APPLICATION OF THE PRINCIPLES OF BUDDHIST PSYCHOLOGY TO CONTEMPORARY SOCIAL PATHOLOGY

Changing horizons in the field of psychotherapy

Rollo May, discussing the shift of significant 'problem areas' in the field of psychopathology, observes that at the beginning of the twentieth century the most significant question was the 'person's difficulty in accepting the instinctual and specially the sexual side of life',[15] the problem that dominated Freud's mind; next, with Rank and Adler, there was a shift of interest to the problems of inferiority, guilt and inadequacy; for neo-Freudians like Horney the dominating theme then became the conflict between individuals and the group; and today the focal issues are those of anxiety, loneliness and emptiness.

May's grasp of the situation is interesting: '. . . the most common problem now is not social taboos on the sexual activity or guilt feelings about sex itself, but the fact that sex for so many people is an empty, mechanical and vacuous experience.'[16] He feels that in formulating goals people do not base them on strong conviction and a sense of reality. He points out that this 'inner emptiness' is not restricted to the consulting room of the psychiatrist, but that the available sociological data confirm the presence of the phenomenon at a broader social level.

Our concern in this section will be with the manifestation and roots of social pathology which find miniature expression in the consulting room of the psychiatrist. Two large labels which were used to express this uneasiness in a specific way were that of 'anxiety' emerging out of clinical data and that of 'alienation' as, manifested in sociological studies. Today, forms of social pathology have been given a kind of technical coherence by Erikson's concept of 'identity crisis'. The concept of 'identity crisis' offers interesting possibilities in the application of the Buddhist principles of psychology. Thus in this section of the work, we shall make a study of the human person in the face of the identity crisis, and we shall attempt it in the light of Buddhist psychological analysis.

Faceless Person in a Changing World

The depersonalising tendencies of the social and economic scene are varied and many: the growth of automation and the division of labour have converted the worker into such a slave of the machine that work has become drudgery for him, boring and stultifying; the growth of gigantism in industry, ever-increasing bureaucratisation and the development of a routinised life are combined with periods of leisure that drown people's deep discontent with their work. People get used to forms of entertainment which dull their sensitivity to the lack of joy in their jobs; and convergence on the cities and the degree of mobility add the further factor of rootlessness to the problem.

Exposure to a never-ending variety of stimuli increases the sense of diffuseness which invades the self. Absence of an inner purpose directing one's life makes it possible for parasitic desires and artificial life-styles to eat into the soul. By a consistent refusal to look at ourselves closely, we create blocks and barricades which prevent the growth of self-knowledge. Lack of genuine *self-knowledge* and *self-direction* are the clearest features of persons emerging in this context.

Not only does this situation create fragmented and crippled personalities, it also nullifies for ever the possibility of any warm encounter between people. Though there is no significant communication between two faceless men, paradoxically people become 'other-directed' in an almost pathological manner. People run to others in this way because deep within themselves they feel lonely and there is a need to find an escape from the vacuum. In this way both faith in oneself and the ability to engage in meaningful communication with others are lost.[17] This, in brief, is the predicament of the people who live in 'sick cities'.[18]

The physical, social and psychological space in which these people live produces a kind of social pathology. Psychopathology, which originally dealt with specific behaviour disorders, needs to widen the base as well as the goals of therapy if it is to be useful in such a context. We shall now briefly present a Buddhist analysis of this crisis in identity produced by lack of genuine self-knowledge and self-direction.

Identity Crisis in the Light of Buddhist Psychological Analysis

The application of the principles of Buddhist psychology has to be worked out in two phases. In the first phase, it would be necessary to emphasise the regeneration of the 'authentic person'. It was mentioned that the lack of genuine self-knowledge and self-direction are the two besetting ills in the predicament of man we have just outlined. The Buddhist upholds sincerity and genuine self-knowledge in contrast to shame and deception; personal decisions and self-direction instead of being tied to the impersonal and the mechanical; and a basically honest attempt at self-understanding without searching for diversions and escapes to temporarily submerge one's inner conflicts. This reattainment to the authentic person offers parallels with existential, humanistic and Freudian psychotherapy. Once the regeneration of the human person is achieved, the specific ethical and spiritual directives for development and growth will take firm root. This would be the second phase in the application of the principles of Buddhist psychology. However, unless the inner blemishes within an individual are fully comprehended there is no possibility for development of the person.

There are two significant suttas which illustrate our point. The *Discourse on the Simile Of the Cloth* points out that it is futile to graft spirituality on to a person who has a defiled mind. If a cloth that is dirty is dipped into a colourful dye, the dirty cloth will not emerge in a clear colour; but if a cloth that is quite pure and clean is dipped into a dye, it will come out very clear.[19] The discourse on *No Blemishes* also conveys a similar idea by means of a different analogy. There is a difference between a person who has a 'subjective blemish' and thinks 'I have a subjective blemish' but does not *comprehend* the nature of the blemish as it is, and a person who thinks 'I have a subjective blemish' but does *comprehend* its real nature. This is compared to the difference between a bronze bowl brought from a shop which is dirty whose owner neglects cleaning it, and the same article bought by a person who constantly cleans it. The dirt in the bronze bowl represents the presence of attachment, aversion and confusion within us.[20] The Buddha remarked that no amount of external ritual and ceremonial like bathing in the river or lighting fires can cleanse the evil person. To use a modern idiom, no amount of hectic other-directed activity and palliatives that temporarily camouflage our inner vacuity can help us. Diligent and honest self-analysis is the first step in the regeneration of the crippled, alienated and unhappy person.

The doctrine of the Buddha presents us with a way to break through the transient identifications that prevent us from getting a true picture of ourselves, and to comprehend the nature of the basic *indeterminacy*, *ambiguity* and *formlessness* that run through contemporary society. According to Jacobson, the contemporary predicament to which the doctrine of the Buddha has relevance may be described thus:

> the basic indeterminacy of the human creature, the ambiguity and formlessness at the center of their lives, and with their tendency to try to fix their identity upon some cluster of transient identifications with which they become involved in learning to live in a particular time and place.[21]

He also says that the 'Buddha's brilliant and unique grasp of this predicament is found in his teachings about *anatta*.'[22]

If the concept of 'identity-crisis' embodies the central focus of social pathology in the west, what are the therapeutic implications of the doctrine of egolessness (*anattā*) as a key to diagnosis and remedial measures? The fact that there is a basic formlessness and indeterminism within man and that this is covered by transient identifications should not imply that the Buddhist has no base for the development of a 'life-style'. A Buddhist style of life intended to solve the identity problems in our society has to be steered across a sharp razor's edge, without falling into the extremes on either side. If there is a built-in torn-asunderness in man, it does not imply that the Buddhist has to build a life-style on the rocks of eternalism or the shifting sands of anarchism and nihilism. The Buddhist doctrine of egolessness (*anattā*) steers clearly through both eternalism (*sasatadiṭṭhi*) and annihilationism (*ucchedadiṭṭhi*). As a life perspective it rejects the ways of both pure sensuality and extreme asceticism. The Buddha exalts a way of life unhindered by either self-love or self-hatred.

Now that the basic standpoint in relation to the problem of the identity crisis has been presented, it would be necessary to examine in detail some facets of the issue in relation to the material found in the discourses of the Buddha.

Whatever facet of the crisis in identity we examine from the standpoint of Buddhist psychology each will be seen to be woven round the central doctrine of egolessness. This point can be well presented with the help of a graphic image that the Buddha uses to describe man's attachment to the ego:

> Just like a dog, brethren, tied up by a leash to a strong stake or pillar – if he goes, he goes up to that stake or pillar; if he stands still, he stands close to that stake or pillar; if he squats down, he squats close to that stake or pillar; if he lies down, he lies close to that stake or pillar.[23]

This image of the dog tied to a leash expresses in a picturesque manner how whether the matter in question is self-love or self-hatred, the same obsession with the ego remains; whether it is the lure of sensuality, the depression of the religious melancholy or the punitive self-punishment of the ascetic, each is circling the same post to which it is tied, namely the ego; wounded narcissism, self-pity and conceit are also manifestations of ego-attachment. States like boredom and the fear of loneliness cannot be comprehended while there is inability to accept and understand the doctrine of egolessness. We shall now examine some of these issues against the background of the doctrine of *anattā* (egolessness).

Narcissism

Orrine E. Klapp, examining the common symptoms related to identity problems, considers excessive self-concern and narcissism as significant causative factors in problems of identity.[24] We know that according to Greek mythology Narcissus fell in love with the reflection of his own body in water. This idea was developed by Freud, who found in the clinical situation a type of patient exhibiting a pathological fixation to his own body. However, the narcissistic person is not only proud of his own body, but attempts to fix his identity by transient identifications with such symbols as social status or wealth or with fads and fashions, ideas and ideologies, and so on.

> The suttas describe the situation in this manner: Suppose, friend Ananda, that a woman or a young lad fond of self-adornment, should gaze at the image of his face in a mirror that is clean and spotless, or in a bowl of clear water – he would behold it owing to a cause and not otherwise. Even so, friend Ananda, through the cause 'body' comes the conceit 'I am', not otherwise. So also as to feeling, perception, the activities and consciousness – owing to a cause comes the conceit 'I am', not otherwise.[25]

There is of course a semantic problem involved in the concept of self-love. We have to make a distinction between self-centred motives and self-devoting motives. For example, the practice of *mettā-bhāvanā* (meditation on loving kindness) is the finest example of the fusing of self-love and love for others. The meditation of loving-kindness is first developed towards oneself and then radiates towards others. One starts with the thought, 'May I be happy' and extends this to the happiness of others. Even where a person makes a sacrifice and forgoes certain material benefits, it merely strengthens his self-development. The very nature of the good is such that no one can seek his liberation without seeking the liberation of others. Such mature, self-devoting motives have to be distinguished from narcissistic self-love, craving for admiration, self-conceit and excessive self-concern. This subtle dialectic of 'self-love' embedded in the psychology of Buddhism helps us to understand the forms of social pathology which emerge from excessive self-concern.

Self-hatred, depression and melancholy are negative aspects of wounded narcissism. Wounded narcissism gives way to depression and melancholy as well as leading to rage. Self-hatred betrays paradoxically an excessive concern with the self. The most distressing form of self-hatred may be referred to as 'identity despair'. Such despair comes to a man who is dissatisfied with his own image of himself, what he has been, what he has achieved and his ideals. Such despair can come to a man late in his life, and even to one 'Who has two cars, two homes, two television sets, and still is not what he wanted to be. . . .'[26] While identity despair may lead even to suicide, many people lead lives of 'quiet desperation'.[27]

Loneliness

David Riesman in his book *Lonely Crowd* refers to a kind of compulsive gregariousness in man (like joining clubs) and a frantic endeavour to fill one's leisure time cram-full with activity.[28] Here we find the strange phenomenon of 'running away from the self' and an attempt to lose oneself in the anonymity of the mass. Rollo May feels that this kind of pathological other-directed behaviour exhibits a fear of solitude.

According to the Buddhist analysis there is a difference between 'being alone' and 'being lonely'. The inability to experience solitude and delight in a short spell of being alone is due to the fear of loneliness.[29] Loneliness itself has various facets: it can be the culturally conditioned loneliness of isolation, the loneliness of a person who has lost someone dear to him, the forced state of loneliness due to a temporary sickness, and so on.[30] But the loneliness of a man who is running away from himself is a more basic kind of loneliness.

We may compare these states with those of the man who enjoys solitude; of the man who needs to be alone to experience the infinity of nature of the mountains and the ocean; with the seclusion which inspires artistic and literary activities; and so on.[31] While the Buddhist considers the experience of solitude as the way to obtain deep religious insight, this experience is distinct from that of the nature lover or the artist. The *Dhammapada* recommends:

> A lonely seat – a lonely bed
> And faring alone untiringly
> Alone subduing himself he might –
> In sylvan solitude find delight.[32]

Sitting alone is the resort proper to a recluse and oneness (solitude) is called sageship. Even for the layman who practises meditation and self-analysis, the ability to sit alone, meditate and experience the bliss of solitude is commended. The therapeutic value of this is reflected in the need for 'moratoria' and 'quiet places' in society pointed out by Erikson, the most celebrated writer of the twentieth century on identity problems.

Another solution that the Buddha offers for the layman living in society is the development of mature interpersonal relations based on both respect and concern for others. Such interpersonal relations, as clearly presented in the *Sigālovāda Sutta*,[33] can be distinguished from symbiotic attachments of domination or dependence and pathological other-directed activity. Even for the layman, it may be said that a component of the meditative life could always enrich his social relations and give them depth and meaning. A society that appreciates the social value of a 'meditative life' will not be prey to spiritual decay, monotony and boredom.

Sensuality and Boredom

We have already mentioned that the drive for sensuality is a dominant goal that pervades human life.[34] However, the degradation and the dehumanisation of the pursuit of pleasure and man's sexual life today have escalated the crisis in identity. Any attempt to develop a Buddhist life-style today cannot ignore this problem.

The obsession with identifying oneself with fast-changing and transient objects, the restless search for diversity and the consequent boredom is nowhere given such graphic expression as in Soren Kierkegaard's *Either/Or*.[35] This portrait of the pure romanticist, pleasure lover and hedonist embedded in the character of Don Juan is precisely what is conveyed in the Buddhist context by the phrase '*kāmasukhallikānuyoga*'. The kind of person who is struck by this kind of passion and cupidity is one who belongs to a group of people referred to as the 'lustful type' (*rāgacarita*).

Young people in the modern world who are drawn into tinsel love-relationships without any warmth and depth of feeling are already rebelling against their predicament. The degradation of sexuality and the aridity in human relations lacking genuine concern, affection and tenderness is a crucial source of the identity crisis. One's sense of identity is enhanced by productive and creative human relations, whether these relate to love, work or amusement. When mechanical, compulsive or pragmatic functions replace such life-giving relations they become parasitic on the essentially human attributes of man. The ethics and the psychology of human relations in Buddhism are grounded in the cohesive emotional factors of genuine affection, kindness, respect and a deep sense of compassion for others.

Though the Don Juan type of character (representing the very personification of sensuality) has a temporary appeal for the young, it leaves them changing their objects of desire by a kind of 'rotation method' until boredom, melancholy and despair sets in. The Don Juan ideal is not one that could become a consistent philosophy of life. Pure pleasure as a way of life fails not only because pleasure is followed by pain, but because of the dissonance of this kind of life and its total unreality. The pure hedonist is finally drawn down into a horrifying state of boredom. By planning further means of diversion to avoid his boredom, he runs into the oncoming ruin with greater force.

Boredom is one of the most profound symptoms of identity problems today. There are really two kinds of boredom: a person's mood may be directed to a particular object like a play or a book and he might get bored with it; one can also be bored not with any specific object, but with oneself. People like Kierkegaard feel that at this very moment of the emergence of being bored with oneself a real metamorphosis is possible, but people drown it with diversions. If one could only grasp with insight the nature of this 'nameless emptiness' one could come within the very doors of wisdom (the *anattā* doctrine). So let us now look at the philosophy of emptiness in Buddhism.

Negative and Positive Encounters with Emptiness

The experience of 'inner emptiness', boredom, loneliness and nausea is part and parcel of contemporary art and literature.[36] Prototypes of these experiences in the clinical situation are becoming common, but the literary and even the current philosophical writings provide an encounter with what may be called an 'emptiness' which is merely negative.

In the context of Buddhism, there are two approaches to the experience of 'emptiness'. One is the negative encounter with the vacuity and boredom in one's life, the other is the positive realisation of this as an insight into the nature of reality, the lack of an inner essence and permanent self along with a spiritual experience of the 'void' and the 'signless'. It is due to a kind of spiritual poverty that modern man is incapable of converting this negative encounter into a more positive insight into the nature of reality.

Edward Conze, analysing the Sanskrit term for emptiness, *Sūnya*, says that the Sanskrit root helps us to understand how the 'word *empty* becomes a synonym for Not-Self'.[37] This subtle connection between the self and emptiness is a central feature in the Buddhist doctrine. The question is raised, 'Void is the world! Void is the world! they say, O Lord Pray, Lord how far does this saying go?' Then the Buddha replies: 'Because the world is void of the self, Ānanda, or of what belongs to the self, therefore it is said, 'Void is the world'.[38]

In the light of this context, the world is referred to as 'void' because the world does not have or is devoid of a permanent and eternal self. Conze also makes another interesting point, regarding a double meaning found in the word '*sūnya*': The Sanskrit word *sūnya* is derived from the root *svi* to swell. *Sūnya* means, literally, relating to the swollen. In the remote past, our ancestors had a sense of the double meaning of words. They often deliberately used verbal roots with two opposite meanings. Conze says that *svi* conveyed the idea that something which looks 'swollen' from outside is 'hollow' from inside. Thus our personality according to its constitution by the five *khandhas* (groups) is swollen, but is hollow inside, for there is no self.

Unless the so-called self receives positive identifications, it manifests itself as a void or hollow. In this context T. S. Eliot's reference to the *hollow men* and *stuffed men* of our age is interesting.[39] If the etymological meaning of the word *dukkha* (as suggested by Horner)[40] connotes the idea of 'an evil hollow', the link between *anattā* and *dukkha* presents us with a significant existential dimension to understand the philosophy of the void. It is by a deep insight into the nature of reality, by understanding the doctrines of *dukkha* and *anattā* that we transcend a purely negative submergence by boredom and emptiness.

There is even a yet more positive grasp of 'emptiness' in the two discourses on emptiness.[41] Here the gradual path to the understanding of the nature of emptiness is presented in stages:

> As this place of Migāra's mother is empty of elephants, cows, horses and mares, empty of gold and silver, empty of assemblages of men and women, and there is only this that is not emptiness, that is to say the solitude grounded on the order of monks; even,

> so, Ananda, a monk, not attending to the perception of village, not attending to the perception of human beings, attends to solitude grounded on the perception of forest.[42]

When the monk is pleased with this, he comprehends that the disturbances that exist in the perception of a village or of human beings does not exist here; the only thing that is here is the solitude grounded on the perception of the forest. Then the monk moves on to the solitude grounded on the perception of earth, then to the plane of infinite consciousness, perception of nothingness, perception of neither-perception nor non-perception and finally the concentration of the mind that is signless. Now he is freed from (or empty of) the cankers of sense-pleasure, becoming and ignorance. The only disturbances are those that emerge due to the fact that he is living and endowed with a body.[43]

In this manner the Buddhist monk as a lover of solitude practices the 'meditation on emptiness', and thus the empty, hollow and the vacuous need not disturb him. We might rightly say of him, 'He is filled because he is empty.'[44]

6 Health and Sickness in Buddhist Perspective

In examining the concepts of health and sickness, in Buddhist perspective, there are three important questions which call for analysis and discussion. Firstly, in what sense can we talk of concepts of mental health and sickness in Buddhism? Secondly, if Buddhism has significant insights on the nature of mental health and sickness, in what way can Buddhism be regarded as a 'therapeutic system'? Thirdly, what are the most central therapeutic strategies of Buddhism and some of the specific techniques? In discussing these issues, material will be drawn basically from the early Buddhist tradition.

In one sense everyone is subject to 'mental disease', except the *arahants* who have destroyed the *āsavas*. The word *āsava*, literally meaning 'influxes', is a figurative name for the four biases – sensuous bias (*kāmāsava*) bias for eternal existence (*bhavāsava*), the bias of views (*diṭṭhāsava*), the bias for of ignorance (*avijjāsava*). In the *Gradual Sayings* it is said that diseases are of two kinds, diseases of the body and diseases of the mind.[1] The Buddha presents the proneness to psychological conflicts and disturbances in the following words:

> Monks, there are to be seen beings who can admit freedom from suffering from bodily disease for one year, for two years, for three, four, five, ten, twenty ... who can admit freedom from bodily disease for even a hundred years. But, monks, those beings are hard to find in the world who can admit freedom from mental disease even for one moment, save only those in whom the *āsavas* are destroyed.[2]

Again, in another context, in the *Kindred Sayings*,[3] the Buddha, speaking to an old man in the last stages of life, advises him:

Wherefore, housefather, thus you should train yourself:- 'Though my body is sick, my mind shall not be sick.' Thus, Housefather, must you train yourself.

Thus in this sense everyone who is dominated by craving and subject to the delusion of a permanent ego generates different degrees of anxiety, depression, discontent etc. In those who take these to an excess, they come on the limits of mental and behavioural disorders.

There is also another approach to the concept of mental health, where we can talk of a well-adjusted and balanced person, though he is not one who has achieved perfection. For the person who does not commit himself to the life of renunciation, the Buddha recommends the life of the righteous householder. While the recluse seeking ultimate release from suffering will obtain inner peace (*ajjhatta-santi*), the righteous householder aims at harmonious living (*dhammacariya, samacariya*).[4]

So we can speak of a certain degree of mental health and harmony in the well-balanced, righteous householder and yet a more perfect concept of mental health in the *arahants*.

The idea that the abnormal is not restricted to a closely labeled group of neurotics and psychotics, but that the average person is liable to a great deal of anxiety, depression and fears is a theme which has emerged in the West, in recent times. Even Sigmund Freud, who often labours to point out that he is not seeking an absolute ideal of normality but merely to transfer 'hysterical misery into common unhappiness',[5] sometimes claims that 'we are all hysterical at times'. It is in this context that those like Anthony Store remarked that the process of analysis is sought rather as *a way of life rather than as a form of treatment.*[6] This would be the perspective to view the Buddhist insights on health and sickness.

Though Buddhism offers interesting techniques to deal with certain forms of mental and behavioural disorders, it is more a way of life for one who copes with the general run of anxieties and delusions.

Thus we see number of dimensions in the therapeutic stance of early Buddhism:

(1) The notion that mental diseases are completely overcome by the *arahant*;

(2) That the concept of the well-adjusted man living the righteous

and harmonious life, also displays a dimension of mental and physical health;

(3) The therapeutic process that Buddhism advocates is more a way of life than a form of treatment;

(4) That there are therapeutic resources in Buddhism which can be used to deal with people who have psychological problems, some of whom are converging on breakdowns of a neurotic nature.

However, we can overdo the metaphor of therapy:

> To consider meditation from the standpoint of its therapeutic action is only one way of describing this technique of living. Seen from another direction, meditation transcends the merely therapeutic ...[7]

In fact, it has been almost paradoxically expressed:

> Meditation is most therapeutic when it is not looked upon for therapeutic effect, but is put into practice as an end in itself...[8]

While conceding all these points and specially emphasising the fact that there is a risk of overdoing the metaphor of 'therapy' in Buddhism, it can be said that there is a great therapeutic potential in Buddhism, part of which has already been theoretically examined by scholars and empirically and clinically explored by therapists.

In general it may be said that psychological and social conflicts are almost an in-built feature of the human predicament, which the Buddha describes as *dukkha.* As Marie Jahoda says in her work, *Current Concepts of Positive Mental Health*:

> If it is reasonable to assume that such conflicts are universal, we are all sick in different degrees. Actually, the difference between anyone and a psychotic may lie in the way he handles his conflicts and in the appearance or lack of certain symptoms.[9]

As yet, as she points out, there is no reasonable agreement regarding the usage of the term 'sick'.

However, in developing a Buddhist perspective, while emphasising the point that all of us are 'sick' in a certain sense, that we are subject to different forms of conflicts, it would be useful to explore the more positive conceptions of mental health rather than merely rest with the idea that health is the absence of disease. The value of these conceptions is that they could be placed in a spectrum, with different people approximating to them to different degrees.

POSITIVE CONCEPTS OF MENTAL HEALTH

Reality Orientation

Reality orientation in the Buddhist context has a specific focus, which can be different from the Western context. In the Western context efficient perception of reality is clarified in the following manner: 'The normal individual is fairly realistic in his appraisal of his own reactions and abilities and what is going on in the world around him.'[10] It is a via media between over-evaluating one's skills and running away from a situation. This is perhaps an adjustment oriented criterion.

In Buddhism there is a deeper encounter with certain core realities: impermanence (*anicca*), unsatisfactoriness (*dukkha*), and egolessness (*anatta*). By understanding these core realities, we discern the nature of time, change, process, the relative patterns in change, the arising, the emergence and the vanishing of phenomena; we also see the meaning of the deeper grounding of human tragedy with equanimity, understand losses, sickness, death, anxiety and dread; we get a clear grasp of the types of identities to which we develop attachments and onto which we project delusory beliefs, the identities of the self, other people and the external world.[11]

Attitude Towards the Self

Along with a deeper reality orientation it becomes possible to shed the delusory beliefs about the self, and the loosening of the psychological grip of narcissism. In fact, Erich Fromm, searching for a viable concept of mental health and well-being comments:

> Well-being is possible to the degree to which one has overcome one's narcissism; to the degree to which one is open, responsive, sensitive awake, empty. . . . Well-being means, finally, to drop one's Ego, to give up greed, to cease chasing after the preservation and the aggrandizement of the Ego, to be and to experience one's self in the act of being, not in having, preserving, coveting, using.[12]

It must be emphasised that both the reality orientation and its transformation in generating a new attitude to the self is not merely an intellectual change as such, but an experiential change brought through the practice of *vipassanā* meditation.

Self-knowledge

As the metaphysical and psychological frontiers of the wrong notions about the self break down, space emerges for the development of greater self-knowledge. By the continuous practice of mindfulness, hidden crevices of the mind open, rigidities disappear and a greater receptiveness to the present becomes possible. It also becomes possible to see the past for what it is. A deep and penetrating awareness, which can break through distorting conceptual, intellectual and semantic baggage, emerges. It is with this clarity of perception that one can sort out ones' thoughts as well as emotions.

Voluntary Control and Autonomy

As the mind becomes open, flexible and pliable, it becomes easy to break through automatic, conditioned and compulsive behaviour. Voluntary decisions become easy and a great degree of freedom and autonomy in our volitional activities emerges.

Ability to Form Sensitive and Satisfying Relationships with Others

With the greater self-knowledge, satisfying relations with others become possible. Thus instead of developing relations based on greed, domination, dependence, and power, there are productive relationships of care, friendship, trust, and compassion. The psychology of troubled relationships is something very central to Western psychotherapeutic concerns,[13] an area which we have investigated in the study of human emotions in Buddhism, of conceit, jealousy, care and compassion.[14]

Body-mind Integration

The importance of body-mind integration is a concept that has been highlighted in the West during the last few decades, due to the findings that many diseases have a psychosomatic dimension, specially those which were singly labeled as somatic. Also, with this interest, there was a growing enthusiasm for the development of psychosomatic, or what is called holistic, medicine. In this context Buddhism has some unique contributions to make.

It is often thought that many philosophies with a religious orientation generate a body–mind dualism, where the body is looked upon as something to be tortured, rejected and eliminated. This attitude is often combined with a kind of Cartesian dualism of body and mind. Though in certain contexts the Buddha refers to body and mind as independent variables, ('Subdued in body but not subdued in mind, unsubdued in body, but subdued in mind...'),[15] the deeper emphasis is on the notion of mutual dependency and reciprocity. This perspective is well ingrained in the practice of the 'way of mindfulness' (*satipaṭṭhāna*), for instance in the practice of the mindfulness in breathing, leading to both physical and mental health.

THE NEGATIVE FACTORS – GENERATORS OF MENTAL ILLNESS

Now that we have outlined some of the more basic conceptions of positive mental health, it is useful to pay attention to the negative factors, those generating disease or to put it in another form, those that are obstacles to the attainment of mental health. The Buddhist term for this is 'hindrance' (*nīvaraṇa*).

The five hindrances generally mentioned in the discourses of the Buddha are the following:

(1) Sense desire (*kāmacchanda*)
(2) Ill-will (*byāpada*)
(3) Sloth and Torpor (*thīna-middha*)
(4) Restlessness and Worry (*uddhacca-kukkucca*)
(5) Sceptical Doubt (*vicikicchā*)

These are called hindrances because they obstruct the development of the mind (*bhāvanā*). According to the Buddha's teachings there are two central forms of meditation (*bhāvanā*). They are, tranquility meditation (*samatha-bhāvanā*) and insight meditation (*vipassanā-bhāvanā*). Tranquility meditation leads to the complete concentration of the mind in the meditative absorptions (*jhāna*). For achieving these absorptions, the overcoming of the five hindrances is a preliminary condition.[16]

These five hindrances are explained with the graphic imagery of a pond of water: sense desire is like the water being merged by a variety of intricate colours and one cannot see the image of ones' own face in the pond; ill-will is like boiling water, indicating a turbulent mind; sloth and torpor are like the pond covered by moss and vegetation, too dense to break through, as is the mind; restlessness is like a pond that is wind-swept, an agitated mind; and, finally, doubt is like muddy water, an obscure and cloudy mind.

Their emergence has to be first noticed and recognised and they can be overcome by the development of mindfulness. Strong desires generate strong attachment and anxieties, while ill-will can bring about antagonism, discontent and even depression; sloth and torpor means a mind that lacks zest, enthusiasm and energy and can succumb to weariness and boredom; restlessness creates an agitated mind, swinging from greed to aversion and attachment to discontent. Doubt blocks directional movement and clarity of purpose. While these five can be considered as the roadblocks to spiritual development and mental health, they also provide, structurally, the ground that creates different types of mental conflicts and pathology.

There are different kinds of antidotes which are recommended for these maladies. To deal with sense desires, different levels of therapeutic techniques are recommended. They range from meditational exercises like meditating on impure objects which can break through a lustful personality orientation, to others, like guarding the sense doors, moderation in eating, noble friendship and engagement in suitable conversation.[17] Ill-will can be handled by the antidote of the meditation on loving kindness. Also, reflection on the doctrine of *kamma* is useful. If we are dealing with a virtuous man, we cannot destroy him by anger; if he has vices he has to reap what he has sown; if one's own position in life is irritating, one can remind oneself, one is the master of one's journey through *saṃsara*. Indignation and anger at the universe, people or symbols will not help. Without falling into fatalism, the doctrine of *kamma* provides valuable therapeutic resources.[18] Noble friendship and suitable conversation are also recommended.

In the same way, laziness, drowsiness, sluggishness and boredom can be handled by simple dietary rules; not to over-eat; a change of bodily postures; an open air walk mindfully done; noble friendship; suitable conversation; and, the perception of light as a meditational exercise with a high degree of concentration. Shaking or stirring oneself (*saṃvega*) by the tragic aspects of life, death, suffering and impermanence, is also a way to break through sloth and torpor. The tragic aspects of life add a sense of 'urgency' described by the graphic image, like the man 'whose turban is on fire'. Also, the practice of sympathetic joy, and reflection on the great qualities of the Buddha, are recommended.

An agitated mind should develop quietude by study of the doctrine and keeping company with those who possess dignity, restraint and calm. Also meditational exercises leading towards joy, concentration, tranquility and equanimity are recommended. All these are helpful in mastering restlessness and worry, and generates a tranquility of mind. Doubt has to be overcome by developing firm conviction – in the Buddha, the doctrine and the *sangha*. When doubt is present, one has to notice it, without identifying oneself with it. A good intellectual understanding without grasping will provide the background to develop meditational exercises.

What is of central importance is that, while these hindrances point to some of the negative factors which generates a 'sick mind', they also form a central concern of the fourth part of the *Mahā-Satipaṭṭhāna Sutta*, The Greater Discourse on the Foundation of Mindfulness.[19]

The foundation of mindfulness has four aspects: the Contemplation of the Body, (*kāyānupassanā*), the Contemplation of Feeling, (*vēdanānupassanā*), the Contemplation of the State of Mind (*cittānupassanā*) and the Contemplation of Mental Contents (*dhammānupassanā*). The objects of right-mindfulness cover the entire man and his full range of experience. It provides the foundations of what may be called a Buddhist therapeutic system.

We have examined the contextual meanings of the terms 'sickness' and 'health' in terms of our own understanding of the Buddhist conception of mental health. In doing this we discerned three dimensions: the one on the path towards perfection, or the *arahant* conception; the one which, while dealing with the routine anxieties and conflicts of the householder, aims at the righteous and harmonious life; and finally that which indicates different types of breakdowns, adjustment problems of a radical variety, or psychosomatic illnesses. This last group may not always be that actively within the Buddhist fold as such, but may benefit from the therapeutic resources which have been given a more secular orientation, so they are accessible to people with diverse world-view orientations. For instance, we have Fromm's claim that rejection of narcissism can form a point of convergence for the major religions of the world.[20] In fact, a worthwhile forum on the 'therapeutic resources across religion' is a project for the future. It is also an area where cross-cultural psychologists are interested in examining the socio-cultural boundaries of mental health resources.

But our task in what follows is limited to pick out an area of interest in the *satipaṭṭhanā* technique – an area which will cut across the different levels of sickness and health cited above – and make an intensive analysis of it in the rest of this chapter. This would be a more rewarding venture in a short analysis, than making summary presentations of the *satipaṭṭhanā*, as such works are any way available.

The chapter will examine the Contemplation of Feeling (*vedanānupassanā*)[21] with some reference to the Contemplation of the Body, and Mind and Mental Contents. The Buddhist analysis of feeling (*vedanā*) and emotions is a veritable gold mine in the search for therapeutic resources to deal with the conflicts and anxieties of our times. But, surprisingly, it is a much neglected field, and some of the initial (almost pioneering) studies in the area point towards some useful and creative insights found in the discourse of the Buddha.[22]

The Contemplation of Feeling as grounded in the *satipaṭṭhāna* is undertaken within the framework of the meditative practice, the goal being the growth of insight (*vipassanā*). But as Nyanaponika Thera points out in his *Contemplation of Feeling*, 'It is, however, essential that this Contemplation should also be remembered and applied in daily life whenever feelings are prone to turn into unwholesome emotions.'[23] He goes on to comment: 'If the vanishing point of feelings is repeatedly seen with increasing clarity, it will become much easier to trap, and finally to stop, those emotions, thoughts and volitions, which normally follow so rapidly, and which are so often habitually associated with the feelings.'[24]

It is from the basis of feelings that emotions emerge. While we can concentrate on the entry point of feelings which later get converted into emotions, we can also make a detailed observation of the emotions, which in the *satipaṭṭhāna* technique will be to direct attention on the mental states. In this way we avoid the development of emotional problems. The Buddhist method is not the method of repression but that of detailed observation, watching, and non-judgemental recognition.

Such observation helps you to *understand* the logic of the emergence of emotions, and can be done in many ways. One can focus attention on the three forms of feeling – pleasant, unpleasant and indifferent – or one can examine the roots of emotionality in greed, hatred, and delusion. Greed, hatred and delusion are associated with the three forms – anxiety, resentment and self-assertion – through which a large facet of our emotional life can be understood.[25] They are the tension-producing factors and lie at the root of many developed, neurotic life-styles.

FEELINGS AND EMOTIONS

The neglect of emotion studies in religions, and even in the context of Buddhism, is due to the popular view that emotions interfere with man's moral and spiritual life. They are unwholesome states to be eradicated and road-blocks to be cleared in the weary battle between reason and feeling. As far back as 1914, a pioneer Buddhist scholar, Mrs C. A. F. Rhys Davids, referred to the lack of sufficient discussion of emotions in available Buddhist writings as one of the 'archaic silences.'[26] From a Buddhist perspective, as far as the negative emotions are concerned, they have to be undestood, their complex structures explored, and, we have to, in more popular terminology, 'become friends with them'. As far as the positive emotions are concerned, compassion, care, and benevolence should be cultivated and developed with a refined sensibility, and strengthened by the practice of meditation so that they take deep roots within ourselves.

Feeling (*vēdanā*) is the central category in terms of which we can understand emotions. The term '*vēdanā*', translated as 'feeling', refers to a sensation which can have a 'physical' or 'mental' origin and is described as pleasant, painful or indifferent. An emotion occurs when an object is considered as something attractive or repulsive. There is a felt tendency impelling people towards suitable objects or impelling them to move away from unsuitable or harmful objects. The individual also perceives and judges the situation in relation to himself as attractive or repulsive. An individual thus, possessed of 'like' (*anurodha*) and 'dislike' (*virodha*), approaches pleasure-giving objects and avoids painful objects. When we make a judgement in terms of the hedonic tone of these affective reactions, there are excited in us certain dispositions to destroy it (anger), possess it (greed), to flee from it (fear), or to get obsessed and worried over it (anxiety).

While the 'entry points' where feelings get converted into emotions can be discerned by a sharp focus on the span of attention, there is a deeper layer of nourishment which feeds our emotional life. Pleasant feelings, for instance, induce an attachment to pleasant objects, as they rouse latent sensuous greed (*rāgānusaya*). Painful feelings rouse latent anger and hatred (*paṭighānusaya*). States like pride, jealousy, and elation could be explained in terms of similar proclivities. When we refer to these proclivities as 'a deeper layer', it is merely a figure of speech and such metaphors can give the impression that they have a spatial location. It merely indicates the strength of their dispositional quality, and to break through such traits need resources of many types. Some intellectual and theoretical grasp of the nature of emotions, in an impersonal form, is useful. More introspective and personal approaches become useful when developing self-analysis, but again these have to be gradually seen and observed as 'impersonal processes', leaving out any projection of one's own ego. Then it is the meditative framework of understanding and experience, at different levels, which can develop more refined and stable insights. In terms of the five aggregates, feeling has to be grasped in terms of the '*vēdanā-khanda*' and emotions in terms of the '*saṇkhāra-khanda*'.

A fuller understanding of these emotions and their related feeling-tones, by contemplation as well as reflection in our routine lives, widens and refines our understanding of ourselves, breaks through the barriers we have built between ourselves and others and thus opens up a pathway for reducing inter-personal stress and conflict. The psychology of 'troubled relationships', which we have cited under our concepts of positive mental health as a problem to be examined, will find some greatly relevant therapeutic resources in the Buddhist analysis of emotions. We have made a careful study of some of the emotion profiles as found in the discourses of the Buddha; those like fear and anger, sadness and happiness, and the more complex ones like jealousy and pride as well as the great altruistic emotions of compassion, loving kindness, and sympathetic joy, along with the role of equanimity in emotional experience.[27] The ability to form sensitive, satisfying and productive human relationships is one of the positive criteria of mental health, and very relevant to our times.

An interesting study of the psychology of troubled relationships from the perspectives of Buddhism in relation to the five hindrances of lust, anger, sloth and torpor, restlessness and doubt has been made by Seymour Boorstein.[28] In this work the following observation is made: 'Psychotherapy of troubled relationships usually involves clarification of communications and learning of constructive communication.'[29] In addition, in insight therapy (*vipassanā*), 'the fears, angers, and tensions that arise are used to focus on the transference distortions, thus making conscious those forces, usually of an infantile nature, that have been unconscious. Once they become conscious, these forces can usually be dealt with by the more rational and adult aspects of the personality.'[30]

Thus greater self-knowledge through understanding feelings and emotions can be a useful instrument in a clinical context in building a productive doctor–patient or an analyst–patient relationship, as Boorstein explains in his study. But this aspect of the *satipaṭṭhāna* has wider social ramifications in offering a corrective to what Fromm calls the 'pathological society' as such. Greater self-knowledge through the understanding of emotions generates pliability and flexibility with our own thoughts and emotions, and a sense of transparency (as seeing one's image in an unruffled, tranquil pond),[31] in regarding the many half-thoughts and unarticulated feelings which pass through in quick succession. The development of mindfulness generates this sense of clarity in our emotional lives.

Apart from the social and inter-personal aspects, the understanding of emotions through the practice of mindfulness has other implications. If we study the structure of an emotion, there are the physiological and cognitive aspect of emotions, which are equally important in the light of the *satipaṭṭhāna*.

Let us briefly look at the facets which are ingredient aspects of emotions. First, it is necesary to emphasise the concept of rationality linked to our emotional life. Emotions are so often presented as irrational and fickle, that we fail to see the complicated logic which is embedded in our emotions:

> We are not afraid of X unless we take X to be dangerous; we are not angry at X unless we take X to be acting contrary to something we want; we do not have remorse over having done X unless we regard it unfortunate that we did X . . .[32]

Thus people can appeal to understanding and knowledge to change the attitudes of others – they can get people to see things differently. Whether in the clinical context, a social context or a context of understanding one's own complex thoughts, the fact that emotions have a logic of their own makes this task possible.

Not only do people have reasons but they display standard patterns in their behaviour, namely dispositions. Here is such a description of vanity or conceit:

> We expect a vain person to do a number of things: namely to talk a lot about himself; to cleave to the society of the eminent; to reject criticism; to seek the footlights and to disengage himself from conversation about the merits of others.[33]

Thus, what we call conceit or the Buddhist call *māna*, will have certain behavioural and dispositional aspects.

In general, emotions have a cognitive aspect (the noise that we hear across a forest and the black shape that we see is a bear and the belief that the bear can attack us), an evaluative aspect, (it is a 'danger'), and behavioural dispositional aspects (we can run or hide; a tendency for flight). In the same way that the emotions have *an implicit rational structure*, there are many significant *physiological changes* in emotions. While their rational aspect provides a footing for the development of the Contemplation on states of Mind and Mental Objects, and their evaluative element can be laid bare by the Contemplation of Feelings, their physiological aspect can be grasped and related to the physiological rhythms of emotional experience by the Contemplation of the Body.[34]

EMOTIONS AND PHYSIOLOGY

Emotions have two aspects, a cold and a hot part. One component consists of *evaluative cognitions* – our valuations characterising how we see the world. The other component represents the *arousal aspect* of emotions. Given that any one emotional experience is a product of these two components, a multitude of emotions become possible.[35] The human body has two parts, the somatic part and the autonomous, nervous system. The latter has two parts, the sympathetic part (concerned with the expenditure of energy and coping with excitement) and the parasympathetic part (dealing with the conservation of energy and relaxation). The sympathetic nervous system is responsible for a number of changes in emotional experience; blood pressure and heart rate increases; respiration becomes more rapid; the pupils of the eyes dilate; electrical resistance of the skin increases; blood-sugar level increases to provide more energy; the blood becomes able to clot more quickly (in case of wounds); motility of the gastrointestinal tract decreases or stops; the hairs on the skin become erect.

It must be mentioned that, as a number of psychologists and philosophers have pointed out, physiological changes may not help us to differentiate one emotion from another and the changes are *conceptually not identified with particular emotions*, but yet physiological changes are part of occurrent emotions.[36] For instance, the physiological changes which occur in fear (increased heart and respiration rates, and flushing or paling of the skin) also occur in anger. But they are extremely important to the intensity with which the emotions are experienced. Bodily sensations become more important for positive emotions in an indirect way: decreased pulse, respiratory rates can be found when there is joy and tranquility. The possibility of physiological differentiation of emotions is yet a live issue in ongoing research, but at the level of available knowledge it is only the cognitive and evaluative factors which help us to understand the logic of different emotions.

The Contemplation of the Body (*kāyānupassanā*) is a central part of the practice of mindfulness (*satipaṭṭhāna*). The nature of this chapter does not give us sufficient room to go into this matter in detail from a Buddhist perspective. Elsewhere, in a forthcoming work, more detailed study of the emotions and physiology is being made.[37] For the present, briefly, the Mindfulness of Breathing provides a useful area to see the link between physiology and emotions.

Nyanaponika Thera in his *Heart of Buddhist Meditation*[38] points out the positive benefits of meditation, both in the psychological and physiological realms:

> These instances will show that Mindfulness of Breathing is very active in quietening bodily and mental unrest or irritation.[39]

Meditation can always help to cut across the ideogenic as well as the physical and physiological facets of negative emotions. The impact of meditation on patterns of breathing, blood circulation, heart beat and so on, is being experimentally explored, and there is a fair amount of experimental evidence of the beneficial bodily consequences of meditation. This is also linked to a new interest in psycho-somatic medicine. Based on the Zen Buddhist tradition in Japan, experimental work has been done to generate new concepts in psycho-somatic medicine. When people lose sensitivity about how their bodies feel (alexisomia), Zen meditation has been considered as an approach to restore innate potentials for self-control based on mind-body non-dualism and the dissociation between intellectual and emotional activities.[40]

THE PHILOSOPHY OF THE MIND-BODY RELATIONSHIP

In the final analysis, the background philosophy for the link between emotions and physiology and for psycho-somatic medicine is found in the Buddhist conception of the relationship between the body and mind. While upholding the notion that the person is a psychophysical unit (*nāma-rūpa*), Buddhism does not subscribe to the identity hypothesis, that the mind and the body are one and the same entity, or the dualistic hypothesis that the mind and the body are entirely different and separated. Both the *nāma* and the *rūpa* groups derive their respective designations depending on each other. There is reciprocity and mutual dependency. Both mentality and materiality are inextricably interwoven into a 'tangle-within' and a 'tangle-without'. They are sometimes referred to as the 'two bundles of reeds supporting each other'.

More than anything found in the West, the law of dependent origination gives the Buddhist perspective on the mind-body relation its unique context. The closest that we can find as a basis for East–West communication and cross-cultural understanding is C. D. Broad's Compound Theory presented in his work, *Mind and Its Place in Nature.*[41] The Compound Theory emphasises the notion of mutual-dependence:

> Might not what we know as a 'mind' be a compound of two factors, neither of which separately has the characteristic properties of a mind, just as salt is a compound of two substances, neither of which by itself has the characteristic properties of salt? Let us call one of these factors the 'psychic factor' and the other the 'bodily factor' . . .[42]

Broad even says that the Compound Theory leaves an open stand on the question of survival after death and its implications for the psychic factor.

While Buddhism upholds mutual dependency and reciprocity as its deep philosophical framework, where necessary the Buddha encourages a pragmatic and practical usage, taking into account the relative sense in which body and mind may be considered as independent variables. In fact Yujiro Ikemi in his discussion of, 'The Concept of "Ki" in Oriental Medicine and Psychosomatic Medicine',[43] says:

> . . . as a methodology, we need a kind of paradoxical logic that expresses 'the mutually independent and, at the same time, dependent relationship' that mind-body has.[44]

THE INTEGRATION OF POSITIVE MENTAL-HEALTH CONCEPTS

In the preceding sections, we examined the Buddhist conceptions of mental health and sickness, then outlined six concepts of positive mental health, and then moved into the examination of negative factors generating mental sickness. These negative factors or hindrances (nīvarana) consist of the fourth part of the *satipaṭṭhāna sutta*, the Contemplation of Mental Content.

Then we moved to a closer examination of feelings and emotions, which brought together the first three parts of the *satipaṭṭhāna* of the Body, Feelings and States of Mind. In discussing the importance of understanding emotions, we discussed therapeutic resources for the therapy of troubled human relationships and the importance of body-mind linkages in emotion studies.

But yet the central concept which can unify the six facets of mental health and the integration of emotion studies is the Buddhist analysis of the self, the *anatta* doctrine. It is a notion central to reality orientation and our attitude towards the self and self-knowledge, and the formation of healthy human relationships – the less we are under the delusion of the ego, the more autonomy we have.

In an attempt to explore the value of the *anatta* doctrine in terms of Buddhist therapeutic resources, we have made a detailed study of its relevance for emotion studies, which will be found in a forthcoming work, *Emotions and Their Shadows*. In the concluding section of this chapter, it is expected that a close study of one of the emotions, with a strong orientation towards the self and which will bring out the ambiguities of the self-world relation, will be a useful supplement to this study.

There are some emotions which have a central focus on the self like pride, conceit, jealousy, depression and anxiety, and others like fear, anger and sadness are related to the self but in a more indirect manner. Emotions like compassion and loving kindness and all wholesome emotions are severed from the grip of the ego. Out of the many attempts which have been made to find principles to organise emotions, an important question is how we separate negative from positive emotions, or, in more familiar Buddhist terminology, the wholesome from the unwholesome – the self-transcending from the self-centred emotions. In doing this, the emotions–self linkage provides an interesting basis to view emotion phenomena. Though there have been piecemeal attempts by philosophers and psychologists to examine the nature of jealousy, pride and humility in terms of the self and related issues of identity formation, Buddhism offers a more self-conscious and structured methodology to view the self–emotions relationship in terms of wholesome states leading to mental health, and unwholesome states leading to mental sickness.

As this project is being worked out in detail in our *Emotions and their Shadows*, here a sample case study of an emotion profile is presented to conclude this analysis, namely, an analysis of the relationship between emotions and the self as seen in the emotion of jealousy.

EMOTIONS AND THE SELF IN THE EXPERIENCE OF JEALOUSY

The ego–emotions relationship has certainly emerged as a problematic concern in recent writings in the philosophy of emotions.[45] Jealousy has been one of the emotions which has been cited as an interesting emotion to help understand the role of the self in emotional experience. Another emotion of interest discussed in relation to the self is pride.

The emotion of jealousy in the Western philosophy of emotions has been viewed from various levels of generality:[46]

(1) Ones position as a favoured individual is threatened.
(2) It may be understood in terms of 'possessive' behaviour.
(3) It may be understood in terms of a crisis in personal identity, as a wound to self-esteem and self-love.
(4) It may be understood in terms of the reality and the unity of the concept of self.

Therapeutically it has been observed that the difficulty in overcoming jealousy lies in the strong problems of personal identity it generates:

> But like other emotions that concentrate on the self, jealousy raises questions about whether there is, at the core of traits that are central to us, an irreducible *me* that would remain even if the most central traits were altered. . .[47]

> But precisely because jealousy does raise crucial issues of personal identity and its survival, there are strong blocks in the way of overcoming jealousy.[48]

The Buddha faces the questions squarely and clearly and says that a futile attempt to preserve a false concept of the self with its related identifications generates the emotional conflicts. Corporeality, feeling, perception, disposition and consciousness work reciprocally to generate a relative sense of serial unity. But to build strong permanent identities and project permanence to the stream of experience is to create a false facade. The other false path is to consider this relative unity as a protoplasm without directionality and project a doctrine of chaos. The Buddhist middle path between eternalism (*sassata diṭṭhi*) and nihilism (*uccheda diṭṭhi*) provides the middle ground to face identity issues whether they may be metaphysical, ethical or emotional. As we have observed elsewhere:

> Somewhere within the narrow ridge between the path of chaos and nihilism and the traps of identity illusions, one has to penetrate through a razor's edge a realm of interim and critical unities, dissolving as we cross them, transcending them as we cut across their inner dialectic. The reality of personal and group identities all flounder on this narrow ridge, and to steer clear of the trap is the greatest challenge.[49]

This is the Buddhist answer to the challenges of the identity issues.

In the therapeutic context, the Buddhist would reject both the profile of the man with the overdone, heightened and bolstered identity and the other without any coherence and directionality, heading towards chaos, disorder and nihilism. The doctrine of egolessness does not mean that people should not struggle with the notion of 'who am I?' But it has to be done in the critical and mature way as recommended by the Buddha.

Ernest Jones, who made a very clear analysis of the concept of jealousy, observed three elements which go to make jealousy: fear at the thought of losing the loved object; hatred of the rival; and the wound to self-esteem (narcissism).[50] An idea linked to the damage to self-esteem is the possibility of developing a feeling of diminished self-worth. Spinoza adds to this texture of jealousy the mechanism of ambivalence, the vacillation between love and hatred directed to the beloved and also sorrow regarding the absence of what we love.[51]

All these features make jealousy an interesting 'blend emotion' fed by other emotions like fear, anger, love, sorrow, feelings of prestige and humiliation, and self-love.

The pāli term *issa* in Buddhist texts is rendered both as envy and jealousy. It is considered as one of the defilements of the mind (*upakkilēsa*) along with others like greed, ill-will, malice, contempt etc. *Issa* emerges as a form of hateful consciousness with a strong undertone of possessiveness and may be understood in terms of the *upādāna* which, although often translated as 'clinging', may more properly rendered as 'entanglement'. This refers to a kind of obsession with what we like or dislike or have ambivalent feelings toward. With strong and obsessive attachments, loss and sorrow and complex blends of anger and sorrow are possible in the Buddhist analysis. In the final analysis and at a more deeper though a general level, jealousy in the Buddhist context illustrates the strong identity problems of the ego.

To conclude, jealousy is a complex and rich emotion: jealousy develops strong fixations in love, excites a strong dose of anger in competition and failure, doubles-up one's instinctive avarice by holding on to what one might lose (at least in the imagination), and plays on ambivalence by tolerating strong emotions of love and hatred towards the same object. It falls abruptly into an empty abyss of loss, and as the circuitous process of identification develops, self-destructive impulses emerge: for it is by rallying against oneself that the melancholic preserves identification with the lost object.

From the perspectives of its philosophical, psychological and therapeutic contributions, Buddhism does make a very significant attempt to understand, unravel and solve man's emotional conflicts.[52]

7 Mind–Body Relationship and Buddhist Contextualism

'Is it "I" who draw the bow, or is it the bow that draws me into the state of highest tension? Do "I"hit the goal, or does the goal hit me? Is it spiritual when seen by the eyes of the body, and corporeal when seen by the eyes of the spirit – or both or neither? Bow, arrow, goal and ego, all melt into one another, so that I can no longer separate them. And even the need to separate has gone. For as soon as I take the bow and shoot, everything becomes clear and straightforward and so ridiculously simple. . . . '[1]

'Sound is not a thing that dwells inside the conch-shell and comes from time to time, but due to both, the conch-shell and the man that blows it, sound comes to arise. Just so, due to the presence of vitality, heat, consciousness, the body may execute acts of going standing, sitting and lying down, and the five sense organs and the mind may perform various functions.'[2]

The Buddha denies the existence of any permanent entity either physical or mental. He considers the human person as a psychophysical complex. There is also no attempt to reduce mental processes to physical processes or vice versa. The mind and body have a conditioned existence and they emerge within a dynamic continuum of a variety of relations. Basically a Buddhist does not accept a dualistic position or a monistic position (whether it is the materialistic or the idealistic type). Within this framework, the discourses of the Buddha make relative distinctions between the 'physical' and the 'mental', as when the Buddha refers to feelings which are physical or mental. The Buddha presents a contextual discourse of issues pertaining to the mental and the bodily facets of our experience, discouraging any excessive entanglement in metaphysical concerns. In a more, deeper sense, the question whether the mind is identical with the body or whether they are independent of each other is a question that the Buddha left aside, as an undetermined question.

We shall first deal with the metaphysical issue pertaining to the mind–body issue, then with the ethical facets of the issue, which has led to a fair amount of distortion of the Buddhist perspectives, and finally present the insights of Buddhist experientialism. This last facet may be referred to as its epistemological strand, though experientialism in the Buddhist context is different from the kind of rationalism and empiricism found in the Western philosophical traditions.

Schopenhauer described the mind–body issue as a knot, and the Buddhist texts discourses describe it as a 'tangle within and tangle without'.[3] But yet the Buddha has presented his analysis of the subject with precision and clarity within the bounds of the four noble truths, which is basically an attempt to deal with human suffering.

METAPHYSICAL ISSUE

'Just as friend, two bundles of reeds were to stand one supporting the other, even so consciousness is dependent on name-and-form and name-and-form is dependent on consciousness; and the six sense-spheres on name-and-form, contact on the six sense-spheres, feeling on contact, craving on feeling, grasping on craving, becoming on grasping, birth on becoming and decay-and-death, sorrow, lamentation, pain, grief and despair are dependent on birth. This is the arising of the entire mass of suffering. But, friend, if one of those two bundles of reeds is drawn out, the other one would fall down, and if the latter is drawn out the former one will fall down.'[4]

The term 'name-and-form' is quite crucial for understanding the Buddhist analysis of mind and the body. There are two important contexts of their usage. First, name and form, which is a translation of the pali term nāma-rūpa, are often associated together as a reference to the five aggregates: feeling, perception, disposition and consciousness associated with nāma and rūpa associated with the material shape derived from extension, cohesion, heat and mobility. All five are also referred to as aggregates of attachment which generate the false notion of a pure ego. Feeling (*vedana*) is the affective basis of experience and perception (*saññā*) the cognitive basis and *sankhāra* (a difficult term to translate) may be considered as the volitional and dispositional strands in our personality. Consciousness (*viññāna*) is also one of the aggregates. But *nāma* and *rūpa* are also considered as the fourth link in the wheel of dependent origination and that is the reference given above, where they are compared to two bundles of reeds supporting each other. This is the context that will form the focus of the present analysis.

In this context, the aggregates of feeling, perception and dispositions provide the manner in which one becomes conscious of matter. Thus in the context of the dependent origination, matter, feeling, perception and dispositions may be rendered as name and matter (*nāma-rūpa*) and thus having any experience would involve name-and-matter, as well as consciousness (*viññāna*) (*nāmarūpa saha viññāna*). Matter may be considered as internal (*ajjhattika*) and external (*bāhira*). In our experiences we cognise both, the internal in the form of 'this body of mine', and the external as the 'tree I see outside'. Thus the most important relationships are made of the linkages of name-and-matter plus consciousness. They arise together and cease together. That is the central message of the context cited above, from the description of the dependent origination links. They are reciprocal, depend upon each other and they also emerge simultaneously and cease simultaneously. Dependent on consciousness there is name and matter and dependent on name and matter there is consciousness.

After we understand the point about reciprocity, dependence and simultaneous origin and cessation, it becomes easy to free ourselves from the traps of ontology like dualism and monism. As will be discussed later in this chapter, this point is made more strongly in the anti-ontologising context of meditation, where the phenomenal nature of the experiential process is seen, and also we realise the 'designation' like nature of the terms we use like feeling and the body.

'When, friends, there is no eye and there is no form and there is no eye-consciousness, it is impossible that he will point out a designation of contact. When there is no designation of contact, it is impossible that he will point out a designation of feeling. When there is no designation of feeling, it is impossible that he will point out a designation of perception.'[5] We of course do make sensible distinctions between feelings, perceptions and thought, but all these emerge from a synthetic process and are linguistic devices that describe this process. Practice of meditation constantly helps us to move away from our ontologising dispositions and pay more heed to the designations we use and the pragmatic nature of language. Thus the body–mind linkages are also seen as processes of this sort.

In general, the Buddha did not push the questions like the body–mind issue towards the obtaining of theoretical finality. While drawing clear distinctions for the purpose of conveying his message concerning the alleviation of human suffering, the Buddha had a practical and pragmatic approach to problems. He steered clear of metaphysical traps. He considered the communication of ideas as a pragmatic and linguistic issue which should help the individual to follow the Buddhist experiential path and discover the nature of 'things as they are'.

After having cleared the metaphysical mist, it is necessary to say that the relative use of terms like 'mental' and 'bodily' are found in the discourses. The Buddha says for instance that if a perfected one (*arahant*) is struck by some physical injury (injured by a bamboo splinter), the feeling he experiences will be a bodily one and not mental : 'O Monks, when he is touched by a painful feeling, he will not worry nor grieve and lament, he will not beat his breast and weep, nor will he be distraught. It is one kind of feeling he experiences, a bodily one, but not a mental feeling. It is as if a man were pierced by a dart, but was not pierced by a dart following the first one.'[6]

To cite another context where relative distinctions between 'bodily' and 'mental' are made: 'Monks, there are to be seen beings who can admit freedom from suffering from bodily disease for one year, for two years . . . twenty . . . even hundred years. But monks those beings are hard to find in the world who can admit freedom from mental disease even for one movement, save in whom the passions (*āsavas*) are destroyed.'[7] Also, the Buddha says in another context: 'Though my body is sick, my mind shall not be sick.', 'Thus householder, must you train yourself.'[8]

But there are other contexts, where the reciprocity is emphasised, others where their designation like character is emphasised. We shall yet find another important strand, when we discuss Buddhist experientialism in this chapter. It is with this kind of contextual stance that the Buddha looks at the mind–body issue, which Schopenhauer described as a knot, and the Buddha described as a tangle.

ETHICAL PERSPECTIVES ON THE BODY

Buddhist discourses describe the consequences that can befall a person with an excessive attachment to the body. The body in certain contexts was symbolic of sensuality and deliverance is seen as getting out of the spell of the body. There are many metaphors from the discourses that have been cited by scholars, like that of the body being a wound, a sore, that it is fragile like a jar and so on. Meditation on disgust would focus on the death, sickness, old age and the fragility of the body. 'The eye of flesh', the 'body as burning with passion' and such descriptions do emphasise the point that the body may be a hindrance to the leading of a good life.[9]

But then in other contexts, we find that suicide is condemned, extreme asceticism is considered as a futile endeavour and the basic necessities of food, shelter, health, cleanliness, fresh air, clean water, good environment and so on are emphasised. The Buddha clearly states that liberation is not achieved by matted hair, starvation, nakedness and living in a degrading environment. One who reads the discourses in a piecemeal fashion, as to what the Buddha said about the body, may miss the point that there is a sense of balance and harmony about the body and the mind which is necessary and that is the basic Buddhist attitude. When we focus attention on the Buddhist meditative path and the place of the body in the practice of Buddhist meditation this point will be seen.

The Buddha advocates restraint of body, speech and thought. What this implies is the cultivation of gentle ways of body, speech and mind. Refinement and composure, erect physical posture, mindfulness when standing, sitting and walking, all involve an important role for the cultivation of norms for a sensibility for the body too. At this point we see a strong link between the ethics and the meditative life in Buddhism. If we overdo this image of the body as a wound, we may miss this more integrated body–mind perspective, which of course goes well with its philosophy. The section that follow, will go more deeply into this point.

BUDDHIST EXPERIENTIALISM

Some of the philosophical knots like the body–mind issue have a spell on us, when our knowledge is limited to book knowledge (*sūtamaya*) and intellectual knowledge (*cintāmaya*). It is only through experiential knowledge (*bhāvanāmaya*) that one can break through these knots.

The Buddhist practice of mindfulness has four divisions: the practice of mindfulness in relation to body, feeling, thoughts and the working of the mind and the body together.[10] In Pali they are referred to as *kāyānupassanā*, *vedanānupassanā*, *ciftānupassanā* and *dhammānupassanā*. In the context of meditation, the body has a central place and basically the body and the mind may be seen as the two sides of the same coin. In systematic meditative practice, whether it is tranquillity meditation or insight meditation, only one's own mental and bodily processes become the foci of mindfulness practice, as what is aimed at is knowledge by direct experience. External objects or the mental activities of others are reached through perception or inference.

The meditation on the body starts with that of breathing and is extended to bodily postures, activities, parts of the body, elements and so on. The practice of mindfulness begins with mindfulness on breathing in and breathing out, which in Pali is rendered as '*ānāpāna-sati*'. Though the development of physical and mental health is not the primary target of the practice of mindfulness, (the primary goal being the development of insight into suffering, impermanence and impersonality), the mindfulness practice generates conditions for both physical and mental health. The development of such insight also refines the Buddhist understanding of the mind–body relationship, viewing experience in terms of conditionality and relativity.

Breathing has both physical and mental facets and is the finest base for body–mind integration and health. If we link up the mindfulness on breathing with the mindfulness on feeling, we enter a rich territory of 'emotions-and-the body'. When initial pain signals get converted into anger and fear, breathing patterns change – there is bodily turbulence and agitation. When there is calm and collectedness and joy breathing patterns and their rhythm are different.

As one moves into the mindfulness of bodily postures like sitting, walking and standing and extend them to the whole body, we become aware of body language linked to emotions like for instance, when we are angry, our hands tend to close into fists. The simple point about the different ways in which we use our hands or the more symbolic way in which we display anger by close fists or the more receptive and open gestures found in meditative postures with upturned palms – all these open up a whole universe of body–mind discourse.

In general the linkages between psyche and soma that is seen in the links between the practice of mindfulness on the body and feelings has been one of the central areas of our recent research[11], and this is the reason for emphasising the value of Buddhist experientialism as providing an avenue for insights on the mind–body relationship. As we have discussed elsewhere, the nature of what is called '*alexithymia*' is interesting. The word comes from the Greek, a: 'without', lexis: 'word', thumos, 'heart' or 'affectivity'. It can refer to people who have difficulties in describing affective states or distinguishing one emotion from another. It has been pointed out by Joyce McDougall in this context that affects provide the closest links between psyche and soma, and in this situation there is a failure of the linking of psyche and soma.[12]

The Buddha's Discourse in the Middle Length Sayings, 'Discourse On Mindfulness of Body' may be considered as the Buddhist Charter for experientialism in the context of the mind–body relationship.[13] In this discourse the Buddha raises the question, 'And how, monks, when mindfulness of body has been developed, how when it has been made much of, is it of great fruit, of great advantage?' No attempt to review this discourse is made here, as we have already focused on the essential spirit of the dialogue in the above analysis in relation to the body–mind issue. We shall at this point refer to a few instances of the bodily facets of the experience of rapture and joy cited in the discourse.

When the five hindrances of sense-desires, ill-will, sloth and torpor, restlessness and worry, and sceptical doubt have been eliminated, one enters the first jhanic state (state of absorption). Describing this state as a state of harmony of body and mind, it is said that the person's whole body is pervaded, drenched, permeated and suffused with joy: 'Monks, as a skilled bath-attendant or his apprentice, having sprinkled bath-powder into a bronze vessel, might knead it while repeatedly sprinkling it with water until the ball of lather had taken up the moisture, was drenched with moisture, suffused with moisture. Even so monks, does a monk drench, saturate, permeate, suffuse this body with rapture and joy that is born of aloofness. . . . Thus does a monk develop mindfulness of body.'[14] All the states of absorptions are described in terms of graphic images and metaphors which illustrate the integration of mind and body in the experience of these states.

There are also vivid descriptions of bodily expressions when one is overtaken by anger and lust. An interesting episode where Saccaka the Jain went to debate with the Buddha is a good case in point. While the Buddha maintained an unruffled countenance and a relaxed body and mind, Saccaka was so excited and agitated that sweat was pouring and soaked his robes. It is said that at the end of the debate, Saccaka became ashamed, his shoulders drooped, his head downcast and brooding. It was a 'loss of face'.[15]

We have emphasised the experiential stance of Buddhism. The Buddha did engage in debate and argument when people came to him with wrong views or distortions of the Buddha's teachings. Two views which were currently debated were the view of *Sati* that consciousness was identical with the self and the materialist view that the body was identical with the self. *Sati* upheld that the continuity of consciousness was identical with the self: he maintained that one and the same consciousness continues unchanged and is reborn.[16] *Sati* also maintained that this was the view of the Buddha. The Buddha referred to it as a wrong view, as consciousness is generated by conditions and so dependent on them. Visual consciousness for instance depends on the sense organ eye and material objects and through contact emerges eye-consciousness. The same may be said about consciousness of sounds, smell, taste, touch and ideas. Ideas involve memory and images.

Though he did engage in debates he said in the final analysis, there were three groups of thinkers, rational metaphysicians who used logic, the traditionalists who merely based their views on scripture alone and the experientialists who belonged to the meditative tradition. Regarding the traditionalists, of course, the Buddha said that even his own doctrine should be tested in the light of experience and critical reason. But even reason had its limitations. There may be theories which are logically coherent but not true of the world. The Buddha was critical of speculative reason and did respect critical and analytical reasoning. But they had their limits. Ultimately the person who wishes to test the veracity of the Buddha's teaching has to go to experience.

It is on the basis of his personal experience that the Buddha made one of the most intelligible and sane analysis of the mind–body relationship – that the mind and body are neither separable nor identical, not even alternatives, but that they are inseparable. They are like two bundles of reeds supporting each other. To use a metaphor – the bow, arrow, goal, and ego, all melt into each other, so that I can no longer separate them

CONCLUDING THOUGHTS ON THE BODY–MIND ETHIC

We mentioned above that the metaphors of the 'wound', 'sore' and the 'fragile jar' to describe the body, though they have their point may give an unbalanced perspective about the place of the body image in Buddhism, to those who do not have a holistic comprehension of Buddhism, and this may be rectified by turning to the meditative tradition. Buddhism is basically a middle path between extreme asceticism focused on self-torture and excessive sensuality. The life style worked out for the householder, as different from the monk, of the harmonious and righteous life (*sama cariya*, *dhamma cariya*), again do show that there is a legitimate place for the metaphor of the body for the householder.

In a sense the 'body' is an image representing in compressed form the biological and physiological inheritance of the humans. In the way that a railway track provides certain frameworks for the engine driver to chart the train, the physiological, biological and in Buddhism the *samsaric* and *karmic* psyche too, provides the track to chart our way. We cannot do violence to the body and achieve liberation from suffering. The Buddha's arguments against suicide, even on religious grounds betray this point. Even the kind of 'disgust' recommended in meditation has to be placed in the context of the pali word – *nibbida* (translated as 'disgust'). Meditation on the foul and disgust have to be worked on a kind of razor's edge, so that they are filtered through the way of equanimity, rather than aversion, hatred and revulsion. As Nyanaponika Mahathero quite rightly points out, 'When insight is deepened and strengthened, what has been called disgust (in rendering the pali term *nibbida*) has no longer the emotional tinge of aversion and revulsion, but manifests itself as withdrawal . . . .'[17] It is a turning away from worldliness, as well as an attempt to rid of defilements that remain as a residue. The development of the stance towards the body emerges from the cultivation of the most refined experientialism and meditative practice.

Take for instance the sensation of pain. Pain has a sensory aspect to it, unlike for instance grief, which is more psychological. In meditative practice we work on pain, and when pain emerges in the body you shift your stance of mindfulness from breathing to the sensation of pain. As you make friends with pain, as the discontent and anger goes to the background you begin to see that you may feel differently about this experience. The instructions would perhaps go in this manner: 'Go into the body, go into the shoulder, go into the lower back, breathe with it, and try to penetrate the pain with your awareness and with your breathing.'[18] Such practices have been described as '. . . an inner science that marries the subjective and the objective, in which you become more familiar with the workings of your own body.'

Perhaps recent trends in the sciences and Western medicine are also focusing on the body, as they discern important links between the nervous system and the immune system. Recent work in the area of the brain sciences, perhaps indicate that feelings are not just elusive psychic qualities but rather very much linked to the landscape of the body. Sections of the brain that integrate body signals appear to play an important role in emotional experiences. During the time that the Buddha lived neurology was not a live concern. These developments are interesting and perhaps fit in well with the Buddhist perspectives on the body and emotions, as emphasised in this chapter. The interaction between body and mind appears to be an idea that has brought in new perspectives to modern medicine.

The path of Buddhist experientialism and its framework is based on the body–mind integration, and one has to be cautious in seeing that the ethics of the body in Buddhism does not go off these rails, in the same way that excessive metaphysical queries concerning the body–mind relationship may turn out to be an exercise that is counterproductive. What I refer to as 'Buddhist experientialism' may be the platform to generate the most productive and positive framework to understand the body–mind relationship in Buddhism.

In the way that the body is important in Buddhist thought, consciousness takes a pre-eminent place in the psychology of Buddhism. It may be an error to think that the ontology of the mental is an objective study for science. The neglect of consciousness in modern psychology is to be regretted, specially in view of the point highlighted in this article, that the body and mind work together in actual experience. The recent work by John R. Searle, emphasising the importance on 'consciousness' and 'intentionality' is an important contribution to the philosophy of mind. 'A dominant strain in the philosophy of mind and cognitive science has been to suppose that computation is an intrinsic feature of the world and that consciousness and intentionality are some how eliminable . . . .'[19] He says that the Cartesian tradition and the vocabulary that the West has inherited conditioned thinking on these matters and the vocabulary includes apparent oppositions like, physical versus mental, matter versus spirit, materialism versus mentalism and so on. He observes that, 'Consciousness is a mental, and therefore physical property, property of the brain, property of the brain in the sense in which liquidity is a property of systems of molecules. The fact that a feature is physical does not imply that it is not mental.'[20]

Searle also says, that the deep mistake is to suppose that one must choose between materialism and monism, and that his own view is not a form of dualism. Searle feels that in discussing the mind–body issue 'we are captives of a certain set of verbal categories'. At this stage of the analysis, there is no attempt to go all the way with John Searle and say that his position on the mind–body issue exactly fits in with the Buddhist position, as there are possible framework differences between him and the Buddhist view, which goes beyond the analysis attempted in this chapter. But his diagnosis of the mind–body 'tangle' as the Buddha described or – the mind–body 'knot' as Schopenhauer described, falls very much in line with general stance on the mind–body problem taken in this chapter. Buddhist contextual discourse is the way to avoid the dialectical traps of the mind–body problem, but to understand the real nature of what we call the mind–body complex, according to the Buddha, each of us, (if we wish to) need to explore the way of Buddhist experientialism.

8 A Holistic Perspective on Emotion Theory and Therapy in Early Buddhism

Hysterics behave as if anatomy did not exist.

Sigmund Freud

I now proceed to urge the vital point of my whole theory, which is this: If we fancy some strong emotion, and then try to abstract from our consciousness of it all the characteristics of bodily systems, we find we have nothing left behind, no 'mind-stuff' out of which the emotion can be constituted, and that a cold and neutral state of intellectual perception is all that remains.

William James

Just as, friend, two bundles of reed were to stand one supporting the other, even so consciousness is dependent on name-and-form (physical and mental phenomena) and name-and-form on consciousness. . . . If friend, I were to pull towards towards me one of those sheaves of reeds, the other would fall.

(*Samyutta Nikāya*, II, 114)

PRELUDE

The Buddha's strategies for managing emotions are directed towards the goal of reducing human pain and tribulation, as well as a complete liberation from the basic human predicament of *unsatisfactoriness* (*dukkha*). Today, noteworthy research influenced by Buddhist techniques of meditation in the domains of psychology, medicine and neuroscience have opened up the question *can the mind heal the body?* According to the hypothesis of 'neuroplasticity' developed by Richard Davidson the brain continually changes as a result of experience (Goleman, 2003, 21–3). This hypothesis has opened up new vistas for research on meditation. The claim that the brain, immune system and the emotions are interconnected point towards the emergence of new insights into health and emotional well being. Against the backdrop of the current interface of Buddhism and science on emotion studies, this presentation is designed first to attempt a clarification of the intricate relationship between the body and mind in emotional experience. In the light of these new developments, a viable conceptual map of the mind–body relation in Buddhism would be very relevant. Why is this task important? As I have mentioned in a previous study, the Buddha has discouraged people from pushing the logic of the body–mind relationship into extreme limits and getting entangled in metaphysical debates. 'The Buddha presents a contextual discourse of issues pertaining to the mental and bodily facets of our experience, discouraging any excessive entanglements in metaphysical concerns. In a more deeper sense, the question whether the mind is identical with the body or whether they are independent of either is a question that the Buddha left aside, as an undetermined question' (de Silva, 2000, 142–3). The present analysis carries this contextual discourse into both the analysis of theories as well as therapies of emotion. In both the philosophy and psychology there is a conflict between the body-based theories and cognitive appraisal theories of emotions. While till recent times such conflicts existed in the area of therapy, there are now new cross-cutting frontiers of therapy and a convergence of interest in mindfulness practice. Also, while insightful discoveries in neuroscience are important, a Buddhist analysis needs to make a critical appreciation of the findings without falling into the trap of any reductionism. Thus in many respects this presentation develops a holistic perspective on emotion theory and therapy.

The second task is to compile the different techniques for managing emotions dispersed in the Buddhist *suttas* and assess their value, both in the context of therapy as well as their place in a Buddhist lifestyle. This study presents four types of strategies found in the *suttas* as well as Buddhist practice for regulating emotions. Thirdly, towards the latter part of this chapter some illuminating metaphors to understand the nature of emotions are clarified. These metaphors drawn from the *suttas* help us to capture the notion of *momentum* in emotions, as well as see emotions as a series of *preparations* to act, reminding us of the psychologist Frijda's definition of emotions as 'action readiness'.

The Interface Between Contemporary Science and Emotion Studies

It may be said that especially during the last two decades there has been a significant revival in emotion studies due to new developments in neuroscience, biology, psychology and medicine. As a result of these developments, an important thesis emerged in cognitive science that *understanding emotions is central to understanding intelligent systems.* The first important insight was the need to locate emotions within the interacting systems of *cognition, motivation* and *emotion.* In our normal access to the sensory world, we see things as red, round, tall, dense and so on. We identify sensory stimuli as apples, trees, and rivers. But if our sensory stimulus is an unexpected and disturbing one – that something we see is a dangerous snake, the meaning of the sensory stimulus is strongly *affective* – fear. The difference between seeing red and 'seeing fear' is important. In fact, though conscious thoughts and conscious feelings appear to be similar, they are produced by different subsystems.

The second important point was a discovery of Joseph Ledoux who examined the single emotion of fear, was about the speed of the affective process. As a neurologist, he found, that the emotional meaning of a stimulus might be appraised by the brain before the perceptual systems have fully processed the stimulus. In like manner, emotions like that of the fear of the snake, for example, occur with tremendous speed, then, the appraisal we make – the snake is poisonous and it is a danger – occur in a very quick and automatic manner. In more simple terms, the emotional brain works faster than the rational brain. Another emotion that is registered very fast is anger, which like fear is partly a survival signal. The foregoing gives us an opportunity to develop an insight into a good deal of behaviour by using an explanation from Buddhist psychology. According to Buddhism, the attempts to use reason to control emotions like anger and lust does not *often* work. Buddhist mindfulness practice helps us to focus on the present without the burden of past memories, which emerge as conceptual summaries and automatic thinking. As will be shown later, recently Western therapeutic traditions have found an effective instrument to deal with recalcitrant passions in the use of the practice of mindfulness practice. Meditation is a process by which we deepen our attention and awareness and helps us to be calm even when encountering unexpected situations like encountering a snake on a forest track. If we do not have that degree of mindfulness we become subject to emotional hijacking. The following passage describes the process of emotional hijacking by the amygdala:

> Imagine walking in the woods. A crackling sound occurs. It goes straight into the amygdala through the thalamic pathways. The sound also goes from the thalamus to the cortex, which recognizes the sound to be a dry-wig that snapped under the weight of your boot, or that of a rattlesnake shaking its tail. By the time the cortex has figured this out, the amygdala is already starting to defend against the snake.[1]

This study is very much concerned with the question of why passions, or negative emotions invade us in such a quick and mechanical manner. Of course, some emotions like guilt and jealousy and certain forms of anger develop as a more complex and gradual process. Thirdly, Ledoux had an important point about the levels of consciousness, both our cognitions and emotions seem to be operating at subliminal levels. In the Buddhist analysis of negative emotions like lust and anger these are invariably coloured by ignorance or lack of awareness. We can make sense of this point by referring to the occurrence of the dormant proclivities at a subliminal level (*anusaya*). In the discussion on anger as recorded in the book *Destructive Emotions*, the Dalai Lama observed: 'In Buddhist psychology, there is an understanding that many of the emotions need not necessarily be manifest. In fact, the emotions themselves may be felt or experienced, but they are also present in the form of habitual propensities that remain unconscious, or dormant, until they are catalyzed.'[2] These tendencies lie dormant (*pariyuṭṭhāna*) but have the potentiality to provide the base for the emergence of greed, anger and conceit. The arousal of these tendencies is due to stimuli in the sensory field, from the body or thoughts. These stimuli, if pleasant, condition the emergence of a tendency to greed (*rāgānusaya*) and if unpleasant a tendency towards anger (*patighānusaya*).

While these findings on emotions of Ledoux and also similar noteworthy findings of Damasio (Damasio, 1994) present to us interesting findings, they tend to be exclusively amygdaloid-centric and neglect higher level interpretations which are cortico-centric. These interpretations slide more towards the arousal theories of emotions neglecting the role of appraisal theories : 'When the brain receives some emotion-laden stimulus, it will seek to interpret that, just as it would any other stimuli. Amygdala activitation is part of the interpretation; so is cortical activation' (Hardcastle, 2003, 245). The neocortical areas of the brain bring a more analytic and appropriate response to our emotional responses, modulating the amygdala and other limbic areas. In fact, the importance of the pre-frontal areas in navigating us through decisions that matter in life is an important concern.

Emotion Concept in Buddhism

As our main interest is the wise management of emotions, we need to clarify the Buddhist concept of an emotion. An emotion in the context of Buddhism is a construction, an interactive complex within a causal network. This concept may be understood as having its structure in the five aggregates. When the practice of mindfulness becomes sharper and clearer, it is possible to discern the nature of the five aggregates: matter or physical form (*rūpa*); feeling (*vedanā*), the affective tone of experience, either pleasant, painful or neutral; perception (*saññā*), the factor responsible for noting, distinguishing and recognition; volition (*sankhāra*), the intentional aspect of mental activity; and consciousness (*viññāna*), the basic awareness operating through the senses. Thus within the five aggregates, we discern the three dimensions of the *cognitive, affective* and *conative* or volitional aspect of human consciousness. These three dimensions along with the activity of the body provide the background for emotional activity, both wholesome and unwholesome. In more detail, it may be said that *emotions emerge as a joint product of perceptions, feelings, desires, beliefs, appraisals and physiological arousal.*

Cultural and social filters as well as interpersonal interaction are also factors related to emotions. Thus within the course of managing emotions, the focus of attention may be any one or more of those components of an emotion. In the current state of philosophy and psychology of emotion, we see an emerging chasm between cognitive theories of emotions and physiological arousal theories of emotion.[3] Buddhism provides a more holistic approach accepting the importance of both facets of emotions. In the course of the analysis, I shall give a number of reasons why Buddhist psychology is enabled to move into a more holistic position.

In the management and control of defilements (*kilesa*) or negative emotions, the earliest point where one may 'apply the brakes' is at the point of feeling, so that you do not activate the subliminal tendencies (*anusaya*). Nyanaponika Thera has made a complete study of the *vedanā-samyutta*, which with the *satipaṭṭhāna* and the law of dependent origination provide a kind of charter for emotion studies. Nyanaponika Thera said, 'It should be first made clear that, in Buddhist Psychology, "feeling" (Pali: *vedanā*) is the bare sensation noted as pleasant, unpleasant (painful), neutral (indifferent). Hence it should not be confused with emotion, which, though arising from the basic feeling, adds to it likes or dislikes of varying intensity, as well as other thought processes.'[4] Out of the five factors cited above, *sankhāra* provides the framework for placing the operative factors in emotional experience together. This point is well confirmed by Nyanaponika Thero who declared, 'The specific factors operative in emotion belong to the aggregate of formations (*sankhāra-khanda*). Feeling is one of the four mental aggregates which arise, inseparably, in all states of consciousness; the other three are perception, mental formations and consciousness.'[5]

In the structural analysis of the five aggregates, such constituents as perception, feeling, volition, consciousness and body are revealed in their differentiating characteristics. Compared with this analytic approach, in the dependent origination analysis, we get a more synthetic approach, which shows the dependence and interdependence of phenomena. In the standard dependent origination analysis presenting the mind–body complex as a dynamic continuum, it is said that sense impressions condition feeling (*phassa-paccaya-vedanā*), while feeling is the condition for craving (*vedanā-paccaya-taṇhā*), and then craving conditions the more intensive form of clinging (*taṇhā-paccaya-upādāna*).

In the *Madupindika Sutta* (M. 109ff.), there is an interesting variation as pointed out by Nanananda Thero: 'what one feels, one perceives; what one perceives, one reasons about; what one reasons about, one proliferates' (Nanananda 1971).[6] The phrase, 'what one feels, one perceives' (*yam vedeti tam sañjānati*) adds an interesting variation, as this indicates that it is possible for feeling to precede perception (de Silva, 1992, 43). This context helps us to illuminate the thesis developed by Kitayama and Niedenthal in the book, *The Hearts Eye: Emotional Influences in Perception and Attention*, 'emotional states and emotional traits influence basic processes of attention and perception' (1994, 1). They say that at times, the result of perception may be an emotion rather than a cognitive state, such affective perceptions play an important role in our psychic life. Robert Zajonc who is also a contributor to this book, upholds the thesis that preferences for stimuli can be given immediate responses without previous cognitive appraisal, while Richard Lazarus, the psychologist who upholds an appraisal theory of emotions, says that the appraisals involved in emotions need not always be conscious (Lazarus, 1984). In fact, Cheshire Calhoun presents the same point from the stance of a Western philosopher:

> Our cognitive life is not limited to clear, fully conceptualized, articulated beliefs. Instead, beliefs constitute only a small illuminated portion of that life. The greater portion is a rather dark, cognitive set, an unarticulated work for interpreting our world, which if articulated, would be an enormous network of claims not all of which would be accepted by the individual as his beliefs (Calhoun, 1984, 338).

In Buddhist discourses the term *diṭṭhi* refers to a deep state of existential confusion regarding one's identity and is basically a distorting cognitive schema. Goleman, refering to the role of such distorting schemas in Buddhism (*moha* which is often used in place of *diṭṭhi*), says that such cognitive schemas can dim our awareness and create blind spots (Goleman, 1997, 237).

A different sort of contexts from the one cited above, is one that brings out the motivational factors in emotion. A textual passage which describes the dynamic setting in which emotions emerge is the following:

> Thus it is Ananda, craving comes into being because of feeling, pursuit because of craving, gain because of pursuit, decision because of gain, desire and passion (*chandarāga*) because of decision, tenacity because of desire and passion, possession because of tenacity, avarice because of possession, watch and ward because of avarice, and many a bad and wicked state of things arising from keeping, and watch and ward over possessions.[7]

These are different ways of understanding the emergence of what may be broadly called *affective* processes influencing perception and motivation, as well as the impact of motivation and cognition on emotion. The observation made at the beginning, that today cognitive science accepts a closer linkage between cognition, motivation and emotion, illuminates the different approaches of looking at emotions in the Buddhist discourses. A crucial point about the Buddhist analysis is the very close link between craving and affective processes like emotions. The above quotation on the emergence of passion brings out an important quality of emotions – the development of a momentum. I shall come back to this quality of emotions (p. 172), where volitional actions are described with the metaphor of 'an impulse that sets a wheel moving' (*abhisankārassa gati*). Though I have used the translation of the term *chandarāga* as passion (in the above quotation), the term passion used for over two thousand years, from the ancient Greeks to mid-eighteenth century, is a derivation of the Latin, *pati* (to suffer) and Greek *pathos*. But this derivation gave emotions a notion of *passivity*: 'gripped by anger', 'plagued by remorse', 'drowned by sorrow' and in the context of love, 'struck by a Cupid's arrow'. A rendering of this sort helps people to abjure responsibility for their actions. Responsibility for emotions is a quality that permeates the moral dimensions of emotions in Buddhism. When a person acts within the framework of full mindfulness (*sati*) and *yoniso manasikāra* (wise reflection) the person's commitment to the action is very clear. This does not mean that the person who acts under the influence of greed, hatred and delusion is not aware of his or her actions. Such a person acts with intention (*cetanā*) and responsibility. *Cetanā* is a mental factor (*cetasika*) common to all states of consciousness, *karmically* neutral ones and even the weakest. Thus the 'quality of awareness' runs through the whole moral dimension of emotions in Buddhism.

The body is important, because in many of the basic emotions like anger, fear and sadness, physiological arousal is a basic quality of the emotion. Also bodily calm is a feature in emotions like happiness born of contentment and joy in meditative states. In fact, William James's classic statement on the subject quoted at the head of this chapter brings out the importance of the body in emotions: 'if we fancy some strong emotion, and then try to abstract from our consciousness of it all the feelings of its characteristic bodily symptoms, we find we have nothing left behind . . . and a cold state of intellectual perception is all that remains'.[8] But as Gerald Myers[9] and Robert M. Gordon have pointed out,[10] James appears to have been careless in formulating his theory. We can always find good examples that fit his theory (that we first cry and then become sad): for example the feeling of sudden fright we have if we miss a step in a long winding staircase. But to move from the position that the *emotional quality of consciousness* is caused by bodily feelings – to the position that our *emotions are caused by bodily symptoms* is a long road indeed. The work on facial expressions and emotions, well presented in the writings of Ekman,[11] is important research. This work on facial expressions brings to our mind a graphic passage from William James, where he says that giving way to the symptoms of grief increases the passions, that each fit of sobbing makes the sorrow more acute until we get exhausted. He also says that by suppressing automatic body changes you can gain control of that state.

But we are also very interested in not merely the more basic emotions like anger and fear, but also in the more complex emotions like jealousy, guilt, and conceit, where the facial expressions are not as manifest as in anger and fear. Also the face is more *often* a mirror of emotions than an instigator or an antecedent of emotional behaviour. In fact, in his recent work Ekman had some very useful insights on re-evaluating appraisals using the Buddhist technique of 'attentively considering our emotional feelings'.[12] The most important point about appraisals in Buddhism is the moral dimension of emotions. A significant point often missed, ignored or insufficiently dealt with in emotion studies in the scientific tradition is the moral qualities of emotions. The new studies under the guidance of the Life and Mind Institute have been more sensitive to the moral facets of emotions. Buddhism considers emotions that spring from the affective roots of greed and hatred, as well as the cognitive root of delusion as unwholesome, and those that emerge from generosity, loving kindness and wisdom as wholesome. The qualities of liberality, loving kindness, renunciation and unselfishness involve a whole range of appraisals, not the working of the mechanical automatic pilot but a whole range of wholesome values and perspectives. The Buddhist perspective on emotions is very much focused on following *right view* as well as freeing our minds from cognitive distortions.

Some Critical Issues Concerning the Jamesian Theory of Emotions

While accepting the important role of the body in emotions, there are critical issues that make it difficult to uphold a fully pledged Jamesian theory of emotions. James claimed that emotions are basically somatic disturbances consequent on the perception of an exciting fact. An emotion is not the somatic changes as such but the perception of these changes. Some of the problematic issues are as follows:

(1) It is necessary to recognize a distinction between an emotion as an episodic emotional perturbation and a long standing emotional attitude. According to a recent study by a philosopher and neuroscientist, James 'has systematically, but unwittingly, screened out the attitudinal, as well as the motivational, cogitative and fantasy aspects of the emotions' (Benett and Hacker, 2003, 203). A person's judgements may be clouded not only by the distress and agitation of the moment, as for instance when one is engulfed with grief, but also by long-standing resentment and jealousies. Especially in the context of Buddhism these dispositional dimensions are important.

(2) A person's emotions cannot be simply measured in terms of the frequency of emotional agitations. The strength of motivational patterns and behaviour over time are more complex factors that resist exact quantification.

(3) There is no single emotion prototype as the conceptual complexities of emotions vary from the nature of fear of physical harm, grief and anger to others such as hope, remorse, compassion and pride.

(4) A great deal of experimental work done on emotions is on animals and the distinction between emotions in humans and animals is often lost.

(5) Some emotions have characteristic somatic accompaniments,

some are emotional perturbations with behavioural manifestations; yet some of these are expressive reactions like facial grimaces and others are voluntary, done with a purpose.

(6) Above all emotions are linked to volition. This is a point James valued in his ethics yet this point has to be related and fully integrated to his analysis of emotions. It has been observed that James had hinted at a way out of getting entrenched in a biologically programmed mind, when he said, 'The faculty of voluntarily bringing back wandering attention over and over again is the very root of judgment, character and will' (James, 1950, 424; Schwarz and Begley, 2002).

Mind and Body Relationship in Emotions

Apart from the holistic conception of emotion outlined above in terms of the material found in the *suttas*, there are other important philosophical and practical reasons which emphasise the need to move towards a more balanced perspective: accepting the thesis that there can be feedback mechanisms by which the body can affect the mind and the mind can affect the body.

(1) The Buddha used contextual discourse, when he made a relative distinction between 'physical' and 'mental' in referring to feelings. But he discouraged any metaphysical entanglements about their ultimate status, which he left as an *undetermined question*.

(2) In the more dynamic setting in which the Buddha discusses the nature of consciousness and body, they are reciprocal, depending upon each other, and they also emerge simultaneously and cease together. Thus we need to free ourselves from the traps of dualism, monism or any form of reductionism. It is said that mind and body are like two bundles of reeds supporting each other.

(3) The point is conveyed in more practical terms in the anti-ontologising context of meditation, where we see the phenomenal nature of the process, and the 'designation-like' nature of concepts like feeling and body.[13]

(4) While requesting us to be cautious of not falling into the net of wrong views (*diṭṭhi*), at times the Buddha considers the body as a trap that obstructs liberation but in other contexts emphasises the importance of the composure and sensibility of the body. In fact the

Four Foundations of Mindfulness (*satipaṭṭhāna*) provide avenues towards the path of liberation based on both the body and mind.

(5) Looking at the area of current therapeutic approaches which have integrated the use of mindfulness practice, Jon Kabat-Zinn's ground-breaking programme indicates the value of mindfulness of both the body and mind. In general I take the position that according to Buddhism, it is possible to view our body/mind as a feedback loop, where both the physical and the cognitive facets play important roles.

Making a reference to the Cognitive Somatic Anxiety questionnaire prepared by Daniel Goleman and Jon Kabat-Zinn, Kabat-Zinn commented on the relative uses of body scan, yoga and sitting meditation in his clinic: 'The sitting meditation is the most cognitive of these techniques, because you're just watching the mind without doing anything with the body. The body scan is more somatic; you're moving through the body, and it helps them because usually they are so much in their heads.'[14]

Bridging the Chasm Between Cognitive Theories of Emotions and Arousal Theories of Emotions

The release of a recent book *Thinking about Feeling* is an important landmark in the history of the philosophy of emotions.[15] The work, edited by Robert C. Solomon, brings the frontier lines of the above debate up to date. John Deigh, who has written the first chapter of the volume, presents two conflicting programmes in psychology, one emerging from William James and the other from Sigmund Freud. To quote Deigh, 'James's ideas are the sources of the view that one can fruitfully study emotions by studying the neurophysiological processes that occur with experience of them. He identified them with feelings.'[16] Deigh also said, 'Though Freud often described emotions as flows of nervous energy, his view of them as transmitters of meaning and purpose was nonetheless implicit in his notion of an unconscious mind and the way he used this notion to make sense of his feelings, behaviour, and physiological maladies that seems otherwise inexplicable.'[17] What Deigh pointed out is that Freud gradually moved from a *somatogenic* to an *ideogenic* explanation of human behaviour. He concluded his chapter by saying that the central problem for the philosophy of emotions is to develop a theory that reconciles these two facets of emotion studies.

We have already presented the outlines of a holistic approach to emotion studies in Buddhism. Another area in emotion studies where this apparent chasm between the Jamesian and Freudian approach has been bridged is the new therapeutic orientations in the West, influenced by the efficacy of Buddhist mindfulness practice. The work on behaviour modification by Padmal Silva,[18] the more recent development of mindfulness based cognitive therapy by Segal, Williams and Teasdale,[19] Erich Fromm's posthumus publication, *Art of Listening*,[20] Mark Epstein's *Thought Without a Thinker*[21] – all these point to a significant domain of convergence of Western systems of therapy and Buddhist practice. Padmal Silva's work has been greatly influenced by the early Buddhist tradition in Sri Lanka. Jon Kabat-Zinn has created a veritable revolution in therapy as seen not merely in the work done in the Massachusetts stress clinic but also the impact he had on Teasdale and his colleagues and others. While Erich Fromm had some important correspondence with Nyanaponika Thera of the forest hermitage in Sri Lanka, Mark Epstein came under the influence of the *vipassanā* meditation teachers, especially Joseph Goldstein and Jack Kornfield.

These therapeutic traditions have crossed frontiers from their early insular base in the West and developed a flexibility to deal with practical problems of mental health and sickness. The Buddha had been greatly critical of people who clung to pedantic doctrinaire views and fell victim to the entrapment of partial views and categories. The Buddha pointed out that anger and confusion arise when they get hooked to opposing views, partial views and speculative views, and that the recluse who has developed insight has gone beyond partial views. The *Kalahavivāda Sutta* in the *Sutta-Nipāta* is a very illuminating sermon on the futility of getting entangled in views, and the wisdom in following the path of practice.[22] Even right-view (*sammā diṭṭhi*), which is the starting point of the Noble Eightfold Path, is compared to a raft used for crossing the river. The raft is not meant to be carried over one's shoulders after crossing the river. The conception of right-view is an aid and a perspective for practice rather than a theory for disputation and debate. The *Sutta-Nipāta,* which contains the very early strands of the Buddha's message, also finds a close echo in the *Discourse on the Snake Simile* in the *Middle Length Sayings.* It is in this discourse that the Buddha compares the *dhamma* to a raft, and says that it is not meant for embellishment, gossip and excessive debate. It is against this background that we need to understand Buddha's approach to the relationship between the mind and the body.

The Domination of a Metaphor

Though some of the Western therapeutic traditions have crossed frontiers with a new wisdom to deal with the practical problems of the alleviation of human pain, there is yet a stumbling block in the philosophical studies of emotion. This is largely due to the 'domination of a metaphor'.[23] Due to the recent impact of Buddhism on the therapeutic traditions, Western psychology (in the area of emotion studies) is likely to be more responsive to Buddhist psychology in the future. Western philosophers from Plato and Spinoza, coming down to recent times, see the management of emotion in terms of a metaphor: *reason as the charioteer and passions as the unruly horses.* David Hume turned the metaphor upside down by saying that reason is and ought to be the slave of the passions. Even the Buddha has been referred to as 'an incomparable charioteer for the training of persons (*anuttaro purisa dhamma-sārati*)'. But Buddhism replaces this dualism of reason and passion with a three-factor analysis: *passion, reason and mindfulness.* We often over-intellectualise the emotions in our attempts to deal with the chaos of passions around our lives. It is our contention that the battle between our logical perceptions and emotions found in the Western philosophical traditions might be taken to a more effective level – the practice of mindfulness.

The simple point is that emotions do not *often* fit neatly into the mould of logic: Ajahn Sumedho observed, 'The mind relishes the way it is logical and controllable, the way it makes sense. It is just clean and neat and precise like mathematics – but the emotions are all over the place, aren't they? They are not neat and they can easily get out of control.'[24] What meditation does is to mature on a different level. One should not get caught in fluctuations and vicissitudes and one needs balance and clarity. We do not try to destroy the passions but try to contain them through a process of silent listening, deep compassionate listening. When the mind is silent and its internal dialogues and chatter subside, the deeply ingrained patterns of automatic thinking become transparent. The following words from Mark Epstein recognise without any ambiguity the value of Buddhist contemplative practice for understanding and regulating emotions:

> Bare attention is the technique that best defines the Buddhist approach to working with our minds and emotions. It is impartial, open, nonjudgmental, interested, patient, fearless, and impersonal. In creating a psychic space analogous to, but not identical with, Winnicot's transitional space of childhood, it facilitates the ability to transform psychic disturbances into objects of meditation, turning the proverbial threat into a challenge, and is therefore of immense psychotherapeutic benefit. There is no emotional experience, no mental event and no disavowed or estranged aspect of ourselves that cannot be worked with through the strategy of bare attention.[25]

Emotion and Thought in Early Buddhism

Having presented the perspectives for a holistic theory of emotions in Buddhism, I shall now briefly explore the place of thought in early Buddhism. Then I shall get back to one of the primary concerns of this chapter, the role of wisdom in the management of passions. This is broadly the *ideogenic* dimension of emotions as distinguished from the equally important *somatogenic* dimension of emotions. Earlier in our discussion, it was mentioned that in Buddhist psychology, an emotion is an interactive complex of perceptions, feelings, desires, beliefs, appraisals and physiological arousal. In this section I turn to the non-somatic factors as Buddhist resources both as therapy and as path for liberation.

Emotions are usually considered to be different from drives like hunger, thirst and the sexual drive, and from objectless moods like irritation. Some of the important states considered as emotions are anger, fear, love, grief, envy, jealousy, guilt, pride, shame, sympathy and compassion. Traditional philosophers like Aristotle and Spinoza included greed in this group and it is also found in Buddhism. Some philosophers have developed accounts of emotions close to the image of appetites: 'emotions are surges of affect or energy in the personality, unreasoning movements that push people into acting without being very much connected to their thoughts about the world'.[26] The second type of philosophical theory upholds that emotions involve interpretation and belief. 'Thus we are not afraid of X unless we take X to be dangerous; we are not angry at X unless we take X to be acting contrary to something we want; we do not have remorse over having done X unless we regard it as unfortunate that we did X; we are not grief-stricken over X unless we see X as the loss of something we wanted very much; we do not have pity for X unless we take X to be undesirable; and so on.'[27] Emotions depend on our interpretations of situations in terms of their significance to our lives.

Among the traditional Western philosophers, while Aristotle presented the first cognitive theory of emotions, Spinoza stands preeminent in working out the thought components of emotions.[28] Among the contemporary philosophers, Martha Nussbaum's recent work, mainly focused on the emotion of grief, presents a thesis that 'emotions are upheavals of Thought'.[29] In the therapeutic tradition, Albert Ellis's 'Rational Emotive Behaviour Therapy' (REBT) examines people's core irrational beliefs. He also notes the importance of automatic thoughts but assumes that they stem from their basic unrealistic, illogical and dysfunctional core philosophies.[30] He does not use anything like mindfulness practice as is done by Kabat-Zinn in looking at automatic thoughts. Within the current therapeutic trends, 'Mindfulness-based Cognitive Therapy for Depression' is one system which comes close to having a therapy focused on thoughts.

Buddhist Contemplative Practice and Mindfulness in Everyday Life

I have in the preceding discussion developed what may be called a holistic theory of emotions in Buddhism based on the analysis of the emotion concept, the material in the Buddhist discourses, especially based on Nyanaponika Thera's study of the *Vedanā Samyutta,* the convergence of the mindfulness-based therapeutic traditions dealing with the different facets of the emotion concept and also an analysis of the body–mind relationship. Lastly, I am looking at the *Satipaṭṭhāna* as a frame of reference. In this context, based on Thannisara Thero's analysis of the *Satipaṭṭhāna,* it is necessary to recognise, how, when one makes the body the frame of reference, whatever feelings and thoughts one experiences are related in terms of the body as a primary frame of reference; the same pattern is followed when the primary frame is a mind state. This approach also emphasises the anti-ontologising approach of contemplative practice in Buddhism.

In the Buddhist contemplative tradition, the mind-defiling passions or negative emotions are described by the term *kilesa* and the *Middle Length Sayings* has a list of sixteen under the term *upakkilesa*: covetousness, illwill, anger, malice, hypocrisy, spite, envy, jealousy, deceit, fraud, obstinacy, impetuosity, arrogance, pride, conceit and indolence.[31] A mind that is tarnished by these defilements is compared to a discoloured cloth with stains and one that needs a complete washing, so that the stains disappear.

The *Satipaṭṭhāna* has four Frames of Reference for Mindfulness Practice: body, feeling, mind and mental qualities, but in each of these states one can focus on the body and then feelings related to the body or thoughts related to the body and so on. These four frames of reference for the practice of mindfulness fall into two classes. The first class – the body (*kāya*), feelings (*vedanā*) and the mind (*citta*) function as the given objects of meditation practice – what experience presents as the given objects of meditation. The meditator takes one of these objects as his *frame of reference*, relating all his or her experience to this frame. This process can be understood using an analogy of someone holding something in his or her hands. For instance if one experiences feelings and mind states in the course of taking the body as a frame of reference, one tries to relate them to the body as the primary frame of reference. A feeling is related to the way it affects the body and it is the same with mind states. The second class of object which belongs to the fourth frame of reference, *dhamma* – represents the qualities of mind, which are developed and abandoned as one masters the meditation.[32] But the list of *dhammas* include not only the five hindrances and the seven factors of awakening which are mental qualities, but also the five aggregates, six sense media and the four noble truths, and some scholars have used terms like 'phenomena' to describe this collection. Thanissaro Thero says that the other items actually 'deal with variant forms of abandoning the hindrances and developing the factors of awakening'.[33] The important point is that the frames of the *satipaṭṭhāna* give the practitioner the freedom to develop body-based concentration, mind-based concentration or a combination of both.

Now, we shall direct our analysis and discussion to the five hindrances as placed in the *dhammānupassāna* with some reference to greed, hatred and delusion in the *cittānupassanā*. We wish to use the discussion on the following five hindrances as an ideal context to emphasize the place of emotions in the Buddhist contemplative life. These hindrances are major obstacles to the successful practice of meditation. They may be temporarily suppressed in the experience of *jhana* and insight but they are fully overcome through the complete development of the noble eightfold path.

Five Hindrances

(1) Sensual desire (*kāmacchanda*)
(2) Ill-will (*byāpāda*)
(3) Boredom (sloth and torpor) (*thīna-midha*)
(4) Restlessness and Anxiety (*uddhacca-kukkucca*)
(5) Uncertainty (*vicikiccā*)

Meditation is not thinking about things, as it is a discursive level that we try to avoid in meditation. But discursive thinking pervades our lives, and as meditation involves silent observation without either attachment or reaction to thoughts, by focusing attention on the intrusive thoughts triggered by sensual desires or anger, we can develop clear awareness of thinking. The *Vitakkasanthāna Sutta* (Discourse on Forms of Thought) may be considered as a kind of charter for the methodology of dealing with intrusive thoughts. This discourse mentions five techniques.[34] The first is the method of *aññanimitta* (different object): ideational activity (*vitakka*) associated with desire, aversion and confusion is to be eliminated by reflecting on a wholesome object. This method is compared to a carpenter driving out a large peg with a small peg. The second method, that of *ādiñava,* aims at scrutinising the peril of these harmful thoughts. This is compared to a man in the prime of life who is fond of adornment and beautifying the body seeing the disgusting sight of a carcass round his neck. The third is *asati amanisikāra* (not attending or letting go) where unwholesome thoughts are eliminated by not paying attention to them. The fourth method is *mūla bheda,* going into the causal roots of the bad thoughts. Lastly, if these techniques fail, the method of *abhinnaggaha* should be followed. According to this method, one uses one's will power to subdue, restrain and dominate the mind. By repeated practice one could emerge as some one who has *mastered these pathways of thought.*[35]

In addition to dispositions of the body (*kayasankhāra*) and dispositions of speech (*vacisankhāra*), there are also dispositions of thinking (*manosankhāra*). It is possible for us either let go these thoughts or make them objects of meditation (*dhammānupassanā*) and through the process of contemplation, our identification with these thoughts becomes very evident. It also becomes evident that these strong emotions of lust, hatred and anxiety have no essence. The Buddha described three types of people prone to anger. When the contemplative sees through the anger, it is like a footprint in water and in others it may be like a footprint on sand or even a footprint carved on a rock.[36] As described in the *Dhammapada,* our life is a creation of the mind: what we are today comes from our thoughts of yesterday; our present thoughts build our life of tomorrow. How do anger and hatred get attached to thoughts? 'When we hold fast to such thoughts as, "They abused me, mistreated me, molested me, robbed me," we keep hatred alive.' If we release ourselves fully from such thoughts hatred will vanish.[37] So if you are free of such thoughts, anger does not consume you. If we see these thoughts as arising and passing away, they will look like dewdrops that evaporate in the sun. Very often, as we get lost in thoughts, it is good to recognise both unwholesome and wholesome thoughts. A close ally of thought is the tendency to build theories and opinions and get attached to them. Another powerful ally of thought is the automatic pilot of judging others and judging oneself. Thoughts often revolve around our sense of the ego and emerge in negativities like arrogance and conceit, as well as in despondency. Thoughts either move towards things to which one becomes attached, or move away reacting to unpleasant things.

There are also forms of conceit (*māna*) emerging from our inbuilt egocentric perspective, which involves a process of comparing oneself with others. These conceits are often related to blind spots in our cognitions rooted in delusion (*moha*). As a defilement conceits are only mastered in the final stages of liberation. As Goldstein remarked, 'Developing a liberated relationship to thought in all its permutations – such as opinions, judgments and comparing – is a vital and challenging aspect of our practice.'[38] By regular practice of mindfulness of thoughts, it is possible to discipline our thinking patterns and then gradually one becomes able to experience a sense of freedom from the thinking patterns associated with sensuality and anger. Richard Davidson's groundbreaking research into the impact of meditation on the brain illustrates both the effectiveness of meditation to deal with negative emotional states, and the plasticity of the brain. An interesting issue for future research is to explore the impact of wholesome thinking patterns on the brain. In fact, Davidson raises the question whether there could be intentional wholesome thought patterns. Ricard says that there is of course a way ' to stare back at unwholesome thoughts' and though they have the appearance of solidity, you can see them dissolving and melting away.[39]

Emotions do not have clear boundaries and they often come in constellations, and in such contexts, the thought components help us to identify an emotion and distinguish it from others. As we mentioned above fear, anger, remorse and pity are best distinguished from each other by looking at the thought components. In the way that it is possible to agree with James to a great extent that in the most basic emotions physiology gives the 'emotional quality' of the emotions, it is also possible to accept the thesis that the thought components or appraisals best help us to understand the individuation of emotions. Even if more experimental work in the future may give us a more refined version of the physiological basis of emotions, the relationship between appraisals and emotions is something that will continue to provide significant clues in the practice of mindfulness in everyday life. It is also stated in the *suttas* that mental states are translated into sensations in the body (*sankappavitakka vedanāsamosarana*).[40] Though there is no systematic analysis of the role of physiological factors in emotions in the discourses of the Buddha, there are scattered references to facial expressions, behavioural expressions, and especially the rhythms of breathing in the context of wholesome and unwholesome emotions. Breathing has both physical and mental facets and is the finest basis for body–mind integration and health. It is in the area of feeling where we see very well the *psyche-soma* linkage. When initial pain signals get converted into anger and fear, breathing patterns change – there is bodily turbulence and agitation. When there is calm and collectedness breathing patterns are different. The first four hindrances have characteristic bodily and psychological dimensions of expression. The fifth hindrance appears to be fed by a number of factors:

distorted cognitive schemas, an uneven practice of morality and an obsession with theories and opinions (*diṭṭhi carita*).

The five hindrances are explained with the graphic imagery of a pond of water: sense desire is like the water being merged by a variety of intricate colours and one cannot see the image of one's own face in the pond; ill-will is like boiling water, indicating a turbulent mind; sloth and torpor are like the pond covered by moss and vegetation, too dense to break through, and so is the mind; restlessness is like a pond that is wind-swept, an agitated mind; and finally, doubt is like muddy water, an obscure and cloudy mind.

While greed and sensual desires, as well as anger and hatred figure prominently in the practice of mindfulness in everyday life, there is very little discussion of another important emotion – boredom. In the context of meditation, arising of unarisen sloth and drowsiness is considered as a third way of feeding the hindrances. While in the context of meditation, sleepiness, yawning and drowsiness after a meal figure as a description of this condition, it is very rarely that we focus attention on boredom as a part of social pathology, a dimension we also discern in relation to greed, as well as violence. It is important to mention that the five hindrances infiltrate into our social lives in multi-faceted ways. Goldstein (1994, 80) made a very insightful observation, when he said that one should consider boredom as a friend in a meditation setting who is telling you, 'pay more attention'.[41]

'In meditation one develops an understanding of the Five hindrances – how when one of them is present, you investigate it, you understand it, you accept its presence and you learn how to do deal with it. Some times you can tell it to go away and it goes; sometimes you just have to allow it to be there till it wears out.'[42] If there is something unpleasant we have subtle ways of avoiding it, or we try to destroy what is unpleasant. Thus there has to be some honesty about what one feels. It is only when a hindrance emerges in the mind that we can penetrate it and have insight. When the actual situation arises, one has to be mindful without trying to resist, resent or judge.

A more rudimentary form of the five hindrances is found in the objects of reference in *cittānupassana* as passion, aversion and ignorance. The first hindrance is related to passion, the second to aversion and the other three – boredom, restlessness and lack of faith (*saddhā*) to ignorance. Though the five hindrances are principally spoken of in the context of meditation, they have a significant resonance in our life. Sensuality, anger, boredom and apathy, restlessness and anxiety are all part and parcel of everyday life.

From Passion to Wisdom: Navigating Our Emotional Lives

Having completed our analytical study of the mind–body linkage in emotions, it would be most fitting in the last section of this chapter to make a short review of the Buddhist perspectives on the management of emotions. One of the most important areas where Buddhism offers a relevant message today is the value of Buddhist therapeutic techniques in dealing with emotional states. In discussing afflictive and nourishing emotions, Goleman observed that unwholesome emotions in Buddhism are also emotions that make people ill and the wholesome emotions contribute to our health. According to the available scientific research anger or hostility, depression, self-pity, guilt, anxiety and repression are afflictive states in relation to health. The beneficial states are calm, confidence, optimism, joy and loving kindness. He also observes that there are no good studies on greed, though it has taken pathological forms in the culture of the West.[43] Also, practice of mindfulness is a great asset in pain management, and this point is authenticated even in the life of the Buddha. When the Buddha was wounded by a stone splinter it is said he was able to withstand the painful sensation with mindfulness. It is said such people are only struck by one dart (only the physical pain) but many others 'lament, beat the breast and weep' because they are struck by two darts, physical and mental (*vedanā-samyutta*, 6). It may be said that the *harmony of the mind* has a definite impact on the *harmony of the body*. Thus we may say that if we are looking at a normative ideal, in the liberated monk there is a radical transformation of body chemistry. Refined cognitive states like loving kindness, compassion, appreciative joy and equanimity have a great impact on the body.

Working With Emotions, is a fascinating study of emotions presented by a Lama of Tibetan origin, Gendun Rinpoche. This monograph which contains the teachings given by him in France during the summer of 1990 is based on an earlier seventeenth-century study by a very learned lama, Chagme Rinpoche. This exposition by Gendun Rinpoche, which draws many insights from the Tibetan Buddhist tradition, uses a very vivid metaphor to describe *the path from passion to wisdom* – the peacock: 'This refers to the bird's fabled capacity to eat poison and transmute it into the brilliant colours of its tail, a symbol much employed in Tibetan Buddhism to represent the spiritual process of transforming emotional energy into wisdom energy.' According to their analysis of emotions, there are five emotions: desire, anger, pride, jealousy and confusion (ignorance). They consider these as five poisons but that they may be completely transformed as is suggested by the metaphor above. An emotion may be described as the habitual clinging that makes us categorise our emotions according to whether we find our experience attractive (desire), unattractive (anger) or neutral (ignorance). When we consider our own experience as predominant there is pride and when we judge our own position in relation to the perceived objects, there is jealousy.[44]

This analysis offers five methods of working with emotions: (a) abandoning the emotions; (b) remedying the emotions; (c) transforming the emotions; (d) seeing into the true nature of emotions; (e) using the emotions as a spiritual path.[45] In fact, it is mentioned with reference to the first method, 'The methods outlined in this part are used principally in the *srāvaka* tradition, the tradition of the Hearers'. This is of course a clear reference to the early Buddhist tradition and this analysis offers a very useful background to reflect on the early Buddhist perspectives on managing emotions. This work also facilitates a dialogue between the early Buddhist and the Tibetan tradition on managing emotions. The first four methods have parallels in early Buddhism. The early Buddhist *suttas* refer to four kinds of efforts which have some general resemblance to the first four of the above methods: the effort to restrain the senses; the effort to abandon evil and the unprofitable state that arises from time to time; the effort to make become – let positive spiritual skills and energy emerge through investigation, zest, tranquillity and equanimity and lastly the effort to focus attention on selected objects of meditation like repulsive signs.[46]

The Craftsmanship Model

> Thus we can say that the Dhamma – in terms of doctrine, practice, and attainment – derives from the fully explored implications of one observation: that it is possible to master a skill. This point is

> reflected not only in the content of the Buddha's teachings, but also in the way they are expressed. The Buddha used many metaphors, explicit and implicit, citing the skills of craftsmen, artists, and athletes to illustrate his points. The text abounds with explicit similes referring to acrobats, archers, bathmen, butchers, carpenters, farmers, fletchers, herdsmen, musicians, painters.[47]

The development of moral virtues and the mastery of the meditation techniques are often described by the Buddha in terms of what may be called the craftsmanship model. A great deal of what is called the *abandoning of negative emotions or passions,* which involves the exercise of restraint on passions, is well described in the discourses in terms of metaphors. The watchfulness of a door keeper, instilling discipline like a horse trainer, persistence of an army defending a frontier fortress, exerting energy to the correct pitch like a fletcher heating two arrow shafts between two flames, and the balance and vigilance of an acrobat. To give a very good example drawn from music: the Buddha gives advice to Sona regarding the application of energy in the practice of meditation, and says that 'if energy is applied strongly this can lead to restlessness and if energy is lax, this will lead to lassitude'.[48] Keeping a balance in this context is compared to a well-tuned musical instrument.

In the pathways for abandoning passions, restraint of the senses (*indriya samvara*) is the starting point. The Buddha admonished the monks that the path for dispassion has to be followed step by step: the basis for the development of a virtuous character is sense control; the basis for right concentration is virtue; the basis for 'knowledge and vision of things as they are' is right concentration; the basis for revulsion and dispassion is 'knowledge and vision of things as they are'; the basis for knowledge and vision of liberation is revulsion and dispassion.[49]

In the light of the craftsmanship model of developing good skills and healthy emotions, it is possible to develop a more definitive Buddhist concept of emotions, in place of the loose usage of emotion as a category consisting of 'perceptions, feelings, desires, beliefs, appraisals and physiological arousal' (p. 2). The training in the skills for managing emotions 'prepares' us to meet situations and respond to them. A recent interpretation of the term *sankhāra* as a state of preparation is very illuminating in this context. The term *sankhāra* occurs in the five aggregates, in the links of dependent origination and also in the phrase 'all conditioned things (*sankhata*) are impermanent'. Translations also vary depending upon the context. But an important strand of meaning in the context of an emotion is the component of intention, which we preserve by rendering *sankhāra* as volitional activity. In a recent study, Nanananda Thero observed that during the time of the Buddha the word *sankhāra* was already in usage and had the meaning of 'preparation': culinary preparation, back-stage preparation and repairing. But he also points out two other interesting links with the term *sankhāra* as preparation. One is a reference to a state of stress, tension, or activity as preparation for a journey. For example it is said, 'whatever eagerness or tension for making the journey subsided'. The second reference is in the story of the Buddha and Pacetana, the wheelwright. It is mentioned in this context, that the wheel kept rolling so long as the impulse that set it moving (*abhisankhāra gati*) lasted, and then twirled around and fell on the ground.[50] This concept of 'preparedness' and 'momentum' may be used to refer to both wholesome emotions and unwholesome emotions. It is said that bodily, verbal and mental preparations (*kayasankhāra, vacisankhāra, manosankhāra*) are ethically significant. With this very brief clarification of this new way of looking at *sankhāra* as preparations and developing a momentum, we come into contact with a fresh dimension of the meaning of emotions in Buddhism. As the sage reaches a state of liberation this momentum subsides. These insights help us to get a fresh perspective of the abandoning of negative emotions.

The method of rectifying emotions basically refers to the use of antidotes to manage negative emotions and is also clearly a method found in early Buddhism. In dealing with the appeal of a sensual object we are asked to focus attention on its unattractive aspect; and if thoughts of ill-will are aroused in us, then we should dwell on the good qualities of the person who has aroused thoughts of ill-will. Forgiveness, patience and loving kindness are very effective antidotes of anger and hatred. *Mettā* (loving kindness) meditation is the most powerful antidote to several negative emotions. The Buddha first taught *mettā* meditation as an antidote for fear. This meditation was given to a group of monks frightened of shrieks, disturbing visions and foul smells. '*Mettā* overcomes all of the states that accompany this fundamental error of separateness – fear, alienation, loneliness, despair – all of the feelings of fragmentation. In place of these, genuine realization of connectedness brings unification, confidence, and safety.'[51] Remembering the good within us and the good in others, *mettā* leaves out any traces of self-hate or anger towards others. *Karunā* (compassion) is a powerful ally to deal with grief and when joined with gratitude to those who have been separated from us, adds a reflective and dedicatory quality to grief. It is also a context to appreciate the best qualities of people whom we have lost and re-work these qualities into our lives. Though sympathetic or appreciative joy (*muditā*) is hard to cultivate, it is the best antidote for envy and jealousy. Equanimity (*upekkha*) steers us across both undue elation and conceit as well as despondency and dejection. Thus the four sublime states are a very effective resource to deal with the negativities in our emotional lives. There are three forms of pride (*māna*): superior conceits, equality conceits and inferiority conflicts. These conceits emerge on a false valuation of oneself. The cultivation of due humility would be an antidote for conceit and arrogance.

Transforming negative emotions instead of 'demonising' them is a technique common to both traditions, though in the Tibetan tradition this also involves a complex iconography of divinities. But the concept of emotional alchemy is common to both traditions. There has been some misconception that Buddhism advocates 'cutting off the passions'. Even where Buddhism advocates restraint it is more a cultivation of a sensibility. When it comes to transformation, the need to open ourselves to inner experience, our thought patterns and somatic expressions in relation to emotion without denial, repression and escape take a crucial place in the Buddhist path to the wise management of emotions. 'By alienating our own energy, making it "other" and then judging it negatively, we may come to believe that emotions are demonic, that we have "monsters" inside us. By treating emotions as an autonomous power, we grant them dominion over us.'[52]

Denial and feelings of self-importance prevent us from opening ourselves to suffering. Also getting involved in these negativities drains our energy, and we are caught up in the little dramas of anger, fear and sadness. If we drop down a level, go beyond the story and see how the emotion works in our life and do this with mindfulness, it becomes possible to 'contain' such an emotion. 'Becoming literate we can recognize our feelings, tolerate them long enough to learn something from them, and eventually make them more or less an integrated part of our lives and work.'[53] In this manner we contain our anger or fear, take it in its disorganised form and see it with the gift of listening that calms and energises the mind. This is the process of emotional alchemy which Jung describes as converting brass into gold. This theme has been greatly developed in recent times in the writings of Bennett-Goleman, Jack Kornfield and Mark Epstein.[54]

Nyanaponika Thera clarified the method of transforming disturbing thoughts into objects of meditation and thus converting enemies into friends. He quoted a passage from the delightful book, *The Little Locksmith*:

> I am shocked by the ignorance and wastefulness with which persons who should know better throw away the things they do not like. They throw away experiences, marriages, situations, all sorts of things because they do not like them. If you throw away a thing, it is gone. Where you had something you have nothing. Your hands are empty, they have nothing to work on. Whereas, almost all those things which get thrown away, are capable of being worked over by a little magic into just the opposite of what they were. . . .[55]

The Tibetan tradition employs a more complex method for transformation of emotions. There is an exercise for making the five emotions disappear into emptiness by focusing each emotion on the five Dhyana Buddhas. It is a form of creative meditation based on imagery. The technique is described as 'making the emotions disappear by visualisation'.

I shall conclude this study of emotions in Buddhism by explaining the fourth method, the method of seeing into the true nature of emotions. This approach has two facets: one is by developing a reflective turn of mind (*yoniso manasikāra*) in routine life; the second is the development of insight through contemplation. An emotion like anger is normally focused on an object or situation, but if we change the focus from the object to our own consciousness, the anger will thin out. This helps us to catch the anger as it arises. A related quality is the ability to maintain calmness. If we develop this sort of equipoise we are well attuned to use methods like looking at possible consequences; to realise that we are the owners of our deeds and we cannot shirk responsibility; we may be able to realise that people are a mixture of good and bad and not to personalise the wrong that others do and lastly realise that we all share the inevitable mortality of a human being.[56]

Beyond developing this 'reflective turn of mind' towards emotions, it is necessary to discern that emotions have an important hermeneutic role. Emotions have *epistemic* or knowledge-related qualities. Understanding emotions opens up a window to grasp the truths about the human condition. The Buddha has clearly described the nature of things as they are: though the five aggregates give us a false sense of identity, such conditioned phenomena have no permanence (*anicca*); all such aggregates are basically unsatisfactory (*dukkha*); they are not self, not mine (*anatta*). This subtle process of identification with the aggregates accounts for the formlessness, ambiguity and indeterminacy at the centre of our lives. The obsession of identifying oneself with fast-changing and transient objects, the restless search for diversity and the consequent boredom – a graphic description of this predicament is given in Kierkegaard's *Either/Or*.[57] Kierkegaard's description of the pure hedonists captures in essence what the Buddha described as *Kāmasukhalliyānuyoga*. The Buddha located such personalities under the lustful type (*rāga carita*), as different from the anger-dominated personality (*dosa carita*) and the one drowned by opinions and confusion (*diṭṭhi carita*). Such hedonistic personalities have also in them the proverbial 'worm in the apple' and crash with a dissonance they cannot handle.

Kierkegaard said that some people go beyond this simple 'boredom' to a more shattering kind of 'boredom' when their lives go beyond the day-to-day shallowness to a complete collapse of their world. He says just at this movement when tedium, boredom and emptiness are encountered, a real metamorphosis is possible. Some people drown this experience by some trivial diversion like Nero playing the fiddle when Rome was burning. But there are good examples in the Buddhist tradition, examples where people are able to convert such experiences into an object of deep reflection – a positive insight into the lack of essence in persons and things in the world. As Nyanamoli Thera says, 'either in the cool woods which are overgrown or the busy streets', such emptiness and vacuity in its unalloyed forms do not appear, but 'in the desert the doors are open' and such an experience of the void 'provides the backstairs to liberation'.[58] In more general terms, the stories about the transformations described in the stories of Kisagotami and the mustard seed or the robber Angulimala are not mere stories but paradigms of human possibilities. They provide examples of powerful *transformative* insights. It is in this sense that there are *epistemic* or knowledge/insight-related qualities in emotions.

Notes

The following abbreviations occur in the Notes:

A *Anguttara Nikāya*
D *Dīgha Nikāya*
M *Majjhima Nikāya*
S *Saṁyutta Nikāya*
Dh *Dhammapada*
It *Itivuttaka*
Ud *Udāna*

1 BASIC FEATURES OF BUDDHIST PSYCHOLOGY

1 Robert H. Thouless, *Riddel Memorial Lectures*, (Oxford, 1940), p. 47.
2 Mrs C. A. F. Rhys Davids, *Buddhist Psychology*, (London, 1914).
3 Rune Johansson, *The Psychology of Nirvana* (London, 1965), p.11.
4 The material pertaining to the psychology of Buddhism is basically drawn from the *sutta pitaka*.
5. Carl R. Rogers, 'Some Thoughts Regarding The Current Philosophy of the Behavioural Sciences', *Journal of Humanistic Psychology*, autumn 1965.
6 Stuart Hampshire (ed.), *Philosophy of Mind* (London, 1966)
7 Dh., 183.
8 M I, 224.
9 O. H. de A. Wijesekera, *Buddhism and Society*, (Sri Lanka, 1952), p. 12.
10 D III, 289.
11 S V, 168.
12 Wijesekera, op. cit., p. 12.
13 D III, Sutta 26.
14 A II, 16.
15 The *Saṅgārava Sutta* refers to three groups of thinkers: (1) Traditionalists (*anussavikā*), (2) Rationalists and Metaphysicians (*takki vīmaṃsī*), (3) Experientialists who had personal experience of a higher knowledge.
16 Naṇananda, *Concept and Reality* (Sri Lanka, 1971), Preface.
17 For an analysis of the Buddhist theory of knowledge, see K. N. Jayatilleke, *Early Buddhist Theory of Knowledge* (London, 1963).
18 See, K. N. Jayatilleke, 'The Buddhist Doctrine of Karma' (mimeo, 1948) p. 4; The analysis pertaining to the several realms within which the laws of the universe operate is found in the works of commentary, and not in the main discourses of the Buddha.
19 Far a comprehensive study of the Buddhist concept of causality see David J. Kalupahana, *Casuality: The Central Philosophy of Buddhism* (Hawaii, 1975).

20 M I, 520.
21 M II, Sutta 63.
22 M III, Sutta 101.
23 Fromm, Suzuki, Martino (eds), *Zen Buddhism and Psychoanalysis* (New York, 1960).
24 Padmasiri de Silva, *Buddhist and Freudian Psychology* (Sri Lanka, 1973).
25 Erich Fromm, *Psychoanalysis and Religion*, (New Haven, 1961).
26 Rhys Davids, op. cit., p. 133.
27 The beginner who would like to get a bird's eye view of the Pāli canon should read Russell Webb (ed.), *An Analysis of the Pāli Canon* (Sri Lanka, 1975).
28 M II, 211.
29 M I, Sutta 15.
30 Ibid.
31 Ibid.
32 Ibid.
33 Ibid.
34 M II, Sutta 61.
35 See, K. N. Jayatilleke, *Facets of Buddhist Thought* (Sri Lanka, 1971), pp. 79–80.
36 A III, 27.
37 A IV, 448.
38 A II, 186, The story of Kālī the Slave woman in *Majjhima Nikāya*, Sutta 21 also presents an interesting behavioural test. Here the slave woman tests whether her mistress has an 'inward ill-temper' which she does not show.
39 Nyanatiloka, *Buddhist Dictionary* (Sri Lanka, 1956), p. 119.
40 See, Ian Stevenson, *Twenty Cases Suggestive of Reincarnation* (New York, 1966).
41 See de Silva, op. cit.
42 J. C. Flugel, *Studies in Feelings and Desire* (London, 1955), p. 49.
43 See, W. F. Jayasuriya, *The Psychology and Philosophy of Buddhism* (Ceylon, 1963), p. 16; de Silva, op. cit., p.7.
44 M III, 281.
45 Dr K. N. Jayatilleke, 'Some Problems of Translation', *Ceylon University Review*, vols 7 and 8.
46 S III, 60.

2 THE PSYCHOLOGY OF COGNITION

1 M I Sutta, 152.
2 S IV, 9.
3 M I, 190.
4 See, K. N. Jayatilleke, *Early Buddhist Theory of Knowledge* (London, 1963), pp. 433–5.
Padmasiri de Silva, *Buddhist and Freudian Psychology* (Sri Lanka, 1973), p.12.
5 S II, 140.
6 M I, 295.
7 Rune Johansson, *The Psychology of Nirvāna*, (London, 1965), p. 125.
8 Ud 8.
9 S II, 73.
10 M I. III.

11 Ñāṇananda, *Concept and Reality*, (Sri Lanka, 1971), p. 3.
12 S IV, 71.
13 M I, 190.
14 *Middle Length Sayings*, Part I, p. 236.
15 Alex Wayman, 'Regarding the Translation of Buddhist Terms' in *Saññā/Saṃjñā, Viññāṇa/Vijñāna, Malalasekara Commemoration Volume* (Sri Lanka, 1976).
16 Ibid.
17 M I, 415.
18 Mrs C. A. F. Rhys Davids, *Buddhist Psychology* (London, 1914), p. 90.
19 Ibid.
20 See Nayanatiloka *Buddhist Dictionary*, (Sri Lanka, 1956), pp. 114–15.
21 K. N. Jayatilleke, *Early Buddhist Theory of Knowledge* (London, 1963), p. 464.
22 Ibid.
23 S I, 191.
24 Johansson, op. cit.
25 Nyanaponika Thera, *The Snake Simile* (Sri Lanka, 1974), p. 2.
26 D III, 105.
27 M III, Sutta 152.
28 It 24.
29 D III.
30 Jayatilleke, op. cit., p. 423.
31 Ibid.
32 Johansson, op. cit., pp. 23, 90–1.
33 M I, 279.
34 M I Sutta 22.
35 Woven Cadences, 847. P.T.S. (London, 1947).

3 MOTIVATION AND EMOTIONS

1 See C. T. Morgan and R. A. King, *Introduction to Psychology*, 3rd ed. (London, 1966), p. 203.
2 M I, 46–7.
3 S IV, 60.
4 M I, 46–7.
5 M III, Sutta 101.
6 *Kindred Sayings* IV, 87.
7 M I, Sutta 59.
8 *Middle Length Sayings*, II, 67.
9 M I, 303.
10 *Middle Length Sayings*, I, 323–4.
11 *Kindred Sayings*, III, 107.
12 See Magda B. Arnold (ed.), *The Nature of Emotion* (London, 1968), p. 210.
13 Ibid., p. 203.
14 M I, 266.
15 Arnold, op. cit. pp. 206–7.
16 For a discussion of the relationship between belief and emotion, See Alasdair MacIntyre, 'Emotion, Behaviour and Belief' in *Against the Self Images of the Age*, (London, 1971).

17 R. F. Deardon, P. H. Hirst and R. S. Peters, *Education and the Development of Reason* (London, 1972), p. 480.
18 Ibid.
19 Nyanaponika Maha Thera, *Abhidhamma Studies* (Sri Lanka, 1965), p. 79.
20 Dh, 216.
21 M III, 164.
22 J. C. Flugel, *Man, Morals and Society* (London, 1955), p. 197.
23 A V, 193.
24 Mrs C. A. F. Rhys Davids, *Dhamasangani* (translation , London, 1900),p. 20,n. I n. I.
25 Bernard Williams, *Problems of the Self* (London, 1973), p. 222.
26 J. Tilakasiri (ed.), *Anjali*, Wijesekera Felicitation Volume (Sri Lanka, 1970), pp. 20–7.
27 Ibid., p. 27.
28 Ibid., p. 28.
29 Edward Conze, *Buddhism* (London, 1957), pp. 46–8.
30 See Rollo May, *The Meaning of Anxiety* (New York, 1950), p. 8.
31 D. III, 47.
32 See Padmasiri de Silva, *Tangles and Webs*, (Sri Lanka, 1974).
33 Some of the irrational fears related to behaviour disorders have been the subject of psychological analysis, among them the fear of high places, fear of enclosed places, fear of dark places, fear of animals, etc. These are known as the phobias.
34 Leonard A. Bullen, *A Technique of Living*, Buddhist Publication Society (Sri Lanka, 1976).
35 Mrs C. A. F. Rhys Davids, 'Sin', *Encyclopaedia of Religion and Ethics* (New York, 1910–21), vol. II, p. 71.
36 Nyanaponika Thera, *Simile of the Cloth*, BPS (Sri Lanka, 1957).
37 A IV 6–62, translated by Nyanamoli Thera.
38 *Vitakkasanṭhāna Sutta*, M, Sutta 20.
39 See Sigmund Freud, 'Mourning and Melancholia' in *complete Works of Sigmund Freud*, Strachey (ed.), (London, 1953), vol. XIV.
40 *Aṭṭhasālinī*, p. 63.
41 Padmasiri de Silva, 'Buddhism and the Tragic Sense of Life', *University of Ceylon Review* (April – October 1967).
42 A II, 13.
43 See the section on 'Sexuality'.
44 See D III, Sutta 31.
45 D III, Sutta 27.
46 de Silva, *Tangles and Webs*.
47 Dh, 213.
48 Nyanaponika Thera, *Four Sublime States* (Sri Lanka, 1960).
49 See, Gunapala Dharmasiri, 'Principles of Moral Justification in Buddhism and Schopenhauer,' Sonderdruck aus dem 53, Schopenhauer-Jahrbuch, 1972.
50 See Padmasiri de Silva, *Buddhist and Freudian Psychology* (Sri Lanka, 1973).
51 M I, 341.
52 A I, 160.
53 D II, 308.
54 D II, 308–10.
55 Ibid.

56 See Nyanaponika Thera, *The Snake Simile* (Sri Lanka, 1974), p. 6.
57 See Chapter 4.
58 Sigmund Freud, *A General Introduction to Psychoanalysis* (New York, 1965), p. 423.
59 See next section of this chapter.
60 See S III, 1–5.
61 S XXII, 151; see, Nyanaponika (ed.) *Egolessness* (Sri Lanka, 1974), pp. 47–8; also the other extracts dealing with egolessness.
62 A IV, 61–2.
63 S E vol. XIV p. 252.
64 For a comparative study of the Freudian death instinct and the Buddhist concept of the craving for annihilation, see de Silva, *Buddhist and Freudian Psychology*, pp. 148–53.
65 *Middle Length Sayings*, III, Sutta 102.
66 Ñāṇananda (ed.) *Samyutta Nikāya, Part II, An Anthology* (Sri Lanka, 1972), p. 57.
67 M I, 140.
68 M, Sutta 75.
69 See Flugel, op. cit.
70 Morgan and King, op. cit., pp. 235–6.
71 Ibid.
72 Mrs C. A. F. Rhys Davids and W. Stede, *The Pali Text Society's Pāli-English Dictionary* (London, 1953).
73 M I, 433.
74 See de Silva, *Buddhist and Freudian Psychology*.
75 A I, 123.
76 M I, Sutta 2.
77 Ibid.
78 See Chapter I for the meanings of the word *viññaṇa* (consciousness).
79 M I, Sutta 38.
80 S II, 12.
81 D III, 105.
82 A I, 171.
83 A II, 158; S II, 36–41.
84 For a detailed analysis of the concepts of *ālayavijñāna* and *bhavanga* in the light of early Buddhist psychology, See, de Silva *Buddhist dnd Freudian Psychology*, Chapter 3.
85 Bruce Matthews, 'Notes on the Concept of Will in Early Buddhism', *The Sri Lanka Journal of Humanities*, vol. I, no. 1 (1975).
86 See Rune Johansson, *Psychology of Nirvāṇa* (London, 1965).
87 A I, III.
88 The word *Saṅkhāra* of course has a number of strands of meaning, as we mentioned in Chapter 1, but under the heading 'Conative activity' we have cited its central meaning.
89 AII, 14.

4 PERSONALITY

1 C. T. Morgan and R. A. King, *Introduction to Psychology* (London, 1966), p. 460.
2 A II, 186.

3 D III, Sutta 33.
4 As we are working out the psychology of Buddhism as found in the suttas, a certain amount of caution is necessary when we consult works which belong to the later systematisers, those of the *Abhidhamma* tradition.
5 Arthur Danto, 'Persons', *Encyclopaedia of Philosophy*, vol. 6, 1967, p. 111.
6 See Terrence Penulhum, 'Personal Identity', *Encyclopaedia of Philosophy*, vol. 6, 1967, p. 100.
7 See R. Rajapakse, 'A Philosophical Investigation of the Ethical Hedonism and the Theory of Self Implicit in the Pāli Nikayas', unpublished Ph.D. dissertation, (London, 1975).
8 Ibid.
9 K.N. Jayatilleke, *The Principles of International Law in Buddhist Doctrine*, (Leyden, 1967), pp. 49–91.
10 S. I, 135.
11 Rune Johansson, *The Psychology of Nirvāṇa*, (London, 1969), p. 67.
12 Ibid. p. 68.
13 A II, 186; translated in Nayanaponika (ed.), *An Anthology*, Part I (Sri Lanka, 1970), pp. 110–14.
14 *Gradual Sayings* II, pp. 215–18.
15 Ibid.
16 M I, Sutta 7.
17 Edward Conze, *Buddhist Scriptures* (London, 1959), pp. 116–21.
18 See Chapter 3.
19 M III, Sutta 139.
20 A V, 176.
21 M I, 289; S I 101.
22 D III 17, Sutta XXVI.
23 D III, 289.
24 M I, 91, Sn 50.
25 *Middle Length Sayings*, II, p. 186; author's underlining.
26 M II.
27 M I, 85.
28 See Morgan and King, op. cit., p. 474.
29 See Chapter 3 of this work, the section on emotions.
30 M I, Sutta 44.
31 A I, 147.
32 Morgan and King, op. cit., p. 475.
33 M I, Sutta 20.
34 M I, Sutta 20.
35 Ibid.
36 S IV, 118.
37 A II, 146.
38 D II, 307.
39 D III, XXVI.
40 S V 168.

5 BUDDHIST PSYCHOLOGY AND THE WEST* AN ENCOUNTER BETWEEN THERAPEUTIC SYSTEMS

1 L. Wheeler, R. Goodale and J. Deese (eds), *General Psychology* (Boston, 1975), p. 385.
2 Ibid. p. 387.
3 See Padmasiri de Silva, *Buddhist and Freudian Psychology* (Sri Lanka, 1973).
4 L. Wheeler, R. Goodale and J. Deese, op. cit., p. 420.
5 J. C. Coleman, *Psychology and Effective Behaviour* (Bombay, 1969), p. 30.
6 Rollo May, *Existential Psychology* (New York, 1966).
7 Peter Lomas, 'Psychoanalysis Freudian or Existential' in C. Rycroft (ed.), *Psychoanalysis Observed* (London, 1968).
8 R. May, E. Angel and H. F. Ellenberger (eds), *Existence* (New York, 1958), p. 4.
9 K. N. Jayatilleke, *Facets of Buddhist Thought* (Sri Lanka, 1971), p. 88.
10 See Padmasiri de Silva, *Buddhist and Freudian Psychology* (Sri Lanka, 1973).
11 See Chapter 3.
12 See Padmasiri de Silva, *Tangles and Webs* (Sri Lanka, 1976).
13 Ñānavīra Thera, *Notes on the Dhamma* (Sri Lanka, 1964), private edition.
14 Edward Conze 'Spurious Parallels to Buddhist Philosophy', *Philosophy East and West* (1963), p. 112.
15 Rollo May, *Man's Search for Himself* (New York, 1953), p. 13; For an analysis of the concepts of 'alienation' and 'anxiety' in Buddhist perspective see de Silva, *Tangles and Webs*.
16 Ibid.
17 See Rollo May, *The Meaning of Anxiety* (New York, 1950), p. 6.
18 See Mitchel Gorden, *Sick Cities* (New York, 1963).
19 M I, Sutta 7.
20 M I, Sutta 5.
21 Nolan Pliny Jacobson, *Buddhism: The Religion of Analysis* (London, 1966), p. 61.
22 Ibid.
23 *Kindred Sayings*, III, pp. 127–8.
24 Orrine E. Klapp, *Collective Search of Identity* (New York, 1969), pp. 11–14.
25 *Kindred Sayings*, III, p. 89.
26 Klapp, loc. cit.
27 Ibid.
28 David Reisman, *Lonely Crowd* (New Haven, 1950).
29 Frieda Fromm-Reichmann, 'Loneliness', *Psychiatry*, (1959), vol. 22.
30 Ibid.
31 Ibid.
32 See Ñāṇananda, *Ideal Solitude* (Sri Lanka, 1973), p. 14.
33 D III, Sutta 31.
34 See Chapter 3.
35 Soren Kierkegaard, *Either/Or*, vol. 1, translated by Swenson (New York, 1959).
36 See William Barret, *Irrational Man* (London, 1960), p. 54.
37 Edward Conze, *Buddhism* (London, 1957), p. 130.
38 SN IV, 54.
39 T. S. Eliot, *Selected Poems* (London, 1967).
40 *Middle Length Sayings*, I, XXII.

41 M III, Sutta 121 & 122.
42 *Middle Length Sayings*, III, Sutta 121.
43 M III, Sutta 121.
44 See Padmasiri de Silva, *Persons and Phantoms* (Sri Lanka, 1976), Part II.

6 HEALTH AND SICKNESS IN BUDDHIST PERSPECTIVE

1 *Gradual Sayings* II, 143.
2 Ibid.
3 *Kindred Sayings* II, 2.
4 *Middle Length Sayings* 1, 289.
5 Sigmund Freud, *Studies in Hysteria, The Standard Edition of the Complete Psychological Works of Sigmund Freud*, James Strachey (ed.), (London, Hogarth Press, 1966), 2.305.
6 Anthony Storr, 'The Concept of Cure', *Psychoanalysis Observed*, C. Rycroft (ed.), (London: Constable, 1966) p. 53; Also see, Padmasiri de Silva, *Mental Health and the Dilemma of Freudian Psychotherapy; An Eastern Perspective*, in M. Darrol Byrant & Rita H. Mataragnon (eds), *The Many Faces of Religion and Society*, (Paragon House Publishers, 1985).
7 Paul R. Fleischman, *The Therapeutic Action of Vipassanā*, (B. P. S., Kandy, 1986), p. 16.
8 Ibid., p. 17.
9 Marie Jahoda, *Current Concepts of Mental Health*, (New York, 1959) p. 13.
10 E. R. Hilgard, Richard C. Atkinson, Rita L. Atkinson, *An Introduction to Psychology*, (New York, 1975) p. 5454.
11 Paul R. Fleischman, *The Therapeutic Action of Vipassanā*, p. 16.
12 Erich Fromm, 'Psychoanalysis and Zen Buddhism', in Fromm, Suzuki, DeMartino (eds), *Zen Buddhism and Psychoanalysis*, (New York, 1960) p. 91.
13 Seymour Boorstein, 'Troubled Relationships: Transpersonal and Psychoanalytic Approaches', in Boorstein & Deatheridge (eds), *Buddhism in Psychotherapy*, (B. P. S., Kandy, 1982).
14 Forthcoming work, Padmasiri de Silva, *Emotions and their Shadows*.
15 *Gradual Sayings*, II, 137.
16 Nyanaponika Thera, *The Five Mental Hindrances*, (B. P. S., Kandy, 1961).
17 Ibid.
18 Padmasiri de Silva, *The Ethics of Moral Indignation and the Logic of Violence: A Buddhist Perspective*, (Public Trustee Department, Colombo, 1984).
19 Nyanaponika Thera, *The Heart of Buddhist Meditation*, (London, 1975) pp. 73–5.
20 Erich Fromm, *The Heart of Man* (New York, 1964).
21 Nyanaponika Thera, *The Heart of Buddhist Meditation*, pp. 68–71.
22 Nyanaponika Thera, *Contemplation of Feeling*, (B. P. S., Kandy, 1983); Padmasiri de Silva, *The Psychology of Emotions in Buddhist Perspective*, (B. P. S., Kandy).
23 Nyanaponika Thera, *The Contemplation of Feeling*.
24 Ibid.

25 For a discussion on these lines, see, Leonard A. Bullen, *A Technique of Living*, (B. P. S., Kandy, 1976).
26 Mrs C. A. F. Rhys Davids, *Buddhist Psychology*, (London, 1914).
27 Padmasiri de Silva, *Emotions and their Shadows*.
28 Seymour Boorstein, Olaf G. Deathridge, *Buddhism in Psychotherapy*.
29 Ibid., p. 1.
30 Ibid., pp. 1–2.
31 Nyanaponika Thera, *The Five Mental Hindrances*.
32 W. P. Alston, 'Emotions and Feelings', in Paul Edwards (ed.), *The Encyclopaedia of Philosophy*, vol. 2, (New York, 1967) p. 481.
33 Gilbert Ryle, *The Concept of Mind*, (New York, 1964).
34 Nyanaponika Thera, *The Heart of Buddhist Meditation*, section on 'Contemplation of the Body'.
35 See discussion on emotions by George Mandler, in Jonathan Miller (ed.), *States of Mind*, (London, 1983) pp. 138–53.
36 Lyons, *Emotions*, (London, 1980).
37 Padmasiri de Silva, *Emotions and their Shadows*.
38 Nyanaponika Thera, *The Heart of Buddhist Meditation*.
39 Ibid.
40 Yujiro Ikemi, 'The Concept of "KI" in Oriental Medicine and Psychosomatic Medicine', Unpublished Paper, *Proceedings of the ICUS*, Washington D.C., 1986.
41 C. D. Broad, *Mind and its Place in Nature*.
42 Ibid., p. 536.
43 See ref. 40.
44 Ibid.
45 Daniel M. Farrel, 'Jealousy', *The Philosophical Review*, October 1980, pp. 527–60; Leila Tov-Ruach, 'Jealousy, Attention and Loss' in Ameli Rorty (ed.), *Explaining Emotions*, (Berkeley, 1980).
46 Leila Tov-Ruach, 'Jealousy, Attention and Loss'. Ibid.
47 Ibid.
48 Ibid.
49 Padmasiri de Silva, 'The Logic of Identity Profiles and the Ethics of Communal Violence', *Ethnic Studies Report*, ICES, Kandy, January, 1986.
50 Ernest Jones, 'Jealousy', *Papers On Psychoanalysis*, (London, 1950), p. 340.
51 Spinoza, *Ethics*, (New York, 1963).
52 For a detailed comparative analysis of three therapeutic models to deal with emotional conflicts, Psychoanalysis, Behaviourism and Buddhism, see, Padmasiri de Silva, 'Emotions and Therapy, Three Paradigmatic Zones', in Nathan Katz, (ed.), *Buddhist and Western Psychology*, (Boulder, 1983).

7 MIND–BODY RELATIONSHIP AND BUDDHIST CONTEXTUALISM

1 Eugene Herrigel, *Zen in the Art of Archery*, (Penguin Books, Atkana, 1985) p. 85–6.
2 *Dialogues of the Buddha* II, 337–9.
3 *Kindred Sayings* II, 13.
4 *Kindred Sayings* II, 114.
5 *Middle Length Sayings* I, 112.

6 'Discourse On Feelings, Kindred Sayings' translated with a commentary by Nyanaponika Mahathera, *Contemplation Of Feeling*, (Kandy, 1983) p. 15.
7 *Gradual Sayings* II, 143.
8 *Kindred Sayings* II, 2.
9 See J. H. Bateson, 'Body (Buddhist)', James Hastings (ed) in *Encyclopedia of Religion and Ethics*, (New York and Edinburgh, 1932–1936), Volume II, pp. 758–60.
10 See Nyanaponika Mahathera, *The Heart of Buddhist Meditation*, (London, 1975) pp. 57–75.
11 See Padmasiri de Silva, *Twin Peaks: Compassion and Insight* (The Self and Emotion in Western and Buddhist Thought), (Singapore Buddhist Research Society, 1992) pp. 36–74.
12 Joyce McDougall, *Theaters of the Mind*, (London, 1986). p. 159.
13 Discourse 119, 'Discourse on Mindfulness of Body', *Middle Length Sayings*, III, 89–103.
14 Ibid.
15 *Middle Length Sayings* I, 233–4.
16 *Middle Length Sayings* I, 2–271.
17 Nyanaponika Mahathera, *The Wornout Skin*, (Kandy, Buddhist Publication Society, 1977).
18 This point about the confrontation of pain through meditation has been well developed by Jon Kabat-Zinn. See Jon Kabat-Zinn, 'Meditation', in Bill D. Moyers *et al* (eds) *Healing and the Mind*, (New York, 1993).
19 John R. Searle, *The Rediscovery of the Mind*, (London, 1994) p. xiii.
20 Ibid., pp. 74–5.

8 A Holistic Perspective on Emotion Theory and Therapy in Early Buddhism

1 Joseph Ledoux, *The Emotional Brain*, (Weidenfeld and Nicolson, London, 1998), pp. 64–5.
2 Daniel Goleman, *Destructive Emotions*, (Bloomsbury, London, 2003) p. 141. For detailed discussion of the early Buddhist perspectives on the concept of unconscious (or subliminal consciousness), see, Padmasiri de Silva, *An Introduction to Buddhist Psychology*, (Macmillan, London, 2000), pp. 72–5.
3 Robert C. Solomon (ed.), *Thinking about Feeling*, (Oxford University Press, Oxford, 2004).
There have been some attempts in psychology to combine appraisal theories and feedback theories, see, Parkinson, *Ideas and Realities of Emotion*, (Routledge, London and New York, 1995) p. 150: 'appraisal theories and feedback theories may be considered as interlocking and mutually exclusive', also see the papers by Lazarus and Zajonc, in Paul Ekman and Richard Davidson (eds) *The Nature of Emotion*, (Oxford University Press, Oxford, 1994). Parkinson uses the term 'feedback theory' to refer to the theory of William James.
I have also not discussed the socio-cultural theories of emotions: Catherine Lutz's innovative study on a Micronesian culture has great relevance for Buddhism. She says that the term *fago* used in the Ifaluk atoll in the pacific covers both the emotions of sadness and compassion: 'Fago speaks of the sense that life is fragile, that connections to others are both precious and liable to

severance through death and travel, that love may equal loss', in Joel Marks and Roger Ames (eds) *Emotions in Asian Traditions*, (State University of New York Press, 1995), p. 235. Appraisals are often linked to important cultural and social values

4 Nyanaponika, *Contemplation of Feelings*, (Buddhist Publication Society, Kandy 1983), p. 7.

5 Ibid.

6 K. Nanananda, Concept and Reality, (Buddhist Publication Society, Kandy, 1971), p. 5; also see, Padmasiri de Silva, *Twin Peaks: Compassion and Insight (Emotions and the Self in Buddhist and Western Thought)* (Buddhist Research Society, Singapore, 1992), pp. 44–8.

7 *Gradual Sayings* II, 58. Regarding the discussion of *chandarāga* as passion, and the point that emotions imply commitment to consequences and responsibility, James Averill makes the following illuminating comments: 'The self-attribution of emotion allows the individual to abjure, to a limited extent, the responsibility for the consequences of his actions', and he says that 'the experience of passivity is an illusion'; Averill, 'Emotion and Anxiety: Sociocultural, Biological and Psychological determinants', in Ameli Rorty (ed.) *Explaining Emotions*, (University of California Press, Berkley, 1980), p. 80.

8 William James, 'From What is An Emotion', in, Cheshire Calhoun and Rober C. Solomon (eds) *What is an Emotion? Classic Readings in Philosophical Psychology*, (Oxford University Press, Oxford, 1984), p. 131.

9 Gerald E. Myers, *William James, His Life and Thought*, (Yale University Press, New Haven, 1987), p. 240.

10 Robert M. Gordon, *The Structure of Emotions: Investigations in Cognitive Philosophy*, (Cambridge University Press, Cambridge, 1987), p. 92.

11 Paul Ekman, *Emotions Revealed*, (Weidenfeld & Nicolson, London, 2003).

12 Ibid. p. 75

13 *Middle Length Sayings* I, 112.

14 Daniel Goleman (ed.) *Healing Emotions*, (Shambala, Boston, 1997), p. 128.

15 Solomon, *Thinking and Feeling*.

16 John Deigh, in Solomon (ed.) *Thinking and Feeling*, p. 25.

17 Ibid.

18 Padmal Silva, 'Buddhism and Behaviour Change: Implications for Therapy, in Guy Claxton (ed.) *Beyond Therapy*, (Unity Press, N.S.W., 1996), pp. 217–31.

19 Zindel V. Segal, J. Marks, G. Williams and John D. Teasdale, *Mindfulness-Based Cognitive Therapy*, (Guilford Press, London, 2002).

20 E. Fromm, *The Art of Listening*, (Constable, London, 1994).

21 Mark Epstein, *Thoughts Without A Thinker*, (Basic Books, New York, 1995), p. 127.

22 H. Saddhatissa Thero, Translation, *The Sutta-Nipata*, Curzon Press, Richmond, 1998.

23 Padmasiri de Silva, *Buddhism, Ethics and Society: The Dilemmas of Our Times*, (Monash University Press, Clayton, 2002), pp. 188–200.

24 Ajahn Sumedho, 'Rationality and Emotions', in Ajahn Sumedho, *The Four Noble Truths*, (Amaravati Publication, Hempstead, 1992), p. 64.

25 Epstein, *Thoughts Without A Thinker*, p. 127.

26 Martha Nussbaum, *Upheavals of Thought: The Intelligence of Emotions*, (Cambridge University Press, Cambridge, 2004), p. 2.

27 W. P. Alston, 'Emotion and Feeling', in Paul Edwards (ed.), *The Encyclopedia of Philosophy*, vol. 2, (New York, 1967), p. 481.

28 Jerome Neu, *Emotion, Thought and Therapy*, (Berkley, 1977); also see a discussion of three models of therapy, in Padmasiri de Silva, *Emotions and Therapy: Three Paradigmatic Zones*, Inaugural Lecture for the Chair of Philosophy, Peradeniya, 1981.

29 Martha Nussbaum, *Upheavals of Thought*, (Cambridge University Press, Cambridge, 2001).

30 Albert, R Ellis, in Collin Feltham (ed.), *Which Psychotherapy*, (Sage Publications, London, 1997), pp. 51–67.

31 *Middle Length Sayings* I.

32 Bhikkhu Thanissaro, *The Wings to Awakening*, (Dhamma Dana Publications, Barre, 1996), p. 73.

33 Ibid., p. 74.

34 *Middle Length Sayings*, Sutta 20.

35 Also see discussion of 'thoughts' in Joseph Goldstein, *Insight Meditation*, (Shambala, Boston, 1993), pp. 59–67.

36 *Gradual Sayings* I, 283.

37 *Dhammapada For Contemplation*, a rendering by Ajahn Munindo, (River Publications, Belsay, 2001), pp. 3–4.

38 Goldstein, *Insight Meditation*, p. 68; Martthieu Ricard makes an insightful observation on dealing with thoughts: 'The basic way to intervene has been called "staring back" at a thought. When a thought arises, we need to watch it and look back at its source. We need to investigate the nature of that thought that seems so solid, as we stare at it, its apparent solidity will melt away and that thought will vanish without giving birth to a chain of thoughts', in Goleman (ed.) *Destructive Emotions*, p. 214; also see, Daniel Goleman, *Vital Lies, Simple Truths*, (1997), p. 237, a very important book that Goleman wrote on the cognitive schemas which are dimming our awareness and creating blind spots. He refers to Buddhaghosa's analysis of *moha* (delusion) as providing a cure for this ancient malady; see, Goleman (ed.) *Destructive Emotions*, pp. 203–4.

Martha Nussbaum commenting on the upheavals of thought in a context of immense grief shows how our thinking patterns may become deeply 'reflective'. There are background emotions related to our attitudes to death and the world. Also her comments on grief among animals indicate that we need a more complex concept of emotions beyond physiology to understand animal behaviour. Reflective grief of this sort is very much different from the 'automatic pilot' kind of thinking. All this indicates that there is a 'reflective dimension of thinking' which may enhance cognitive theories of emotions. Nussbaum, *Upheavals of Thought*, (2001).

39 Goleman (ed.) *Destructive Emotions*, pp. 214, 216.

40 *Gradual Sayings* IV, 385.

41 Goldstein, *Insight Meditation*, p. 80.

42 Ajahn Sumedho, *Cittaviveka: Teachings From the Silent Mind*, (Amaravati Publications, Hempstead, 1992), p. 57.

43 Daniel Goleman, 'Afflictive and Nourishing Emotions', in Goleman (ed.), *Healing Emotions*, p. 34.

44 Lema Glendun Rinpoche, *Working With Emotions*, (Editions Dzambala, 1992), trans from Tibetan by Anila Rinchen Palmo, p. 4.
45 Ibid., pp. 4–57.
46 *Gradual Sayings* II, 14; also see; *Further Dialogues* II, 120; *Middle Length Sayings* II, 11.
47 Thanissaro, *The Wings of Awakening*, p. 25.
48 *Gradual Sayings* VI, 55.
49 *Gradual Sayings*. VI, 50.
50 K. Bhikkhu Nanananda, *Towards Calm and Insight*, (Karunaratne & Sons, Colombo, 1998), pp. 13–28. Regarding the rendering of emotions as 'preparatory' activity, there is an interesting parallel to N. H. Frijda's notion of emotions as, 'action-readiness', N. H. Frijda, *The Emotions*, (Cambridge University, Cambridge, 1986). It has been commented by scholars that, Fijda has made the most modern discussion of the psychology of emotions in recent times, Keith Oatley and Jennifer M. Jenkins, *Understanding Emotions*, Blackwell, Oxford, 1996), p. 96.
51 Sharon Salzberg, *Loving Kindness*, (Shambala, Boston, 1997), p. 21.
52 John Wellwood, 'Befriending Emotion', in J. Welwood (ed.), *Awakening the Heart*, (Shambala, Boulder, Colorado, 1983).
53 Graham Little, *The Public Emotions*, (ABC Books, Sydney, 1999), p. 17.
54 Tara Benett-Goleman, *Emotional Alchemy*, (Rider, London, 2001; Jack Kornfield, *A Path With Heart*, (Bantam Books, New York, 1993), pp. 71–81; Mark Epstein, *Going On Being*, (Continuum, London, 2001), pp. 163–6.
55 Nyanaponika Thera, *The Power of Mindfulness*, (Buddhist Publication, Kandy 1986), p. 10.
56 For a more detailed discussion of managing anger, see, Visuddhicara Bhikkhu, *Curbing Anger, Spreading Love*, (Buddhist Publication Society, Kandy, 1997); also see, Padmasiri de Silva, 'The Logic of Moral Indignation', in Padmasiri de Silva, *Buddhism, Ethics and Society* (2002).
57 Soren Kierkegaard, *Either/Or*, vol. 1, trans. D. F. and L. M. Swenson, (Anchor Books, New York, 1959), p. 36.
58 Nyanamoli Thera, *Thinker's Note Book*.

Select Bibliography to the Fourth Edition

Benett, M. R. and Hacker, P. M. S. (2003), *Philosophical Foundations of Neuroscience*, Blackwells, London.

Calhoun, C. and Solomon, R. C. (eds) (1984), *What is an Emotion*, Oxford University Press, New York.

Damasio, A. (1994), *Descartes' Error, Reason and the Human Brain*, G. P. Putnam, New York.

de Silva, Padmasiri (2000), *An Introduction to Buddhist Psychology*, Macmillan, London.

de Silva, Padmasiri (1992), *Twin Peals: Compassion and Insight*, Buddhist Research Society, Singapore.

de Silva, Padmasiri (1997), 'The Self and the Emotion of Pride', in Ames, Roger, Dissanayake, Wimal and Kasulis, T. (eds) *The Self as Person in Asian Theory and Practice*, State University of New York Press, Albany.

de Silva, Padmasiri (1997), 'Exploring Vicissitudes of Affect and Working With Emotions', in Pickering, John (ed.) *The Authority of Experience*, Curzon Press, Richmond.

de Silva, Padmasiri (2002), *Buddhism, Ethics and Society*, Monash University Press, Clayton; this work contains a review of Goleman's well known work, *Emotional Intelligence*.

de Soysa, Ronald (1987), *The Rationality of Emotions*, MIT Press, Cambridge.

Ekman, Paul (2003), *Emotions Revealed*, Weidenfeld and Nicolson, London.

Ekman, Paul and Davidson, Richard (eds) (1994), *The Nature of Emotions*, Oxford University Press, Oxford.

Elster, Jon (1999), *Ulysses Unbound*, Cambridge University Press, Cambridge.

Frijda, N. (1986), *The Emotions*, Cambridge University Press, Cambridge.

Goldie, P. (2000), *The Emotions: A Philosophical Exploration*, Clarendon, Oxford.

Goleman, Daniel (ed.) (2003), *Destructive Emotions*, Bloomsbury, London.

Goleman, Daniel (ed.) (1997), *Healing Emotions*, Shambala, Boston

Hardcastle, G. H. (2000), *Journal of Consciousness Studies*, 6, 237.

Kitayama, S. and Niedenthal, P. M. (1994), *The Hearts Eye: Emotional Influences in Perception and Attention*, Academic Press.

Lazarus, R. S. (1984), 'On the Primacy of Cognition', *American Psychologist*, 39, 2, 124–9.

Ledoux, Joseph (1996), *The Emotional Brain*, Simon and Schuster, New York.

Lyons, W. (1980), *Emotion*, Oxford University Press, Oxford.

Marks, Joel and Ames Roger (eds) (1995), *Emotions in Asian Thought: A Dialogue in Comparative Philosophy*, State University of New York Press, Albany.

Nanananda K. Bhikkhu (1971), *Concept and Reality*, Buddhist Publication Society, Kandy; Nanananda K. Bhikkhu (1998) *Towards Calm and Insight*, Karunaratne and Sons, Colombo.

Nyanaponika Mahathera (1973), *The Heart of Buddhist Meditation*, Samuel Wiser, New York; Nyanaponika Mahathera (1983), *Contemplation of Feelings*, Buddhist Publication Society, Kandy; Nyanaponika Mahathera (1986), *The Power of Mindfulness*, Buddhist Publication, Kandy.

Nussbaum, Martha (2001), *Upheavals of Thought: The Intelligence of Emotions*, Cambridge University Press, Cambridge.

Rinpoche, Lama Gendun (1992), *Working With Emotions*, Edition, Dzambala.

Schwartz, J. M. and Begley, S. (2002), *The Mind and the Brain*, Regan Book, Harper-Collins, New York.

Solomon, R. C. (ed.) (2004), *Thinking About Feeling*, Oxford University Press, Oxford.

Thanissaro, Bhikkhu (1996), *The Wings of Awakening*, Dhamma Dana Publishers, Barre.

Zajonc, R. B. (1984) 'On the Primacy of Affect', *American Psychologist*, 39, 2, 124–9.

Primary Sources on Buddhism

This study of emotions in Buddhism is based purely on the discourses of the Buddha found in the *sutta pitaka.* We do not bring any material from the *abhidhamma.* While acknowledging the use of the Pāli Texts and their Translations of the *suttas* published by P.T.S., the author recommends to the reader the following recent translations:

Bodhi Bhikkhu (2000), *The Connected Discourses of the Buddha,* vol. 1 and 2, Translation of the *Majjhima Nikaya,* Buddhist Publication Society, Kandy.

Nanamoli Bhikkhu and Bodhi Bhikkhu (1995), *Middle Length Discourses of the Buddha,* Translation of the *Majjhima Nikaya,* Buddhist Publication Society, Kandy.

Nyanaponika Thera and Bodhi Bhikkhu (1999), *Numerical Discourses of the Buddha,* translation of the *Anguttara Nikaya,* (a selection), Rowman and Littlefield, New York.

Index